THE MATADOR LAND AND CATTLE COMPANY

THE
MATADOR
LAND AND CATTLE
COMPANY

By W. M. Pearce

University of Oklahoma Press : Norman

LIBRARY OF CONGRESS CATALOG CARD NUMBER: 64-11321

Copyright © 1964 by the University of Oklahoma Press, Norman, Publishing Division of the University. Manufactured in the U.S.A. First edition, 1964; second printing, 1982.

To Frances Pearce, my wife
and
Bill and Dick Pearce, my sons

Preface

THIS IS THE STORY of a venture in ranching which began in the 1870's—the bonanza era of the range cattle industry—when land and grass were free and plentiful. Like many other corporations, the Matador Land and Cattle Company, Limited, was founded to take advantage of the fantastic returns from investments in western America which official British documents reported in glowing terms; unlike its fellow joint-stock concerns, however, the Matador survived to the middle of the twentieth century and in this its career was singular, for when its owners sold out to New York investment bankers in 1951, it was the only large foreign-owned company whose operations were devoted exclusively to cattle raising.

To the Scots who purchased the holdings of a small Texas company in 1882 and developed them into one of the great cattle empires of the North American continent, the Matador was primarily a business enterprise; with experience in investment and mortgage banking and a knowledge of animal husbandry, the Dundee directors established policy, exercised close supervision over their agents—the American manager and the ranch superintendents—and determined the annual "financial requirements" which governed the sale of livestock.

The Matador history is largely one of success achieved through the outstanding abilities of the company's agents and strong leadership in the home office. Murdo Mackenzie, the manager in America for thirty-five years, was called by Theodore Roosevelt "the most influential of western cattlemen," and Alexander Mackay, initially the company's secretary in Dundee and later chairman of its board, was rated by John Clay above all other Britishers who visited America in connection with land and cattle investments. In the story, against the backdrop of one of the West's most dramatic episodes, are illustrated the cattle industry's transition from open range to enclosed ranching, the problems of communication in an enterprise whose properties were separated by thousands of miles of land and water, the development and application of managerial techniques, and the gradual loosening of ownership's control over operations as the American managers won the confidence of the shareholders.

That the company was able to survive adversity—the crises brought by overexpansion, erratic markets, depression, drought, and settlement—can be attributed to its staying power, which is to say its capital reserves; that it was able to adjust to changing times can be credited to the foresight, wisdom, and devotion of its leaders, who placed the organization's welfare ahead of their own. An additional consideration here is the long tenure enjoyed by the top echelons of the American agents, for during the sixty-nine years of Scottish ownership only five men filled the manager's position, and during the same period only five men served as superintendent at the "home" ranch in Motley County, Texas.

In view of the Matador's success—the smoothly functioning organization, the fine herds, the substantial profits and high dividend rate announced at mid-century—one wonders why the owners sold when they did. The facts which might provide the answer remain obscure. As one company official pointed out, each shareholder undoubtedly had his own reasons for selling, and among these must have been the price offered for the shares. Certainly taxation—on income and on land as the latter's value increased—was a consideration; in addition, the competition from smaller operators whose flexibility enabled them to react rapidly to changing market and weather conditions was being felt by all large ranches with their huge overhead. At any rate, when the Matador went into voluntary liquidation in 1951, there ended a way of life for scores of people, and the last living symbol of nineteenth century British investment in the western cattle industry passed into history.

Although many people have been of assistance throughout this study, I owe a particular debt of gratitude to W. C. Holden for introducing me to the Matador Papers in the Southwest Collection at Texas Technological College, to John Mackenzie for authorizing the use of the company's records in preparing the Matador history, to R. H. Fulton for donating to the Collection the files at the Alamositas headquarters and for providing the funds for the shipment of the Dundee and Denver records to the College, to W. B. Gates for his interest and encouragement in this project, and to the late Walter P. Webb for his insistence that I tell this story as I have seen it. Maurice J. Reilly recognized, over three decades ago, the importance of preserving the ranch records at the Matador headquarters, and he and his successor in the superintendency at the home ranch, John V. Stevens, have facilitated the transfer of those items to the Collection; Johnny Stevens has been particularly helpful in providing information on the late years of the ranch's history and on the postliquidation period. I am especially grateful to S. V. Connor and R. Sylvan Dunn for locating, collecting, and making available the sources utilized in this study, and to Owen W. McWhorter for reading the manuscript, a document which was typed and checked by Mrs. Mary E. Randal and Myrna Stephenson at no little inconvenience to themselves. Grants from Texas Technological College research funds and from the Texas Tech Foundation gave impetus to the project and sped its completion.

All illustrations not otherwise credited are from the Southwest Collection at Texas Technological College.

WILLIAM M. PEARCE

Lubbock, Texas

Contents

Illustrations

xiii

Maps

The Matador Land and Cattle Company

~1~

Scotsmen and Shorthorns

THE RANCHE seems to me to be quite capable of carrying at least 80,000 cattle . . . and grazing them well. It has abundant supply of water, convenient for grass, and ample shelter for stock during hard weather; is at an elevation where nights are cool and cattle can rest; at a latitude where winters are comparatively safe. It is without doubt one of the best watered, sheltered and healthiest Ranches in Texas.[1]

So wrote Thomas Lawson, a Scottish migrant, following his visit to a cattle range on the plains of western Texas in 1882. Employed by a group of Dundee businessmen to examine and report on lands and herds offered to investors in Britain, Lawson furnished an accurate description of the property inspected and a sanguine prediction that excellent and rapidly increasing returns could be expected from the ranch if it were secured at fair value and managed judiciously.

The wedge-shaped range traversed by Lawson lay within the upper drainage system of the Pease River. Covering most of Motley and extending into Floyd, Cottle, and Dickens counties, its one and one-half million acres included those features of land relief, soils, vegetation, and climate characteristic of the rolling plains of northwestern Texas. From the base of the cap rock[2] the

[1] *Prospectus*, The Matador Land and Cattle Company, 2.
[2] As used here, the term "cap rock" refers to the exposed edge of the foundation rock of the High Plains. Along this line erosion has cut away the surface to

3

land fell away eastward in rolling grasslands, low ridges, and broken, eroded hills, varying in elevation from three thousand feet in the west to two thousand feet along the North, Middle, and South Pease rivers and their tributaries. The red and reddish brown sands and sandy loams, developed under the climatic conditions of the subhumid Southwest, were fairly free of stony material and consolidated formations, although in some places beds of gypsum and limestone accumulation occurred. The combination of soils, elevation, and an annual rainfall averaging twenty-one inches supported the growth of bluestem, buffalo, and grama grasses which, in addition to providing excellent grazing, served as a protective mantle against wind and water erosion.

Actually, the region was little known to civilized man until the decade prior to Lawson's inspection. It is possible that Coronado, misled by the Turk, gazed from the rim of the *Llano Estacado* over the great grasslands, which were to remain untouched by the plow during the next three and one-half centuries; and one might speculate that Juan de Zaldivar's tattooed slave woman, running away "down the barrancas" might have crossed the Pease drainage in her flight toward the rising sun, reportedly only to be picked up by Moscoso's party months later.[3] Certainly the *Comancheros* and Comanches, in their mutually profitable barter during the middle years of the nineteenth century, found the cap rock an ideal meeting place. Here, where the headward erosion of eastward flowing streams had gouged deep canyons into the *Llano Estacado*, the traders could find water and shelter. To these rendezvous the far-ranging Indians brought the products of the hunt and the booty from their forays into Mexican and American settlements; to temporary depots and trading stations—the caves along the canyon walls—rolled the wooden-wheeled carts from the Pecos and the Río Grande.[4]

---

leave an east-facing escarpment with a height of from five hundred to one thousand feet.

[3] Herbert E. Bolton, *Coronado, Knight of Pueblos and Plains*, 271, 356.

With wood, water, and shelter, the traders carried on negotiations in comfort and safety. And when pursuit threatened, the Indians scattered and the New Mexicans took their escape route across the Staked Plain. Doubtless the ill-advised and poorly conducted Texan–Santa Fe Expedition struggled across the range in its search for an ascent to the level of the *Llano* in 1841.[5]

In October and November, 1871, Captain Clarence Mauck, a squadron commander under Colonel Ranald Mackenzie, conducted a reconnaissance in force between the upper Brazos and Red rivers. This was a prelude to his commander's vigorous campaigns of 1872 and 1874, which brought an end to the Indian wars in Texas.[6] With the Comanche menace removed, the buffalo hunters moved in to complete the slaughter of the great bison herd of the southern plains. Operating originally from Dodge City and then from a more convenient base, Fort Griffin, the hunters founded the first settlement in Motley County, a trading post called TeePee City, located at the confluence of the Middle Pease River and TeePee Creek. Located by hide dealers representing Lee and Reynolds of Dodge City, the post never flourished as did Rath City and Hide Town, both of which lay one hundred miles to the south and near the center of the winter grazing area.[7] Even the careers of these settlements were brief, for by 1878 the herds were gone, victims of the Sharps rifle.

With the removal of the buffalo and the confinement of the Indian, the vast grasslands of plains and prairies lay unused, unharvested, safe—a windfall to cowmen who, crowded by settlements and their own expanding herds, sought new space and free grass in the late 1870's. Probing from the leading edge of this movement were the small, independent cattlemen who lo-

---

[4] Robert G. Carter, *On the Border with MacKenzie*, 161.

[5] H. Bailey Carroll, "The Texan Santa Fe Trail," *Panhandle-Plains Historical Review*, Vol. XXIV (1951), 134–143.

[6] Carter, *On the Border with MacKenzie*, 205–206. Cf. J. Evetts Haley, *Fort Concho and the Texas Frontier*, 200–26.

[7] Harry H. Campbell, *Early History of Motley County*, 13, 35. Cf. Carl C. Rister, *Fort Griffin On the Texas Frontier*, 172–73.

cated the water essential to their cattle and established range rights on the grasslands adjacent to streams.[8]

Among the first arrivals in Motley County was Joe Browning, who drove a small herd of Texas cattle from Young County and laid claim to a half-section of land and a dugout at Ballard Springs, named for a buffalo hunter who had made the site his headquarters.[9] Later in 1878, S. R. Coggin and Pitser Chisum, scouting the breaks east of the cap rock, found Frank Collinson, an unemployed buffalo hunter who had lingered in the region, and learning that Collinson knew the country "perfectly, from the Concho to the Arkansas," hired him to drive their recently acquired herd to the head of Tongue River. The eight thousand cattle which they had just acquired from the remnants of John Chisum's herd along the Pecos River in New Mexico were a good grade, a cross between Texas cows and purebred Shorthorn bulls. Earmarked with the "jinglebob,"[10] the eight thousand head were driven in two trail herds from Fort Sumner, New Mexico, by way of Taiban, Portales Springs, the Yellow Houses, Spring Lake, Running Water Draw, and Blanco Canyon to the head of Tongue River. Collinson led the first herd and R. K. (Bob) Wylie the second. Through the winter of 1878–79 the cattle were loose-herded by a crew who lived in line camps, a series of dugouts, and who rode daily to turn back the cattle toward the center of the range. Early in 1879 corrals and a camp were built near Roaring Springs, and a second camp was established near TeePee City.[11]

[8] Frank Collinson, "The First Cattle Ranch on Tongue River, Motley County, Texas," MS, 3.

[9] Through numerous springs and seeps which appear along the base of the cap rock the overflow from the High Plains ground-water reservoir is discharged. By headward erosion, the canyons and ravines forming the headwaters of the Red, the Pease, and the Brazos rivers have cut into the High Plains, exposing the water-bearing strata. Most of the springs occur within three miles of the cap rock, but a few appear along the streams at greater distances. William L. Broadhurst, *Ground Water in High Plains in Texas*, 6.

[10] So called from the effect achieved by cutting the lower portion of the ear so that the ear hung from the head only by a thin strip of hide.

Among the herds which followed was one driven by "Hank" Campbell. Henry Harrison Campbell was born in Cumberland County, North Carolina, on August 31, 1840. With his parents he moved to Texas in 1854; during the Civil War he served with the Twentieth Texas Regiment, seeing action in Texas, Arkansas, and the Indian Territory. Wounded three times, he was invalided home after a severe injury in a battle near Honey Springs, Arkansas. Following convalescence, Campbell became a cowman, gaining experience as a trail hand on drives to New Orleans, Dodge City, and Nevada.[12] By speculation and small drives of his own, he put together a herd which he took to Chicago in 1878 and sold at a handsome profit. This trip proved an eventful one, for while in Chicago, Campbell was invited, along with other cowmen, to a luncheon given by a group of bankers. During the course of the meal, it became known that Campbell had realized a gross profit of fourteen dollars a head on the cattle for which he had paid nine dollars each in Texas.

One of the hosts, Colonel Alfred Markham Britton, was particularly impressed by these figures and by Campbell's bearing and evident knowledge of the cattle business. After the luncheon, Britton made a point of talking with the Texan, and as a result of their conversation an agreement was reached whereby Campbell would secure land in the western part of his state, stock the range through the Colonel's financing, and manage the ranch. With a roll of Britton's money, Campbell hurried back to Texas, bought a small herd, and started in search of a suitable range.[13]

In 1879 the Matador Cattle Company was established and incorporated under the laws of Texas. According to one account, the company was made up of five men, each of whom subscribed $10,000 to create the capital. The five were Britton, Campbell,

---

[11] Collinson, "The First Cattle Ranch on Tongue River, Motley County, Texas," 5.

[12] *Handbook of Texas*, I, 286.

[13] Kansas City *Times*, May 27, 1941.

7

Spottswood W. Lomax, and John W. Nichols of Fort Worth, and a Mr. Cata, Britton's brother-in-law, of New York.[14] Lomax, reported to have been "an enthusiast in Spanish literature," gave the ranch its name.[15]

Campbell's first ranch house was the dugout at Ballard Springs, the rights to which were secured from Browning. Here the first cattle obtained by the new company were received, and here, in December, 1879, John Dawson sold to the Matador a herd of thirteen hundred head branded "V" on the right side. Additional smaller brands were absorbed as they were brought into the country, including the "T41" and "NN" stock driven from Gonzales County in southern Texas, and, in 1881, the Jinglebob herd, purchased from Coggin and Wylie.[16]

With newly acquired herds the purchaser usually "inherited" the range rights claimed by the seller. In the absence of actual landowners, and since statutory laws and the means of their enforcement were remote, a body of custom developed to keep disorder and confusion at a minimum. Range rights and privileges were established by occupation and were recognized as long as a claimant utilized his range and was strong enough to discourage interlopers. It was generally accepted that a rancher controlling a stream or one of its banks held range rights on the land extending away from the stream to the divide separating

[14] Grace C. McDowell, "The Matador Ranch." This unpublished MS, based on information received from Harry H. Campbell, son of "Hank" Campbell, in an interview in 1936, is in the archives of the Panhandle-Plains Historical Society, Canyon, Texas. Cf., Campbell, *Early History of Motley County*, 28.

[15] Lomax's proclivity for Spanish names is illustrated by the fact that in 1883 he and Britton organized and named the Espuela Cattle Company; in 1884, when this company was sold to British investors and became the Espuela Land and Cattle Company, Ltd., Lomax was named resident manager, a post he held until 1889. William Curry Holden, *The Spur Ranch*, 20.

[16] The Matador branded their first calf crop "50M" to suggest the capital of the company. Subsequently, the "50" brand was used only on horses, and the cattle brand became the "V." This "V" is distinctive, so much so that it is called the "Matador V," rather than the "Flying V" or "Running V" or any other standard variation of the "V."

his stream basin from an adjacent watershed. Efforts were made to keep cattle within recognized ranges by a system of patrolling called "line riding," since no fences were present to separate the holdings of neighboring cattlemen and cattle were no respecters of boundaries. Line riders, moving daily along the borders of ranges, drifted the cattle toward the range claimed by their respective owners. The acquisition of title to lands bordering the watering places strengthened range rights by giving to the land owner a legal position on which to base his claims to privilege.

Under this system and with these practices flourishing, Campbell and his associates extended their holdings and by 1882 claimed a range covering the million and one-half acres referred to in the *Prospectus*, with one hundred thousand acres on water fronts held in fee simple. In addition to purchasing cattle and land, Campbell undertook to build a two-room house at Ballard Springs. The lumber was hauled from Fort Griffin, 110 miles to the east, and the window frames from Fort Worth, 300 miles away. The house was completed early in 1880.[17]

With few expenses, ample water, good grass, and high beef prices, the early years of the new ranch's existence were good ones. Between fifteen and twenty thousand calves were branded annually; and when the Texas and Pacific railroad reached Colorado City in 1881, the first cattle marketed by the Matador company were driven to the new railhead, some 110 miles south of Ballard Springs. At the end of the twelve-day drive, Campbell received seventy-five dollars a head for the steers.

With the ranch books showing profit and with more land in western Texas to be "developed" for cattle raising, Britton and his associates prepared to take advantage of the high prices which foreign investors were paying for range interests. British capitalists in particular, lured by the promise of bonanzas in land, lumber, mines, and cattle, were pouring venture money into the American West, and, oddly enough, a generous portion of this flood came from the Scots, a people famous for caution in

17 McDowell, "The Matador Ranch."

money matters. For a small region like Scotland to be able to spare, even for a time, tens of millions sterling was one of the paradoxes in the history of nineteenth-century commerce.[18] Yet the people of this country, familiar with cattle raising, were among the first to foresee the possibilities in western America. As early as 1870 the Scottish American Investment Company was founded; this organization financed a number of cattle companies in the Great Plains, among them the Wyoming Cattle Ranch Company and Western Ranches, Limited. Still another syndicate, the Scottish American Mortgage Company, established the Prairie Cattle Company, one of the largest enterprises in the West, in 1880.

The fantastic earnings reported by these and other companies during the 1870's prompted the British government to send a Parliamentary commission to the United States to investigate the range cattle industry; and when the two commissioners, Albert Pell and Clare Read, reported in 1880 that profits of 33 per cent could be expected in American ranching, the supply of investment money increased.[19] Among the contributors were the Dundee businessmen who were approached by Britton early in 1882 and who, with caution tempering enthusiasm, employed Thomas Lawson to appraise the range and properties owned by the Matador Cattle Company of Texas. Following the receipt of Lawson's report, which placed a valuation on the land, improvements, and livestock at between $1,200,000 and $1,300,000, the Scots entered into a provisional agreement with Britton on September 28, 1882. Signing the memorandum with the Colonel, who held power of attorney to act for the Texas company, were William Robertson, an engineer, Robert Fleming, George Hal-

[18] "Scottish Capital Abroad," *Blackwood's Edinburgh Magazine*, Vol. CXXXVI (1884), 476.

[19] For an excellent account of the British-American cattle companies, see W. Turrentine Jackson's contribution to Maurice Frink, W. Turrentine Jackson, and Agnes Wright Spring's *When Grass Was King*, 135–330.

ley, and John Robertson, merchants, all of Dundee, and William Smith of Benholm Castle, Kincardinshire.[20]

By the terms of the agreement, the Scots undertook to incorporate within three months the Matador Land and Cattle Company, Limited, a joint-stock company, under the Companies Acts, 1862 to 1880, and to purchase on behalf of the new organization the holdings of Britton and his associates for the sum of $1,250,000.[21] Other provisions called for Britton to act as American manager for five years from the first day of November, 1882, and to serve as one of the directors. William Fife Sommerville, a merchant of Dundee, was named assistant manager, and Henry H. Campbell was selected to be ranch superintendent. It was stipulated that Sommerville would engage in no activity on behalf of another cattle company during the period of his employment and that Campbell would engage in no other business, trade, or profession while working for the Dundee corporation.[22] Attached to the agreement was a schedule describing the properties as "about 100,000 acres of land held in fee simple and situated in Motley, Cottle and Dickens Counties, Texas . . . all range and other rights and privileges in or over 1,500,000 acres, . . . 40,000 head of cattle, 14 yoke of oxen, 265 horses and fencing improvements."

Initially it was contemplated that the capital of the company would be £300,000, however, during November, Fleming, Sommerville, and a Patrick Carnegie visited the ranch and placed a valuation of $1,340,525 on the properties. Since this exceeded the purchase price by some $90,000, and since the desirability of adding to the land and livestock in the near future was apparent, the capital was fixed at £400,000 in forty thousand shares at £10 each.[23]

[20] Copy, Memorandum of Agreement.

[21] *Ibid.* In British money, the price was £255,102, since the pound sterling was valued at $4.90 in the negotiations.

[22] Campbell ratified this arrangement involving his personal services in Fort Worth on November 16, 1882.

[23] *Prospectus,* 4.

On December 1, 1882, at a meeting of the directors of the proposed company in Dundee, the Memorandum and Articles of Association were approved. Voting approval were William Robertson, John Robertson, George Halley, and William Smith. These four, along with Fleming and Britton, both in America at the date of signing, were to constitute the first board of directors. Entering the meeting after approval of the Memorandum and the Articles and signing the two documents as "subscribers" were Angus MacIntyre, George Carmichael, William Gibson, and David Halley, all of Dundee.[24]

On December 3, the directors of the Matador Cattle Company of Texas, in session in Fort Worth, voted to dispose of their property, and on December 23, Britton and Lomax signed the bill of sale.[25] On December 4, 1882, the new company was incorporated, and on December 11 the first board meeting was held at the company's office, 104 Commercial Street, Dundee. Here the directors elected William Robertson chairman, appointed Alexander Mackay of the firm of Mess and Mackay, Chartered Accountants, to be secretary, and named James C. Robertson, Chartered Accountant, Dundee, as auditor.[26] The British Linen Company, with offices in London and Dundee, had already been utilized in banking operations and became the official bankers in Great Britain for the new corporation, while all funds exchanged between the United States and Great Britain went through the banking house of Jesup, Paton and Company of

[24] Board Minute Book, The Matador Land and Cattle Company, Ltd., I, 1.

[25] Copy, Bill of Sale, Matador Cattle Company of Texas to Matador Land and Cattle Company, Ltd. The original was filed on February 15, 1883, and was recorded on February 19 at Seymour, Baylor County, Texas, since Motley, Cottle, Dickens, and Floyd counties were then attached to Baylor County. Motley County Records, I, 262–69. In 1891, when Motley County was organized, the records were transferred to Matador, the county seat. Ordinarily, a bill of sale is used to evidence the transfer of the title to personal property and is filed but not recorded; a deed is customarily used to evidence the conveyance of the title to real property and is both filed and recorded. The instrument here referred to conveyed land and transferred cattle, so was a deed and a bill of sale.

[26] Board Minute Book, I, 2.

New York. In Texas an account was opened in the City National Bank of Fort Worth. The office of Hendry and Pollock, Solicitors, Dundee, represented by Andrew Hendry, became the company's law agent in Scotland, while Thomas DeWitt Cuyler, a Philadelphia attorney, served in a similar capacity in America.

The Memorandum of Association stated the objects for which the company was established; and while these were listed in fifteen numbered paragraphs, all bore directly on one purpose—the raising of cattle. The Articles of Association, the constitution, served with few alterations throughout the company's history. This document fixed the capital at £400,000, limited membership in the corporation to those holding shares, authorized each member one vote for each share held by him, with a limit of one thousand votes to a single member, and vested all managerial responsibilities and administrative powers in a board of directors of from four to seven persons. The directors were subjected, in the exercise of their authority, only to regulations prescribed by law and by the company in annual general meetings or in extraordinary general meetings. A significant reservation was the right of the board to approve the party or parties to whom a member wished to transfer his shares and to decline to register any transfer not meeting this approval.

At the December 11 meeting the directors resolved to allot shares in the company to the extent of the capital and proceeded to assign the entire forty thousand shares among the applicants. Ten thousand shares were reserved for Britton and his associates in the Texas company in partial payment of the purchase price, and the remaining thirty thousand shares were divided among 450 applicants. By custom and law, the assignees were not required to pay the full value on each share at the time of purchase. It was proposed in the *Prospectus* that from five to six pounds per share would be called up during the first year and that the balance would be raised by the sale of debenture bonds bearing 5 per cent interest. The Articles of Association limited the borrowing power of the company to the amount of its unpaid capital and authorized the offering of the organization's assets in land and cattle as security for loans obtained through debentures.[27] By February, 1884, the shareholders had paid six pounds per share on the forty thousand shares.

The "installment buying" of stock doubtless encouraged participation in joint-stock ventures on the part of small investors and persons of modest means, for among the list of initial shareholders were persons from a wide range of occupations; included were bankers, clerks, doctors, waiters, ministers, distillers, hatters, spinners, bootmakers, lawyers, auctioneers, and farmers. The greater number of these resided in Dundee and vicinity.[28] William Robertson, with 900 shares, held the largest single block of stock, while several persons held only 10 shares each. Had all the members holding fewer than 100 shares each pooled their strength, they could have controlled the company. However, these people seemed content to leave the management of affairs in the hands of the directors, who held only 3,730 shares among them.[29]

Even before the formal transfer of property took place, Britton and Campbell convinced Fleming that the purchase of additional acreage lying within the range was essential to the protection of the company's range privileges. The fact that several large blocks of land lay within the perimeter of the grazing area brought apprehension to the directors and, fearing that these might be stocked by the owners or by lessees, the board approved the purchase of 203,000 acres and a herd of 22,000 head early in 1883.

Since the substantial outlay for these lands and cattle far exceeded the corporation's cash assets, the board made arrangements with the British Linen Company for a loan of £60,000 on the personal security of the directors. This display of the board

[27] Articles of Association, 13–15.
[28] Board Minute Book, I, 3–16.
[29] In addition to William Robertson (900), these were: Fleming, 825; Halley, 705; Smith, 700; John Robertson, 600.

14

members' willingness to underwrite personally the company's indebtedness was the first of several such occasions and typified the spirit and action which were to sustain the company in years ahead when nothing stood between the organization and bankruptcy but the resolve and reputation of its officials.

The first purchase price and subsequent outlays for land and cattle drove the gross expenditure during the first four months in excess of the authorized capital. To meet this situation, the directors could have followed one of two paths—to sell off as much of the livestock as would be necessary to bring the expenditures within the capital, or to create additional capital in order to square the account. Favoring the latter course, the directors recommended that the capital be increased to £500,000 by the creation of ten thousand new shares at £10 each, these shares to be treated *pari passu* with the shares of the first issue. The resolution to alter the Memorandum and Articles of Association in keeping with the board's recommendation was approved at an extraordinary session of the shareholders following their first statutory meeting on April 3, 1883, at Dundee and was confirmed at a second extraordinary meeting on May 1, at which time the directors were instructed to issue ten thousand new shares at £10 each.[30] Later in the year it was decided to allot the new issue among the shareholders on the basis of one share for each four shares held, and early in 1884 the new shares were offered at par in the proportions named.[31]

Originally, all lands owned by the company were held in the names of William Robertson, Fleming, Smith, and Thomas De-

[30] Report of Proceedings, First General or Statutory Meeting of the Shareholders, Matador Land and Cattle Co., Ltd., 8–10.

[31] First Annual Report, Matador Land and Cattle Co., Ltd., 6. This report actually covered the accounts from November 1, 1882, through December 31, 1883, a fourteen-month period, since the Scots had opened books and assumed tentative control of the ranch on November 1, 1882. The annual reports were published early in each year and covered the accounts for the previous calendar year; they were presented to the shareholders at annual meetings, usually in February or March, held at Lamb's Hotel, Dundee.

Witt Cuyler, the Philadelphia lawyer whose chief functions were to examine land titles and advise the Scots concerning laws which affected the company's operations in the United States. While nothing in the Texas laws in 1882 prohibited the procurement and possession of realty by foreigners, a sentiment hostile to the acquisition and holding of land by aliens was rising in the state; and the directors, with commendable caution, deemed it better that the company's lands be conveyed to and held by trustees, each of whom deposited a declaration of trust with the company to avoid complications in the event of his death.[32]

With the transfer of property to the Scottish directorate, the real headquarters of the Matador Ranch became Dundee instead of Ballard Springs in that the board, meeting frequently, established tight control over all phases of the company's operations and reserved to its members many of the functions and decisions which the boards of other cattle companies delegated to managers and overseers in America. Behind the directors' close surveillance was the fundamental premise that their Texas venture was a business—a long-range one—and that it was deserving of their best professional efforts and vigilance. Knowing well the effects which erratic markets and capricious weather might have on a year's balance sheet, they remained confident of their ability to establish policy and make decisions which would be advantageous to the shareholders. Annually one question was asked: "What are the company's requirements as to income?" The answer, the sum of anticipated American expenses plus payments to retire debts, served as the basic guide to the year's cattle sales and was the goal toward which the year's work was aimed. Favorable weather, good grass, and satisfactory market prices might provide an income to allow additions to a reserve fund and even permit a dividend declaration. However, these last two benefits were of secondary consideration in the determination of the annual requirement.

To effect the desired control by Dundee, an efficient system of

[32] Ernest Wallace, *Charles DeMorse, Pioneer Editor and Statesman*, 203–206.

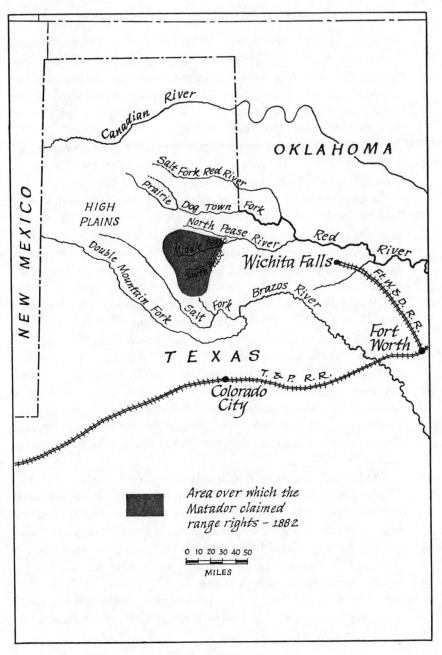

The Matador Range, 1882

communication was created. All official correspondence flowed through the office of Alexander Mackay. To the secretary the board gave its directions, and these were transmitted to the manager in Fort Worth. There the duty of carrying out instructions fell on William Sommerville, since Britton was engaged in new land development schemes and was not in the office regularly. The assistant manager in turn passed on orders to Campbell. Reports from the ranch passed through the same channel to Mackay to be consolidated for presentation to the board.

To Campbell, who had been retained by the new organization because of his experience and intimate knowledge of the range, the change in ownership marked a startling turn from a way of life to which he was accustomed. From complete freedom to run the ranch as he saw fit and with minimum correspondence, he came, after 1882, to operate under a set of principles in bookkeeping, tallying, and reporting which he found, at best, irritating. Held strictly accountable for all sums disbursed and received at the ranch, the superintendent was obliged to advise the Fort Worth office of all payments for stores, wages, and incidentals as they were made, and to forward the ranch payroll to the manager on the first of each month. In addition, the board required frequent reports on the health of the herd, range conditions, and progress in branding, collecting, and marketing cattle—matters to which the directors gave attention in their weekly meetings.

Particularly annoying to Campbell was the board's order that all purchases and contracts exceeding five hundred dollars must have the approval of both manager and superintendent. Prone to disregard this stipulation at first, Campbell purchased 250 bulls in 1883 without assent from Britton's office and, unimpressed by Sommerville's reminder of the company's attitude, bought 34 more graded bulls early in 1884. The latter action, while not repudiated by the board, brought a direct reprimand from the secretary, who stated that "the business must be carried on under certain principles, and all officers of the Company must conform to these."[33]

Unfortunately, such occurrences created animosity between Campbell and Sommerville, a feeling which was heightened on Campbell's part by the board's insistence on sending its instructions through the Fort Worth office. Since these were interpreted and elaborated on by Sommerville, they appeared to Campbell to be orders from the assistant manager. The fact that Sommerville had had some experience in the cattle business in northern Britain mattered little to the superintendent. What did count was the assistant manager's unfamiliarity with the problems of American ranching, a fact which loomed large in Campbell's eyes.

Such circumstances did nothing to lessen the board's difficulties in persuading the superintendent to conform to policy. Campbell's preoccupation with chores on the ranch, his absence from headquarters for days at a time while supervising range operations, and his failure to appreciate the reasons for the directors' interest in detailed information—all contributed to lapses in reporting events at Ballard Springs. An opportunity for Mackay to explain the board's position and to define Campbell's place in the organization came late in 1884. The year had seen prices tumble and confidence in cattle companies shaken; the directors were uneasy when the fall roundup began, and when the superintendent's sole message in November contained only a protest against Sommerville's "interference" with the trail drive and no word regarding the cattle, the uneasiness turned to anxiety. Fortunately, sales were successful, and Mackay's letter to Campbell early in December reflected the board's relief at receipt of good news as well as its insistence on discipline:

> For weeks the Board had been sending enquiries as to sales and pressing for despatches in shipping and [on November 7]

[33] Mackay to Campbell, July 10, 1884.

were without information as to what was being done. They feared that you, in the very laudable desire of having the cattle as fat as possible, were holding them back so long that the chances were some of your herds would be dispersed by storm and we should have had to go to the stockholders with an explanation similar to that of last year. Now that would have been most disastrous for the reputation of the company, for I must tell you that the shareholders of cattle companies in this country are at the present time timid and distrustful, ready to take fright at all kinds of rumours. When I tell you that shares of the Texas Cattle Company which less than two years ago were selling at $25 *premium* are at this moment selling at $1½ *under* par, you will understand that cattle shares are not being strongly held; and while our own are still $2 to $3 above par, any unfavourable rumours regarding dividends on calf branding would send them down. You will understand, then, how anxious the Board were that shipments should be made in good time. Fortunately, you have managed to allay all anxiety by the expeditious manner in which you have shipped after making a beginning, and had you acquainted the Managers sooner of the dates when you would actually drive, the Board would have felt less anxious about the matter. In considering this and all other important points affecting the Company, you must try to put yourself in the position of the Board placed thousands of miles away from a property for the management of which they are responsible, and to recognize that the very fullest information must be continually sent to enable them to have, as it were, the ranch and its workings under their own eyes. . . . The Managers will tell you *when* and *what* to drive, but *how* to drive is your business.[34]

On the first of each month the manager mailed the secretary a copy of the accounts, bank statements, and vouchers for the previous month. The accounts included a statement of petty cash expenditures, deposits, wages, and total ledger footings. These documents, sent by registered mail, were expected in Mackay's office within two weeks, the usual time for mail movements between Fort Worth and Dundee. In the secretary's office

[34] Mackay to Campbell, December 8, 1884.

the accounts were audited again; discrepancies called for an explanation by the manager, even though the amounts involved were less than expenses incurred in establishing corrections.

In order that the manager and the superintendent each might prepare an annual report, the books of the Fort Worth and the Ballard Springs offices were closed at the end of November. In his report Campbell summarized the work of the year, dealt with the condition of the herd and prospects for grass in the coming year, and set forth recommendations concerning the utilization of pastures and installation of improvements on the ranch. Sommerville's communications, occasional and annual, were more comprehensive than Campbell's and revealed a sensitive appreciation of the board's wishes. Systematically arranged, they covered the weather, rainfall, grass, the market, land prices, quarantine laws, transportation facilities, and any development which had affected or might affect the company's properties and operations.

At the beginning of each calendar year, Mackay prepared the report submitted by the directors at the annual meeting of the shareholders. In format this published document varied little throughout the years. It contained first a narrative of cattle sales, followed by a statement on the calf crop, a description of the company's property, and summaries of the range, improvements, land sales, and revenue for the year. This last paragraph held the directors' recommendation concerning dividends. Announcements of a general nature came next; ordinarily these had to do with the issuance of shares, the sale of debentures, and the expiration of terms of directors. Last were the profit and loss account, showing payments and receipts for the year, and the balance sheet, listing the liabilities and assets of the organization.

For the transmission of urgent messages such as the report of a sale, the request for a decision, or the sending of an order, cable service was utilized. Since cablegrams came to be an item of considerable expense, the practice of sending messages in code was begun in 1888. This practice was adopted not only for economy but also for security, and elaborately prepared code books containing hundreds of words were treated with maximum security precautions in each office. Furthermore, frequent revisions of the code were made as new subject matter arose.[35] Each cable was confirmed by a letter in which the content of the message was quoted and its meaning stated. Likewise, the receipt of any message, whether by letter or cable, was acknowledged by the recipient in his next letter to the sender.

Each year Alexander Mackay visited the company properties during the fall shipping season. His journey was in the nature of an inspection, and as a representative of the board, he was accorded every courtesy that the manager's office and the ranch could provide. During his stay in America, he made whatever personal contacts were necessary to the company's business in New York, spent several days in Chicago, where Matador cattle were customarily marketed, and, on the ranch, traveled over the entire range. His acquaintance thus acquired with the people and the land made him invaluable to the company; it is little wonder that he rose from the position of secretary, with a small financial interest in the syndicate—150 shares in 1882—to the chairmanship of the board and the control of thousands of shares of stock in the twentieth century.

Ordinarily one of the directors accompanied the secretary on his annual journey to the ranch. This not only fostered a keener interest in the property on the part of the Dundee people, but gave the employees in America a feeling of belonging to an organization whose governing body had a personal interest in the welfare of those whom it hired. In addition, these visits provided the subject for conversations and the substance from

---

[35] The code was of the simplest kind, with one word standing for a frequently used phrase or figure. As an example, the following cablegram was sent by Sommerville to Mackay on February 26, 1889: "Sold tabret twos tierce delivered Giles net." Decoded, this said that Sommerville had sold two thousand two-year-old steers at $15.00 a head delivered at Giles, Donley County, Texas.

which tales were spun on both sides of the Atlantic. Long after the tweed-clad Scotsmen had left the windy, sun-drenched plains for the windy, chilly shores of the North Sea, the ranch hands had something to talk about—the dress, the manners, and the burry speech of the visitors. And on the banks of the Firth of Tay were displayed photographs of roundup scenes—a crew at the chuck wagon, a calf being branded with the rounded ∨, and always a group picture of the hands, guns and knives ostentatiously revealed. At the next shareholders meeting following his visit, the director gave a report of his experiences and his appraisal of conditions on the range. By such means—frequent letters, cables, and visits—the board in Dundee regulated the business of the company.

As early as 1884 it became apparent that the size of the Matador range was far less than had been assumed originally. By a careful scrutiny of maps, Sommerville found that, even after purchases in 1883, the company could claim grazing rights over only nine hundred thousand acres. This discovery spurred the board to greater efforts toward the acquisition of desirable lands within and along the borders of the range and the securing of grass leases on state and private properties. This escape from the predicament of an overstocked range was preferred to the alternative solution—disposing of a sizable part of the herd.

The consolidation program was characterized by both purchase and exchange of lands. In the former, many parcels were bought from settlers who had pre-empted one-section blocks and who welcomed the opportunity to sell for cash. Values of such tracts varied with location, soil, and terrain, but prices paid averaged $1.50 an acre during the 1880's. In all cases the company required a perfect title in hand before closing transactions.

In 1885 the Scots entered into their largest trade, an exchange of property with the Pitchfork Land and Cattle Company, whose range lay to the east of the Matador. This involved the transfer of 11,840 acres to the Dundee concern in return for 10,933 acres and a payment of $1.25 an acre for the 907 acres difference. Such trades enabled both parties to shorten fence lines and reduce distances from pastures to headquarters.[36]

The rights to graze cattle on the public domain were secured through agents in Austin. With thousands of acres available for leasing early in the 1880's, little difficulty was experienced in obtaining grass rentals on huge tracts of state-owned lands, for which the company paid nine cents an acre a year for a five-year lease. By the end of 1884, Matador cattle grazed on 216,767 acres of Texas school lands. However, as the tide of settlement moved westward, "nesters" took up the more valuable sections, so that at the end of the decade the company's leases from the state covered only 146,000 acres. Correspondingly, lands rented from private owners increased from 36,000 acres in 1884 to about 100,000 acres in 1891.[37]

The cattle industry's transition from the open range to fenced range is nowhere more strikingly illustrated than on the Matador property; until 1884, when the directors voted to erect a fence between their own and the Espuela ranges, the only man-made obstruction to the movement of cattle was a fifty-one-mile barbed wire fence along the northern boundary of the ranch. Within three years a network of wires laced the range, confining various classes of cattle to specific pastures and excluding the stock of other owners from Matador grass. Following their experiences with the Espuela people, the Matador entered into similar arrangements with the Pitchfork and the Kit Carter companies. Ordinarily, construction costs of a common fence were shared equally by both parties. Common or "outside" fences served a purpose in addition to confining cattle to particular ranges: they discouraged trail herds of other brands from crossing the range.

The early fence lines constructed by hands assigned the chore were located with more regard to convenience than to an accu-

[36] Sommerville to Cuyler, January 12, 1886.
[37] Ninth Annual Report, 6.

rate survey or measurement. With instructions to build from a given point toward a distant landmark, the fencing crew sometimes veered in one direction or another as the reference point was masked by hills or vegetation. Likewise, arroyos, steep hills, and bluffs were avoided; the crew merely built around these obstacles and attempted to re-establish the line along its original course. In all likelihood fencing parties little dreamed that their departures from designated lines would result in arguments, lawsuits, and expense later on.

Even before the entire Matador range was enclosed by outside lines, fencing activities were begun on interior lands. The first subdivision to be defined by the dull-barbed, wide-ribbon wire was the horse pasture of some forty sections near Ballard Springs. The beef pasture, proposed as early as 1883, was intended to isolate steers being matured for shipment to market "so they could be freed from the constant disturbance and excitement incident to calf branding." Similarly, cows and their calves would not be disturbed during the fall roundup when the steers were gathered for shipment.

Fencing operations included the construction of corrals for branding and holding purposes. Whereas the stringing of a wire fence was a task which could be given to any ranch hand, the building of a corral required the knowledge and skill of a carpenter. Because of the expense involved in labor, transportation, and materials, and since a corral was a permanent installation, considerable attention was given to the choice of sites and the selection of suitable timbers. When Campbell felt a corral was needed in a particular area, he would bring the matter to Mackay's attention during the secretary's visit to the ranch. If one of the board members was present, the superintendent would emphasize the need and point out the site he had in mind. Upon his return to Scotland, Mackay would present the request to the directors. When a decision was reached, a report would go to Sommerville, who would inform the superintendent. In case of approval, Campbell notified the manager of the material needed and sent along a sketch with dimensions distinctly noted. The Fort Worth office then advertised for bids, requesting that interested parties submit their estimates to include delivery at the railhead nearest the corral. Supplies were then freighted from the railroad to the construction site.[38]

Conflicting claims arising from settlers' efforts to occupy vacant lands plus the belief that railroads would soon cross company property led Sommerville on a search for accurate maps of Motley and Dickens counties. Since existing maps were incomplete and contradictory, the company approved the hiring of a competent surveyor to make as many surveys as necessary to establish control of the country. In 1888, Sam L. Chalk began field work but, plagued by illness, did not complete his notes until 1893. This survey was found later to be unsatisfactory, and R. M. Kenney, a state surveyor, reworked the Matador property. His notes were accepted by the state Land Office in 1905.

While no railroad crossed the Matador range—as Sommerville knew the range—until the twentieth century, the intrusion of settlers on what the company considered to be its lands was a problem from the very beginning. When an interloper appeared, notice was sent to vacate; this failing, a damage suit was filed, and thanks to Cuyler's careful examination of titles, such a suit usually demonstrated the correctness of the company's claim.

Since the Matador corporation's principal and, for all practical purposes, exclusive source of income lay in the marketing of cattle, activities were directed to the raising and maintenance of livestock which could be disposed of at a profit and which would bring substantial returns over a long period of time. "To steadily raise the quality of the herd by the purchase of graded bulls" and "to install improvements which would greatly facilitate the work of the ranch" in leading "to reduced expenses and to better condition of the stock by diminishing the labour of driving and

[38] From 1882 until 1888, Colorado City on the Texas and Pacific Railroad shared Matador business with Wichita Falls, Harrold, Vernon, and other towns on the Fort Worth and Denver line.

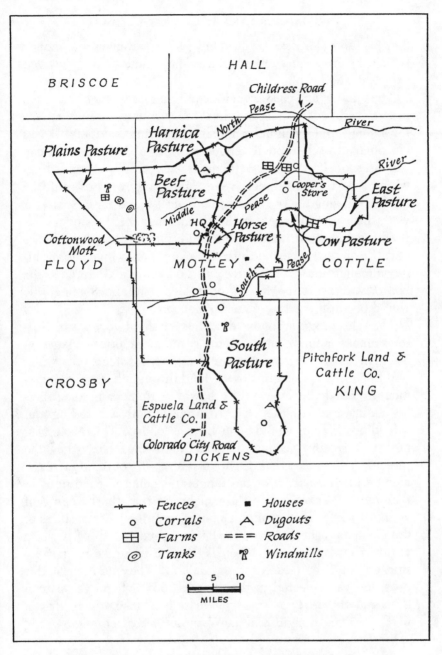

The Enclosed Range of the Matador Land and Cattle Company,
from the Survey by Sam L. Chalk in 1888

herding and the risks of straying" were statements of policy which governed the actions of company officials and justified expenditures.[39]

The number and classes of cattle put up for sale each year were determined by two factors—first, the company's requirements for income, and second, the manager's recommendations. It was customary to sell annually enough cattle to pay the American expenses, declare a modest dividend, and carry over funds from which a portion of the next year's operating expenses could be paid. Following the board's estimate of its needs for a particular year, the secretary would notify the manager of the amount desired; Sommerville, knowing the condition of the various classes of cattle on the range and the market situation, would submit his recommendations to the directors. Following a conference the board would inform Mackay of its decision, and Sommerville would be authorized to sell or hold accordingly.

The sales program followed during the first two years of Britton's managership reflected, in a measure, a practice engaged in by many cattlemen: the custom of marketing steers only while building up the population of the herd through the normal increment of female births. By 1884, however, there came the sobering realization that the range, if used as both a breeding and a feeding ground, would soon be overloaded. This awareness meant a sweeping change in plans following 1884, when the directors announced that "the herd's capability of rapid increase, along with the nature of the range and climatic conditions in that part of Texas led to the conclusion that the breeding of young stock for feeders might shortly form the chief business of the Company, since to produce heavy beeves, four or five years of growth was necessary, whereas the yearlings on a range fully stocked could be cleared off annually."[40] The initiation of this program was reflected in the sales in 1885, when over sixteen thousand three-, two-, and one-year-old stockers were driven north for marketing in Kansas, Wyoming, and Nebraska.

[39] Fourth Annual Report, 6–7.   [40] Second Annual Report, 5.

Customarily, a year's sales activities began in the spring and
ended when the last deliveries were made in November. Early
in the year buyers or their agents would begin their visits to the
range to view the cattle, to see how they had wintered, and to
note the prospects for grass and water. Out of these visits might
come contracts for the purchase of stock to be delivered late in
the summer or in the fall at a designated range, shipping point,
or market. Actually, delivery might take place any time after the
spring roundup when warmer weather and the appearance of
new grass permitted herds to be moved. Cattle marked for delivery to market or distant feeding grounds were collected at a
holding point, then were trailed to the nearest railhead for shipment. Until 1885, cattle collected on the southern portion of the
Matador range were driven to Colorado City, while those gathered in the north were driven to Wichita Falls. After 1885 all
shipments were made from points along the Fort Worth and
Denver Railroad as that line was extended northwestward across
the Panhandle.

When a herd was gathered, a trail boss was appointed to
supervise the work of the trail crew and to assume responsibility
for the herd until the cattle were delivered at market or into the
hands of a buyer. On a rail shipment, once the herd was loaded
in cattle cars, most of the trail crew returned to the ranch, since
only a few hands were needed to accompany the cattle to the
destination.

As early as 1884 the trail boss was required to keep a record of
the herd from the time it left the ranch until it was delivered.
The board felt "it would conduce to carefulness on the part of
the men in charge . . . if the foreman responsible had to narrate
the history of his herd with an explanation of the circumstances
under which cattle escaped or came by accident."[41] This requirement was no novelty, since other companies kept careful records
in like manner, but it set a pattern for Matador employees and

[41] Mackay to Sommerville, December 5, 1884.

focused attention on a foreman's responsibilities. Not only did it "conduce to carefulness"—it enabled the company to present evidence when filing a claim against railroads for losses due to mishandling, carelessness, or slow travel.[42]

Marketing media differed with the classes of cattle put up for sale. Mature steers, for example, were shipped to commission houses in metropolitan areas, whereas stockers and feeders contracted for while still on the range were delivered at an appointed time to their new range or feeding grounds. Until 1893, when the last Matador trail drive to northern ranges was made, cattle scheduled for delivery to buyers or finishing ranges at higher latitudes were gathered near Ballard Springs, where they were thrown into trail herds seldom exceeding two thousand head each and were "lined out" toward the polar star until one of the well-established trails to the north was reached. After 1885, when the quarantine line's extension to southwestern Kansas closed Dodge City to Texas cattle, the Northern Trail was generally used; this route became well defined in the Oklahoma Panhandle and followed a course through eastern Colorado into Wyoming, thence into southeastern Montana.

Once the drives had departed Ballard Springs, the headquarters received only occasional reports of the progress made; these were brief and to the point, usually reflecting the optimism of the trail foreman and sometimes revealing the ingenuity and decisiveness required of a successful boss who was in complete control of his herd for weeks on end. One such message, postmarked Buffalo, Colorado, and dated June 4, 1887, told of a labor problem and its solution:

Boys all made a strike for higher wages so I let 2 men go and

[42] Such a claim was filed in 1886 against the Iron Mountain Railroad. "We give you notice that we claim damages for loss and injury on forty-four (44) head of cattle, three- and four-year-old steers injured by accident on the Iron Mountain Road near Texarkana on the morning of 21st May. The cars were numbered respectively Iron Mountain 1056; Texas and Pacific 5545." Sommerville to Agent, Iron Mountain Railroad, Texarkana, Arkansas, May 24, 1886.

promist the six men that stayed better wages provided it is all rite with the Company. To go through with six men with $5.00 raises will be cheaper than 8 men at the rates at start.[43]

When a herd was due to reach its destination, the manager would travel north by train to the delivery point, hand over the bill of sale to the purchaser, collect the final payment, sell the horses, and pay the trail hands. Of the men, some remained in the north country, while others returned home by rail after seeing the sights in Kansas City, Omaha, or St. Louis.

On one occasion a combination of drought and poor market conditions caused the company officials to approve an undertaking which, while not unique in the cattle business, was a departure from sales practices. In June, 1886, a mixed herd of three thousand old cows, calves, and yearling culls was driven westward across the *Llano Estacado* into New Mexico to be offered for sale in the vicinity of Socorro. The project was exceptionally hazardous from a financial point of view, since there was no certainty that a market could be found at the end of the drive and, once the cattle were in a particular locality, their owners were at the mercy of local buyers. Advertisements of this herd's composition were placed in newspapers, and invitations were extended to prospective buyers to inspect the cattle at holding grounds near Socorro. An advance agent, seeking right of transit across ranges and watering places, sent back word that no grass was available in the Socorro country, so the herd was turned toward Albuquerque, where, at the end of August, the cattle were sold for fifteen dollars a head, three dollars less than the price originally asked.

The drought which made itself felt in 1886 in northwestern Texas was but the forerunner of a prolonged dry period which produced its gravest consequences on the Matador range in 1892. While the damage in its initial year was not too serious in Motley County, a search for water was begun by Campbell. The

[43] C. V. Bailey to Campbell, June 4, 1887.

31

beginning of the dry cycle interacted with the overstocking of the range and the caving in of stream banks as they were trampled by cattle to reduce the supply of live water. The "once clear flowing streams" were reduced to sandy troughs in which occasional pools provided scant water for thousands of animals, and as water points were reduced, the grazing range of the cattle was restricted; good grass distant from water holes was unused, while the areas close to water were overpopulated and overgrazed. Immediate remedial measures involved well-digging and dam-building, but the saving device was the windmill:

> We have seen a wind-mill, which seems to us to come more nearly answering the purposes of cattlemen than anything that has yet been introduced; in order to give the matter a practical test for ourselves we have sent two of these wind-mills to be fitted up on wells which Mr. Campbell has already found. The troughs we use are large wooden tanks, about two and a-half feet in diameter; they are made circular so that the staves may be tightened if necessary. There is an automatic arrangement by which the supply of water to the tanks is regulated; as the water rises in the tank, the wind-mill is thrown out of gear and remains stationary; when the water in the tank is reduced, the wind-mill comes into position again and supplies what has been taken out. In this way the tank is always kept full, but is never allowed to overflow.[44]

Unlike cattlemen on the High Plains, the Matador people were not dependent solely upon windmills for their water supply; the broken country in which the greater part of the range lay was suitable for the construction of tank dams. Thus the importance of windmills was never as great in the prairie region as on ranges lying on the unbroken *Llano Estacado*. Nevertheless, the Dun-

[44] Sommerville to Mackay, May 27, 1886. Early in 1885, Britton asked to be relieved of his responsibilities as manager because of his interest in the Espuela Land and Cattle Company, Ltd. While his contract with the Matador had two years to run, Britton's resignation was accepted, and the sum of £1,500 was paid to him in full quittance of all claims. Sommerville was appointed manager and Campbell was retained as superintendent.

dee board seldom failed to approve the purchase of mills when Campbell submitted a request.

Like many other ranch establishments, large and small, the company held membership in several cattlemen's associations. These organizations, formed to protect the brands of members, to halt rustling, and to influence legislation, were supported by dues levied on the basis of the size of the participants' herds. In 1880, Colonel Charles Goodnight summoned cattlemen in the Panhandle to a meeting at Mobeetie to deal with the problems of thefts and Texas fever carried by trail herds from the southern part of the state. As a result of this meeting, the Panhandle Stock Association was formed in 1881; this organization immediately posted notices of rewards for the apprehension of rustlers and established "Winchester quarantine" to prevent fever-bearing herds from crossing the Panhandle ranges.[45]

By 1886 the Matador had withdrawn from the TeePee and the Northwest Texas associations, but retained membership in the Panhandle Stock Association. This last-named body had been successful in securing the establishment of the thirty-fourth parallel as the Kansas quarantine line in 1885; and while its assessment of a $2,400 membership fee, based on three cents a head on a herd of eighty thousand cattle, was considered by the Scots to be high, Sommerville recommended payment without protest. Although herds originating on the Matador range were always found to be free of ticks carrying Texas fever, the expenses involved in paying inspectors' fees and the loss from shrinkage in weight while cattle were held for inspection made it advantageous for the company to have the quarantine line lie south of its gathering grounds. Since the thirty-fourth parallel ran through the heart of the Matador range, cattle could be collected in pastures lying north of the line and cleared for shipment into and through Kansas without inspection.[46]

Under the hammering blows of drought, blizzards, low prices,

[45] Haley, *Charles Goodnight*, 361–62.
[46] Sommerville to Mackay, December 21, 1885.

and the disappearance of free grass, many foreign-owned cattle companies went out of existence during the 1880's. Certainly profits during the decade failed to approach those anticipated on the basis of the Parliamentary commission's report. But the Matador directors entertained no thought of abandoning their Texas venture, even though some shareholders grumbled because of the small dividends.[47] The board's position was made clear by Chairman Robertson in 1885:

> You are to keep in view that the policy of the Directors has been—and I hope will continue to be—only to pay dividends out of actual sales. This policy, if I mistake not, met with the unanimous approval of the Shareholders at their last annual meeting. I am not, however, to argue from this that your Directors are not to give the subject of dividend—next to the stability of the Company—their very best attention, and to bring every possible effort to bear on the Company's management for that particular purpose.[48]

When the board proposed that a portion of each year's free revenue be placed in a reserve account before dividends were declared, William Mackenzie of Dundee supported the recommendation at the fourth annual meeting of the shareholders:

> I listened with great pleasure to the very interesting remarks of the Chairman, and there is one of the remarks to which I would like to draw attention. He said that if the Directors had been dealing with their own property they would probably have pursued a different policy. Now, I have a very strong conviction

[47] From the Annual Reports for the years listed:

YEAR	PROFIT	DIVIDEND
1883	£15,118	8%
1884	15,893	6
1885	32,430	7
1886	8,834	None
1887	1,763	None
1888	6,632	1⅔
1889	12,140	2½
1890	7,495	None

[48] Report of Proceedings, Third Annual General Meeting of Shareholders, 4.

that all Cattle Companies and all Trading Companies should get themselves into a position so that the Directors can without hesitation deal with their property exactly as if it were their own; that they should be so strong that they should be ready for all contingencies, and prepared to take any reasonable risk. The gentlemen who spoke here [in opposition] labour under the belief that Companies exist primarily for the purpose of paying Dividends. That is a great mistake. (Great laughter.) Companies exist primarily for the purpose of getting themselves thoroughly strong, and into a very excellent and clearly conservative position—so that they may be ready for all contingencies. I certainly admire the courage of the Directors, who are not tempted to pay dividends at the expense of impairing the strength of the Company, and I especially concur in the policy of carrying £10,000 to a special Reserve or Contingent Fund, and I would take the liberty of suggesting that this policy be continued year out and year in until you have at least £30,000, or more than is required for one year's working of the ranche, which will save you getting into debt and incurring any liabilities, or anything of that kind.[49]

While policies regarding dividends, the creation of reserve accounts, and the redemption of debentures could be decided in Dundee, there was little the directors could do to influence the fundamental factors determining income—weather and market prices. By good fortune the winter storms of 1886–87, which brought havoc among the weakened herds on drought-seared ranges from Montana to Texas, spent little of their fury on the Ballard Springs country. Even so, the company wrote off 8,500 head as losses to weather in 1886. For the low prices Sommerville placed primary responsibility on the "Beef Ring":

The Chicago packers have absorbed almost the entire butchering business of the country and by combination have held the balance in their own hands—there has been no competitive buying. All effort is being made to alter this by the establishment of

[49] Report of Proceedings, Fourth Annual General Meeting of Shareholders, 12. Established initially in the amount of £10,000, the reserve account grew to £20,000 by the end of 1890.

stock yards on the west side of St. Louis which will be worked independently of the "Ring" and in which butchers are considerably interested. Western and southern cattle raisers are taking a great interest in this scheme and are giving it hearty support. It is perhaps impossible to foretell the influence it may have but it is one step in the right direction and great hopes of its usefullness are entertained.[50]

In addition to explaining to the shareholders "that the chief market in America, namely Chicago, is largely in the hands of a few individuals whose power of purchase and ease in combining regulate the price of beef cattle everywhere," the board pointed out that "a general trade depression which led to lessened beef consumption on the part of wage earners," the labor strikes of 1886, which disorganized industry in general, and the drought, which caused a flooding of the cattle market, were to blame for the unfavorable situation.[51]

The program of converting the Matador range into a breeding ground, adopted so enthusiastically early in 1885, was never completely carried out. Success in implementing such a plan depended upon a sustained demand for young male stock during the conversion period. Faltering prices following the panic of 1886, the glutted cattle market, and an unwillingness to succumb to the "Beef Ring's" manipulations caused the company to curtail its sales during the period from 1886 through 1889. However, there was no break in the practice of improving the herd. This was done through the spaying of heifers on a limited scale and by the purchase of graded and purebred bulls. Each year following 1883 saw the introduction of several hundred fine sires, most of them Herefords, to the range. In addition, some five hundred of the better male calves born to Matador cows were kept each year. By 1886, Sommerville was of the opinion that all company cows had been bred to Hereford bulls and that the ranch might,

[50] Sommerville to Mackay, November 30, 1886.
[51] Fourth Annual Report, 4.

36

with proper management, raise its own purebred bulls less expensively than it could purchase them.

While the advantages of shipping cattle to northern ranges for "double-wintering" were well known to the Scots, there was no move to carry out such an enterprise during the Britton-Sommerville-Campbell era. The company seemed satisfied to dispose of its stock as quickly as possible after its herds left the home range. An experiment was carried out in 1890, when grasslands in the vicinity of Hymer, Kansas, were leased for summer grazing, but the results of this venture were, in the manager's words, "rather a bitter pill," since the cattle gained no more weight than those which stayed on the home range.[52]

In May, 1890, William Sommerville announced his decision to retire at the end of the year. John Robertson, one of the directors, was in America at the time the board received notice of the manager's action and was authorized to begin a search for a suitable successor. This quest took on added significance when Hank Campbell submitted his resignation, although the superintendent agreed to remain on the ranch until April, 1891, to acquaint the new manager with the company's herds and properties. In October, 1890, after weeks of inquiry and investigation, the board appointed Murdo Mackenzie of Trinidad, Colorado, to replace Sommerville.[53]

[52] Sommerville to O. H. Nelson, November 1, 1890.

[53] Board Minute Book, III, 298. On December 10, 1890, three weeks before he was scheduled to hand over the managerial reins to Mackenzie, Sommerville died of injuries received when he accidentally fell from a windmill tower at his home in Fort Worth.

~2~

The Trail North

MURDO MACKENZIE, destined to become one of the dominant figures in the development of the American cattle industry, was born near Tain, County Ross, Scotland, on April 24, 1850. Following graduation from the Royal Academy at Tain in 1867, he served as apprentice in a law office, was employed as a bank clerk and as assistant factor on the estate of Sir Charles Ross, and, after marrying Isabella MacBain in 1876, returned to the Tain bank as insurance agent. In this last position he attracted the attention of an Edinburgh syndicate whose governing board appointed him manager of the Prairie Cattle Company, Limited, "the mother of British cattle companies," whose extensive range holdings lay in southeastern Colorado, northeastern New Mexico, and the Panhandle of Texas. In 1885 the Mackenzie family moved from Scotland to Trinidad, Colorado, where they maintained their home for the next twenty-six years.[1]

As the Prairie's manager in America, Mackenzie supervised the organization's three range divisions, the shipping and marketing of its cattle, and cared for the company's business in the United States. When, in 1890, he was the target of criticism by one of the Prairie shareholders, Mackenzie decided to resign, though the Edinburgh board urged him to remain in his position. Offered several business opportunities, he chose management of the Matador. Thus there began a relationship between the com-

[1] *Dictionary of American Biography,* XXII, 416–17.

pany and the Mackenzie family which was to endure for more than three-score years.

One of the new manager's first acts—the removal of the company's American office from Fort Worth to Trinidad—was significant in two respects. For one, it revealed something of Mackenzie's character: his action was taken despite the board's contention that the move would be too expensive, but his home and his friends were in Trinidad and he argued that the office would be closer to markets. Secondly, the transfer foreshadowed a new company policy—interest in northern grasslands.

Mackenzie carried with him to his new job two capable Prairie men: Henry H. Johnstone, commonly called the "head booker," who was appointed accountant in the Trinidad office, and Arthur G. Ligertwood, who was named superintendent to replace Campbell. Scots, both Johnstone and Ligertwood had worked under Mackenzie and were known and trusted by the new manager.

The untimely death of William Sommerville placed an extra burden on the incoming officials, but by the end of January, 1891, Mackenzie had closed his affairs with the Prairie people and had visited the ranch at Ballard Springs. Early in February he instructed Ligertwood to take charge of the ranch, relieving Campbell, who had agreed originally to stay until April to acquaint the new superintendent with the range. Mackenzie believed that to prolong Campbell's stay would merely preserve old allegiances and thus delay the establishment of Ligertwood's authority. In the new manager's opinion, the ranch employees were "a demoralized outfit of men"; hence he hastened Campbell's departure and instructed Ligertwood to "make a condition with all your men that they are not to own any cattle and that there is to be no card playing at either the Ranch or Wagons on any pretext whatsoever" and "to strictly prohibit any of our men from frequenting the Saloon." Responsibility for the enforcement of these orders was placed directly on the new superintendent through the statement, "You will understand that I will look to you to have these conditions enforced and that you will dismiss any man no matter who it is who disobeys your order."[2]

The establishment of these rules and the immediate dismissal of men who had the temerity to test them were accompanied by criticism of the manager and threats to his life. That he was not killed was later attributed by Mackenzie to the fact that he never carried a gun:

> That's the reason I am alive today. When I took charge of the Matador, Dan Boone [a foreman] came to me and told me that he'd stay on if we paid him $100 a month and gave him his pick of the horses at the end of the year. I told him that we couldn't do that, and futhermore we couldn't use him at all. He left and later swore all around over the country that he was going to kill me.
>
> The next time I had to go to the ranch I got off the train at Childress and went out to get my buckboard and team. A friend there said: "You can't go to the ranch."
>
> "Why?" I said.
>
> "Dan Boone is swearing he's going to shoot you on sight."
>
> "I've got to go," I said. "If he was going to kill me, he wouldn't be talking about it so much."
>
> I got to the ranch and sent somebody to get him. He came to the round-up and I told him to get up in the buckboard with me.
>
> "I understand you have been saying you were going to kill me on sight. Now if that's what you plan to do, you couldn't find a better place than this. But let me tell you something, as long as I stay with the Matadors, I am going to run them."
>
> After that we became fairly good friends.
>
> He was afterwards killed by the sheriff.[3]

After half a year with the company, Mackenzie confirmed a report which had reached the secretary in Dundee:

> You are perfectly right in surmising that I have had difficulties to contend with which I did not trouble you with, but I am glad to think the worst is past. If, however, I had known what I had

[2] Mackenzie to Ligertwood, February 11, 1891.
[3] Mackenzie to J. Evetts Haley, August 22, 1932. Personal interview.

to go through I would never have undertaken it. My life was threatened on several occasions and even with a good salary a man does not care to take such chances, but having gotten into it once I did not care to show the white feather. $10,000 would not be any inducement to me to face another 6 months of the same kind.[4]

The esteem and respect in which Mackenzie was held by the directors was evident from the beginning of their relationship. Not only did the board defer to the manager in most instances in which differences of opinion arose, but it also put its instructions in the form of requests and its rebukes as suggestions. Like Campbell, Mackenzie was prone to disregard the directors' insistence that reports be made frequently. An attempt to remind the manager of the board's wishes was made in April, 1891:

> I think I explained to you in America that our Board meets every Tuesday and we like to have at the *very least* one letter a week keeping us informed, both as to our own business and as to cattle matters generally.[5]

Apparently this message failed to achieve the desired effect, for two months later the secretary wrote again:

> I am glad you have got a thorough hold on our Matador business. . . . While writing you I think I may give you a friendly hint on the question of correspondence. I remember you saying to me that your Prairie people neither wrote nor sought letters very often. We are the other way. We write a good deal, and we expect a great deal more than we write. We had with Sommerville usually twice a week (always once) long letters as to what was going on, his personal movements, the state of the market and the condition of things generally. You might make it a point to acknowledge on the *first* opportunity every letter which reaches your hand, and *always* confirm by letter a cable sent or received. Anybody can send a message and we not find out its correctness unless confirmed.[6]

4 Mackenzie to Mackay, July 6, 1891.
5 Mackay to Mackenzie, April 8, 1891.
6 Mackay to Mackenzie, June 10, 1891.

Mackenzie's explanation was sincere and dignified:

> I am really sorry my letters do not reach you with the regu-
> larity the Board would wish but my position is somewhat differ-
> ent from the late Mr. Sommerville. He was nearly all the time in
> the office while my time is nearly all taken up from home. For
> instance I have all the past month been from home with the ex-
> ception of four days. I confess I do not write you when away
> from home and the reason is I am often too tired to do so, or have
> so much to attend to that I don't have the time. Take the past
> month as an example. I have either been in the buckboard or in
> the saddle from 6 A.M. till sundown and I am satisfied from your
> own experience that you will agree with me that a man has very
> little inclination to write after a day's work of this kind. I have
> tried however upon my return home to give full details of the
> Company business. . . . I am exceedingly obliged to you for your
> kindness in writing me as you did.[7]

Following this exchange little was said about the promptness
of reports. Johnstone took over the handling of routine messages
and sent information to Dundee when the manager was "from
home."[8]

One stipulation in Mackenzie's initial contract with the company called for the manager to determine the actual size of the
Matador herd. Although the number of cattle purchased from
Britton and Campbell in 1882 was guaranteed to be at least
40,000 head, no actual count had been made. For book purposes,
the herd was rated at 42,000 head in 1882, and subsequent figures for herd totals were based on this number. Branding tallies,
purchases, sales, and losses during the years following the Dundee corporation's acquisition drove the herd strength upward so
that at the end of 1890 the books showed 97,771 cattle burned
with the Matador V.

Unable to undertake a count in 1891 because of his unfamili-

[7] Mackenzie to Mackay, July 6, 1891.

[8] Johnstone became assistant manager in 1897 and served until 1902; from
1904 until 1907 he was manager of the Espuela Land and Cattle Company's
ranch in Dickens County, Texas.

arity with the range, Mackenzie was nevertheless "perfectly satisfied that the number on the ranch [was] considerably short of the number claimed on the books." This opinion was justified, for in 1892, when a fairly accurate tally over the whole range was completed, the herd strength was established at 70,200. In accepting this estimate and in attempting to explain to the shareholders what had happened to the remainder of the cattle, William Robertson stated, "Either the original herd was short of the number at which we bought it, or our calf brand was less than the numbers transmitted·to us from time to time, or the death rate was greater than the figures reported to us from America, or all of these were wrong to some extent."[9] Undismayed by the paper loss of 27,000 head, the shareholders voted to write off £2 per share of the paid-up capital, leaving the shares at £8 each and reducing the authorized capital to £400,000.

By far the most serious crisis experienced by the company during the last decade of the nineteenth century was caused by the "worst drought ever experienced before or since" in the region around Ballard Springs; in 1892 no spring rains fell and summer showers were absent:

> Matters were made worse by the previous overstocking of the range and tramping out of sod. By fall there was not a spear of grass and hardly a settler left in the whole range. Cattle and horses had to subsist on brush, staying mostly in the shinneries [pygmy oak or shin oak forests] which then proved their value to a range. Water holes filled up with drifting sand. Where the land had been cultivated the whole plowed part was blown away until the mark made by the plow point could be seen shining from one end of the field to the other. Prairie dogs died by thousands.[10]

Fearing that there would be no grass, even with fall rains, to carry the cattle through the winter, the management secured

9 Report of Proceedings, Eleventh Annual General Meeting of Shareholders, 4.
10 Murdo Mackenzie, "The Matador Ranch," *Panhandle-Plains Historical Review*, Vol. XXI (1948), 101. This drought was a local one.

permission to lease pasturage from the Home Land and Cattle Company near Panhandle in Carson County, and by the end of the year eight thousand steers had been trailed a hundred miles north to graze where "grass was first class and water plentiful." The arrangement was temporary, however, and since no agreement could be reached with the Home people for a continuation of the lease in 1893, a contract was made with the Francklyn Land and Cattle Company for a two-year lease on the so-called White Deer pasture, a tract of 348,000 acres lying in Gray and Carson counties. For grazing rights on this property, the company paid an annual rental of five cents an acre and secured from the owners authorization to sublease a portion of the pasture in order to reduce costs. During the period 1893–95, over ten thousand Matador steers were kept on White Deer grass; but when the lease expired, no effort was made to renew it, since good rains and fine grass on the home range made leasing unnecessary.

In his first interview with John Robertson and Mackay in 1890, Mackenzie had inquired about the possibility of a return to the company's early program of holding steers until they were three years old. While no definite answer was given at the time, Mackenzie was convinced that a long-range plan should be developed. He had observed that young cattle could not stand the "long hunt"—the roundup—and the hardship of the trail or cattle train as well as mature stock; too, he knew that ranchmen from the northern states and territories—Montana, Wyoming, and Dakota—were sending only mature steers for slaughter and that these animals brought the best prices on the Chicago livestock market.

To convince the directors that the holding and feeding of steers would be profitable, Mackenzie recommended, early in 1891, that pastures in Kansas again be leased for summer grazing and feeding. The suggestion was startling in view of the unfortunate "Kansas experiment" in 1890, but the board's reluctance disappeared when the manager proposed that the herd be placed under a Matador employee. In May, 1891, over 500

44

three- and four-year-old steers were sent to pastures near Strong City in south central Kansas, and in July 600 more were shipped to the same area. To the manager, this action secured a double benefit to the company—grass on the home range was saved and the cattle were "removed from a district where there was a danger at any time of summer of a Texas fever scare which might prevent buyers from handling them." Since satisfactory prices were obtained for these beeves in the fall of 1891, the practice was continued; in 1892 over 1,600 steers were sent to Kansas with Dave Somerville, a Matador foreman, in charge.[11] Under Somerville's supervision, 347 select head were pastured separately, and of these, 250 were placed on full feed for ninety days. The purpose of this project was not to make a profit but to show Kansas farmers that Matador steers were suitable for feeding.

By 1894 the directors were convinced that the "Kansas advertising project" had served its purpose; feeling that Mackenzie's personal expenses and loss of time in traveling were not justified by the profits from the venture, they limited the number of steers shipped to Strong City to three hundred head.[12] Despite this curtailment, Mackenzie continued the project until 1898, when new circumstances caused the practice to be abandoned.

The opportunity for the company to place its steers in sizable numbers on northern plains grass for double-wintering came through a fortuitous meeting between Alexander Mackay and John Clay, Jr., in Edinburgh. Clay, a stockholder in a corporation which controlled Western Ranches, Limited, a huge British-owned cattle company, suggested that his company might be willing to pasture up to two thousand Matador steers for a winter. Specifically, he proposed that two-year-olds from the Ballard Springs range be shipped to lands controlled by West-

11 David Somerville, reported to have been a nephew of William F. Sommerville, was educated for the practice of law in Scotland, but a visit to the Matador ranch in 1890 terminated his legal career. Edward N. Wentworth, "A Search for Cattle Trails in Matto Grosso," *Agricultural History*, Vol. XXVI (1952), 9.

12 Mackenzie to Mackay, December 21, 1894.

ern Ranches in Montana and Dakota, placed under Western Ranches men, and marketed at the end of two years through a livestock commission house, Clay, Robinson and Company, in Chicago.[13] For the use of the grass the Dundee company would pay one dollar a head for the first year, in advance, and one dollar for the second year for each steer delivered at the railhead by Western Ranches hands.

When the board referred the matter to Mackenzie, the manager objected:

> I have fully considered Mr. Clay's letter and while I have no objections to Mr. Clay grazing our cattle, I would not advise the company to turn the steers over to him and give him full control of selling them. I do not wish to insinuate that Mr. Clay would do anything but what would be to your best interest, but life is uncertain and I would consider it unadvisable for the company to turn control of their cattle into the hand of anyone as long as they are company property.[14]

Negotiations were continued, with the result that an agreement was reached in May, 1892; by its terms two thousand two-year-old Matador steers were to be delivered at the Belle Fourche range of Western Ranches in the summer; there they were to remain until marketed in the fall of 1894. The rental fee amounted to one dollar a head a year. Two reservations in the contract satisfied Mackenzie: the beeves could be withdrawn and the contract terminated at the end of one year should the Dundee board feel it necessary to do so, and the Matador owners were to dispose of their cattle through a commission house of their own choosing, though Mackenzie promised that Clay, Robinson and Company could depend on getting the steers to sell if the firm should be in "the same good condition as in 1892."

[13] Since Clay had an interest in this firm, his enthusiasm for the plan is understandable. A valuable source on British influence in the western cattle industry is John Clay's *My Life on the Range* (Chicago, privately printed, 1924; new ed., Norman, University of Oklahoma Press, 1962).

[14] Mackenzie to Mackay, March 19, 1892.

In June the manager went north with two thousand beeves "to get familiar with the country and its ways." The herd was driven to Estelline on the Fort Worth and Denver Railroad and shipped to Belle Fourche, South Dakota; thence the cattle were moved overland some thirty-five miles to the north and were loosed on the Western Ranches range.

Mackenzie's opinion of the Dakota country and his views on northern feeding were reported to Mackay:

> The grass in the North is very good, and as our twos were in good fix when turned loose, I think they should go through the winter in good shape. I did not have time to go over much of the country but what I saw of it I liked well, and am inclined to think that someday the Company will have to extend their business to the North country. I, however, think as you do that we should first try the experiment on a small scale and then if we find it profitable, continue the policy on a larger scale.[15]

During the remainder of the year the manager gave careful consideration to the matter of northern pasturing; and when he went to Scotland for a three months' visit early in 1893, he was able to convince Mackay and the directors that the practice should be not only continued but expanded. As a result, the board authorized Johnstone to arrange with Eugene Holcomb of Rapid City, South Dakota, to pasture two thousand Matador steers under "identically the same terms as in the contract with Clay." Within days after the signing of the Holcomb lease, Mackenzie was back in America negotiating with the railroads for favorable shipping terms; but when the rates were quoted, he felt the cost of rail shipment to be prohibitive and decided to trail the herd north. In so doing, he would save $5,000, or $2.50 a head.

On May 25, 1893, under the care of John Smith and his crew, a herd of 2,068 steers left the White Deer pasture headed slightly west of true north. The trail lay across the Oklahoma Panhandle

15 Mackenzie to Mackay, July 16, 1892.

and entered southeastern Colorado, crossed the Arkansas River at Lamar, and extended to Brush, east of Denver, where Smith mailed his first report and received instructions from Trinidad. He was ordered to proceed to Pine Bluffs and Lusk in Wyoming, and at the latter place to advise the manager by telegraph of the anticipated date of arrival at Middle Creek, South Dakota, where the herd would be turned over to Holcomb's men. On August 6, with Mackenzie and Holcomb present, the steers arrived at Middle Creek; in seventy-three days they had covered a distance of 750 miles, air-line, and had traveled over 800 miles in doing so.

This was the last trail drive of such length to be undertaken by the Matador. In 1894, when the contract for pasturing two thousand steers was renewed with Western Ranches, the Fort Worth and Denver road, eager to get the company's business, quoted a rate of sixty dollars per standard cattle car from Clarendon to Orin, Wyoming. Since thirty-three two-year-olds could be shipped in one standard car, the cost was reckoned at $1.80 a head for the rail portion of the move; from Orin a drive of three weeks would put the herd on the Belle Fourche. John Smith's trail crew could ride the cattle trains north, get return passes, and ship their horses at a reduced rate both ways. The relatively low cost, along with the fact that the cattle could be settled on their new range by July 1, led the directors to favor accepting the railroad's offer.

The first Dakota steers to be marketed as four-year-olds were shipped from the Western Ranches range in August, 1894. At Chicago these beeves netted thirty-five dollars a head, the best average price the company had ever received for its cattle and one which "disposed the board to continue these northern shipments."[16] So profitable was the practice that not only were shipments continued—the number of steers sent annually was increased. In 1903, when over eight thousand Matador cattle went

[16] Report of Proceedings, Thirteenth Annual General Meeting of Shareholders, 5.

to Dakota pastures, the Western Ranches board "unanimously resolved that after that year no cattle should be brought on to the range by outside parties in excess of 6,000 head."[17]

It will be recalled that when the Dundee organization purchased the holdings of the Texas Matador company in 1882, title to the properties was vested in a board of trustees selected by the directors. Subsequent purchases of realty were made in the names of these trustees until 1891, when the directorate experienced a change of opinion about such tenure and gave consideration to assigning all properties to the company. Of the trustees, Thomas D. Cuyler, the Philadelphia lawyer, alone opposed the transfer:

> I am of the opinion that under all circumstances it would not be advisable to convey the lands from the Trustees to the Company; my reasons for saying so are more of policy than law for I can see nothing that would prevent conveyance. . . . The question therefore is simply whether the same reasons of public policy which actuated the Board in deciding to hold the land through the medium of trustees prevails now as it did when the lands were acquired. It is to be borne in mind that the legislation of Texas for the last few years has been hostile to alien ownership of lands. This sentiment found full expression in the enactment of the act of 1891 which has just been declared unconstitutional by the Supreme Court. Undoubtedly, the results to the State of Texas from the enactment and enforcement of this law were extremely disastrous, and in my opinion the danger for another enactment of such law is past unless some action is taken by alien or foreign corporations which will again arouse the spirit of resentment. It seems to me that the conveyance of the large body of land owned by your Company to the Company itself upon the immediate annulment of the alien law will serve as a lever in assisting those who are opposed to aliens in again agitating the subject and attempting their hostile legislation.[18]

Despite Cuyler's objections to a departure from policy, the

17 Mackay to Mackenzie, May 6, 1903.
18 Cuyler to Mackay, December 29, 1891.

board felt that precedent alone was not enough to outweigh the more practical considerations of convenience and complication "should the children or heirs of a deceased trustee not at once comply with the terms of the trust deed." Too, the directors wanted to avoid any appearance of duplicity in connection with the company's manner of landholding, since it was well known in Austin "that the Company actually owned the extensive blocks of land recorded in the Trustees' names and in the counties where the deeds were recorded the officials [were] well aware of the same fact." When Mackay pointed out "that any case which could be made out against the Company could be made out equally against the Trustees" and that the company's right to lease and use other land in its name while title to its own property was vested in trustees might be challenged on technical grounds,[19] the directors' resolution to effect the transfer was strengthened.[19] On March 22, 1892, the board "unanimously resolved that all the Company's lands presently held in the names of Messrs. William Robertson, Robert Fleming, William Smith and Thomas DeWitt Cuyler as Trustees for the Company should be . . . transferred to the Company's own name."[20] Within days the trustees assigned to the company the appropriate deeds, and during the summer the recording of the transfers was completed in Cottle, Dickens, Floyd, and Motley counties.

The action in placing title to the lands directly in the name of the company was a responsibility of the board and was one of several instances in which a major policy change was made without prior approval of the shareholders. Official announcement of the directors' decision was made by the chairman in 1893:

> You have heard that the title to our lands has been taken directly in the name of the Company. This was found desirable in view of changes in the law affecting the question of aliens acquiring land after a certain date. Under legal advice we recorded the Deeds of Trust executed by the Trustees from time to time,

[19] Mackay to Johnstone, April 2, 1892.
[20] Board Minute Book, III, 464–65.

Camp, 1883
H. H. Campbell is in the center, A. M. Britton on the left.

Matador range cattle, 1883

Matador crew, 1883
A Dundee board member is on the right.

Henry H. Campbell

Headquarters, Ballard Springs, 1884

Chuck wagon and crew, Matador range, 1884

Murdo Mackenzie, Alexander Mackay, and Henry H. Johnstone, 1892

Office of the Matador Land and Cattle Company, Ltd.,
second floor of the First National Bank Building,
Trinidad, Colorado, 1903

together with Deeds of Transfer which they executed last year, and the full title to the land is now directly in the name of the Company.

Before leaving the subject of land, let me refer in a word to a recent rather alarmist newspaper article upon the subject of Texas lands. From time to time mutterings have been heard about the confiscation of land held by aliens in America. These rumours have never resulted in any act of confiscation, and we do not believe that they ever will. Foreigners have rights which the laws of every civilised country recognise, and while it is within the right of any State of the Union to change its laws so as to refuse aliens the privilege of acquiring land within its boundaries, it cannot take away by force the property of any alien who has acquired land by legal title before a law of prohibition was introduced. We are well advised that our titles are beyond challenge, and that the Federal Court is a safe defence against any attempt to deprive an alien of his rights.[21]

It was no accident that when Murdo Mackenzie entered the Matador service, the company could lay claim to the use of over 660,000 acres of land on its Ballard Springs range. Ever alert to bargains in real estate and to the acquisition of strategically located sections, the Scots had built up their holdings so that by the end of 1890 they held title to some 445,000 acres and leased 220,000 acres more. The range, as Mackenzie found it, did not consist of a solid block of land over which Matador cattle could graze at will; rather, it was formed by sizable tracts owned or leased by the company interspersed with smaller parcels owned or leased by others.

Until 1891 the company experienced little difficulty in obtaining grazing rights on public school lands; in that year, however, with settlers pouring into the prairie region at the foot of the High Plains and establishing homesteads on these lands, the state's reluctance to permit renewal of the Matador leases became apparent. Only through several personal appearances in

[21] Report of Proceedings, Eleventh Annual General Meeting of Shareholders, 9–10.

Austin and the use of his persuasive powers did the manager succeed in securing new contracts; even then the reservation was made that the company must relinquish any of the leased sections which the state might sell to settlers. Recognition of the problem prompted Mackenzie to set forth his first formal statement regarding the company's land policy:

> All diligence should be used to buy up any section that might help to consolidate Company property. This will be more necessary than ever in a year or two as it will be a short time till all school sections in our pasture are to be taken up and the sooner the company is in a position to keep all their cattle on their own land the better it will be.[22]

If the legislative climate in Austin favored the homesteader, the weather in western Texas was impartial, for the same dry period which brought difficulties to the cattlemen brought disaster to the settler in 1892 and 1893. The drought combined with the business depression following the panic of 1893 to force the abandonment of scores of farms, and the company was provided a brief respite from the nester problem. Considering the low state of its finances, the Matador establishment would have found it extremely difficult to follow Mackenzie's advice to purchase land.

Early in 1894 two contracts covering the leasing of over 103,000 acres were negotiated with the state. This acreage, plus that secured from private landholders, would have been sufficient for Matador needs until 1898. However, in 1895 the state legislature passed a law which was designed to facilitate settlers' use of school lands; had certain parts of this act been allowed to stand alone or to go unchallenged, the company might have been deprived of most of its leased pastures. Two clauses in this measure, sometimes called the "four section lease act," were of particular significance to the large cattle companies which held grazing rights on extensive acreage. One gave the lessee of a

[22] Mackenzie to Mackay, November 30, 1891.

section of school land the privilege of leasing three additional sections; another provided that "any actual settler upon any of the lands mentioned in the act, being the head of a family, shall have the right to buy at any time not more than three additional sections of strictly pasture lands notwithstanding any lease thereof." Of all the Matador officials, Johnstone alone remained undisturbed by this threat to the company's leases. He wrote Mackay, "Section 10 of Article I of the Constitution of the United States reads as follows: 'No state shall pass any law impairing the obligation of contracts.' This seems to me to cover all our case pretty closely."[23]

The land commissioner, A. J. Baker, was disposed to feel that the legislature could and might alter the law dealing with the sale of school lands so as to force the company into litigation with the state in order to uphold its rights under the contract of 1894. Mackay, aware of the hostility to large corporations' holding land in Texas, took advantage of an option granted by the law and instructed Johnstone to arrange for the renewal of the leases on a one-year basis; but before Johnstone could reach Austin, the land commissioner had ruled that the Matador leases were exempt from the law of 1895 and refused to accept a number of applications from persons desiring to file on the company's grass. Baker's actions and interpretation of the law caused the secretary to instruct Johnstone to allow the existing leases to run their course. Somewhat piqued, the assistant manager expressed himself on the vagaries of the land act:

> The land laws of the State of Texas were never in a very clear condition and the efforts of the Legislature last year resulted in worse confusion. The new land law embodies the ideas of so many different people, each wishing to introduce some pet scheme, that ambiguity was almost certain to result.[24]

Baker's forecast that the state legislature might again change the land laws proved correct, for in 1897 a new act threw open

[23] Johnstone to Mackay, January 13, 1896.
[24] Johnstone to Mackay, February 24, 1896.

to settlement, on easy terms, all the public lands within the Matador range. The passage of this measure caused the company to search once more for grasslands, with the result that in 1898 its herds again occupied a portion of the White Deer pasture under an agreement which provided that, beginning in 1899, Matador cattle would have access to the whole tract of 345,000 acres for a three-year period. The "Kansas experiment" at Strong City was discontinued, and Dave Somerville was placed in charge of the White Deer operations; there he received yearling steers annually from the home range and shipped them north to Dakota pastures as they became two-year-olds. Thus it was that, in the last years of the nineteenth century, a pattern was developed which was to be followed for three decades. Since the Ballard Springs range was reduced in size, it became primarily a breeding ground, holding the graded and purebred bulls and cows. From it the yearling steers and spayed heifers were sent to White Deer, to be held for a year; from the northern Panhandle, the two-year-olds were sent to the Dakota pastures for double-wintering before being marketed.

While the circumstances under which this program was developed were somewhat fortuitous, there was nothing accidental in the establishment of the policy; its basis lay in the profitable nature of the practice. Until changing tastes and shrinking grasslands caused another major shift in the 1920's, the company's actions were guided by two requirements—grass in a moderate climate for its yearlings, and ranges in northern latitudes for its mature steers; to meet these, it was necessary to purchase additional land in the Panhandle and to lease millions of acres of grass in the Dakotas, Montana, and Canada during the first quarter of the twentieth century.

The westward movement of settlers and the homesteading of public lands within the company's range during the 1890's was mirrored, in a measure, by the Scots' efforts to purchase acreage which would help consolidate their property inside the range. Between 1891 and 1900, several sections lying "outside the fence" were sold, but purchases of valuable tracts within the range during the same period exceeded sales for a net gain of 38,000 acres, so that at the end of 1900 the assets in land held in fee amounted to 483,609 acres.[25]

Unfortunately, Hank Campbell's departure from the company's service in 1891 was accompanied by misunderstandings and conflicting claims. The fact that the former superintendent took the lead in organizing Motley County and in locating the town of Matador on a section of land one mile northeast of Ballard Springs did nothing to improve relations between himself and the Scots. The directors were interested in raising cattle, not in colonizing the area; and while they realized that land values would increase with the arrival of settlers, they knew that homesteaders would occupy many sections of grasslands which the company had been able to lease from the state of Texas and that taxes would rise as counties were organized. When the citizens of Matador made a tentative bid to purchase a section of land east of the townsite for use as a cemetery, Mackay brushed aside the proposal with the statement that "a square mile solely as a burying ground gives a bad impression of the climate." Not insensitive to opportunities for profit but looking with some disdain on those concerns which fell back on the sale of land to survive, the board summarized for Mackenzie's guidance its policy:

> The Board have not considered that the time is quite come for the Company to sell any of its lands inside the fence, but if a large price were offered for any special section there is no reason why the Company should not sell.[26]

[25] The purchase of a section was reported in 1898: "We got a chance of buying section 275 which is located right at the mouth of Sanders Hollow in Bird Pasture. This section has living water on it, and this land being, as it is, right in the middle of our land and the only water in that neighbourhood, it is a most important section for us, and it would hurt us badly if someone else bought it and fenced it." Mackenzie to Mackay, June 4, 1898.

[26] Mackay to Mackenzie, August 3, 1892.

With the establishment of Cottle County in 1892, the process of organizing all the counties in which the Matador range lay was completed. The company took no part in the organizing activities, nor did it initially make an effort to gain control of local affairs by attempting to place Matador sympathizers in office. This attitude changed, and soon, for tax evaluations placed on the ranch property soared immediately after Motley County's first officials took office. The company, touched in its bank account, plunged into local and regional politics, and in 1894, Mackenzie was able to report on the Motley County elections that "our victory has been splendid as we got everyone of the men we wanted elected." The triumph did result in a reduction in tax costs of $2,000 but was short-lived, for in 1896 the manager wrote that "while the national election has gone our way . . . our local election at Matador has gone against us; Chalk was defeated for County Judge."[27] In consequence, tax payments again went up.

In addition to supporting candidates known to be in sympathy with its interests, the company occasionally made vigorous protests on valuations placed on its lands; Johnstone reported such a remonstrance in 1894:

> As I think I mentioned to you in my letter from the ranch I had arranged while there to go down to Dickens with Judge Browning and see what we could do towards getting the Commissioners to reduce the valuation they placed upon a portion of our lands in that [Dickens] County. We paid the taxes upon all our personal property and upon all land valued at $2.00 per acre but upon all land valued above this figure we refused to pay. The land we refused to pay upon was valued at all the way from $2.25 to $4.00 an acre and the difference this made in the total valuation of the Company's property was $112,000. As there was no saying to what ridiculous figure our lands might be raised in the future we thought we might as well fight the question now as later. We need only fight on the valuation, the tax rate is limited by law.

[27] Mackenzie to Mackay, November 9, 1896.

When we got to Dickens we found that the Commissioners would be in session on the following day and accordingly we asked for a hearing. Judge Browning stated our case very well to the Court but could get no satisfaction from the Commissioners who are in this position. They are certain that any concession made to us means a tremendous outcry from all the nesters and small farmers who have already paid on the $4.00 an acre basis and whose only consolation lies in the fact that the cattle companies are being robbed along with them. The Spur Company has paid its taxes under protest and the Commissioners know that a law suit with one of us means a law suit with both.

The County Judge (who is practically "the Court") is in a quandary and confided to us in private that he had a scheme by which all lands would be valued at $2.00 and under for taxation in 1894. As you are aware the election of County officers takes place next fall and the ridiculous valuations of the present board has destroyed all chances of their re-election unless a radical change is made and the County Judge knows that if he involves the County in a law suit with the Matador and Spur Companies besides, his case will be settled.

We of course declined to give an indication of what our course would be and Browning is now in correspondence with him with the view of getting something definite out of him. In the meantime we hold the law suit over them until they show their hand.

I am of the opinion that if we can be assured of a sufficient reduction in the valuation of 1894 to equalize matters it would be as well to pay the 1893 taxes in full. Although the Commissioners have committed many irregularities in making the levy of 1893 on which we could make a fight still I am always afraid of these State Courts and if we can make any reasonable compromise I would prefer to do so.

I think in the meantime the stand we have taken has done much good especially when it comes on top of the dissatisfaction of the voters so near election time.[28]

Like many other shareholders, those who held stock in the

28 Johnstone to Mackay, February 8, 1894. Judge J. N. Browning was a member of the law firm of Browning and Madden, Clarendon, Texas. Later this firm moved to Amarillo.

Matador company were prone to take an interest in the ranch's operations when a debit balance appeared in the accounts and when no dividends were declared. As profits dwindled and disappeared in the early 1890's, the stockholders made known their dissatisfaction and clamored for a reduction in American expenses, the most convenient remedy they could suggest. The pressure on the board to prune costs was in turn focused on the manager, who received specific suggestions from Mackay on how to reduce charges:

> Your last cable message to us a few days ago was as follows: 'Labian on Cuyler Blacksmith for current expenses.' This message has seven words. Two would have served our purpose— Labian (may we draw) and Blacksmith ($3,000). We knew you could only draw on Cuyler, and we would assume it was for expenses. If the latter had to be made clear, the single word 'expenses' would serve; at the rate of cabling each word counts and in the course of a year the sum is considerable.[29]

Other particular complaints had to do with wages, stores, traveling expenses, and legal charges; and the secretary pointed to the annual reports of other cattle companies—the Espuela, the Hansford, and the Prairie—to show that all three had reduced their expenses:

> It is perfectly clear that our wages bill must yet come down considerably if we are to keep ourselves in the business for any length of time. Charges are so overwhelmingly large on account of the White Deer pasture and the large additions to stores and taxes that the presentation of accounts will prove unpalatable reading to the shareholders. The reduction of charges is the key to the solution and the Board notices with satisfaction that you can promise a substantial reduction this year. You will remember however that we started last year with the hope that the charges would be less than in 1892. Instead of reduction we have a very considerable increase and shareholders who look at the broad facts represented by results year by year are getting ter-

[29] Mackay to Mackenzie, March 8, 1894.

ribly disappointed that this industry shows so few hopeful features and some of them would, I daresay, gladly see the end of it.

What the Board wish to see this year is how charges of all kinds including rents can be cut down. . . . By the new economies which you have introduced your stores, wages and repairs can be reduced largely. The stores account especially will require to come under your eye week by week and month by month. It is one of those insidious accounts which have a tendency to grow larger as soon as attention is drawn off from them for a little. Offers [bids] should be taken for the major part of your supplies and Watson [the stores clerk] should be instructed to keep a tight hand on distribution. The supplies sent to each man in camp should be carefully debited up to an account kept in his name in order to see which of our camp men are economical with supplies. The same should be done with wagons. . . . What is said about stores of course applies to wages, and I fear a lower level of wages will have to be faced by most of your hands excluding perhaps your best men.[30]

Pointing to Mackenzie's travel expenses, Mackay raised a question about the advisability of abandoning the Trinidad office; gained by such a move would be a saving in office costs amounting to £100 a year, travel expense, and the advantage of having someone, either Mackenzie or Johnstone, at the ranch to control expenditures. The fact that Trinidad was "no longer on the natural road" from the ranch to Kansas City and Chicago lent support to the secretary's argument.

The manager's response was immediate:

The only letter that calls for any special notice or remark is your letter . . . where you deal with the expenditures for the past years and make comparisons between my administration and the previous one. At the outset I wish to state that our annual expenses were very materially increased on account of our continued legal struggles and I cannot be held responsible for this. Besides, all the counties we have land in are now organized and

[30] Mackay to Mackenzie, January 24, 1894.

instead of paying $4.50 per section [in taxes] . . . we pay from $13 to $14 per section.

I will now deal with the comparison you made between the Prairie and Espuela and Matador. I will first take the Prairie.

This Company has little or no fence to ride and keeps but very few men during the winter and spring months. We, on the other hand, have to keep from one year's end to the other 8 fence riders at Matador. If we count 8 men @ $30 it comes to $240 per month for wages and for 12 months to $2880. Board for 8 men @ $10 comes for 12 months to $960; total $3840. To this sum falls to be added feed for horses and those riders during winter and fall, and this itself is very material when you have to drive corn as far as we have. I do not mean to say I can run your ranch as cheap as the Prairie Company run theirs, but if I was so disposed I could make comparisons which are common talk in this section. You are well aware of the unprecedented drought which we passed through during the past two years, and the consequent expense we were put to in moving cattle. It is possible . . . our expenses were a little too high last year but you must remember that it is quite possible to economise at the expense of efficiency. The Prairie people since they moved from the Crosselle [Cross L] have the railroad running through their ranges, while we have to drive about 60 miles to the nearest railroad. I could of course reduce the number of our men but I cannot see how I could do so and have our cattle properly looked after. I think at the close of this year the savings in both wages and stores will show up very satisfactory.

Now so far as the Espuela Company is concerned I was at a loss to make out how they managed to keep their wages and stores so low. I consulted with Horsbrugh [Fred Horsbrugh, the Espuela manager] on several occasions and compared wages and price of supplies and could not understand, knowing the number of men, how he manipulated the accounts to keep wages, etc. in his accounts so low. A short time ago on talking the matter over I found that he debited the wages and supplies for his trail outfit to cattle sales. This of course makes a very considerable difference and if you will look at his average for 1892 you will see that he only averaged $10.60 per head while we averaged

$15.00. This shows that it is impossible to make a fair comparison without knowing the full particulars.

As regards the changing of the office it is more difficult for me to explain why there should be no change. If I am to have an office at all I must have it where I reside. I might send Johnstone to the ranch but then there would be no one to attend to the mail when I am away, which, as you know, is pretty much all the time in summer and fall. If I were to live at the ranch it would be different but that is out of the question in the meantime. So far as travelling expenses are concerned you will observe that there is scarcely any charge for train fares and if we were located at any other point I don't see how our expenses could be less than we can make them here.[31]

As credit balances reappeared on the company's books and as profits increased and dividends were paid, demands for a reduction in American expenses became less frequent, then disappeared. The manager, observing this peculiarity in human nature, commented in 1900: "I noticed long ago that if one wishes the average shareholder to take an apparent interest in the cattle business, the only way to achieve this result is to present him with a report showing a large debit balance and otherwise composed of heartrending accounts of famine, pestilence and drouth."

Among the problems with which Mackenzie had to contend during his early years with the Matador the one of the quarantine lines was of some significance; through it the manager was thrust on the national political stage and was given the opportunity to demonstrate his leadership in acting for the interests of the cattle industry. By 1891 the incongruity of restraining lines established by the states and the diversity of laws governing the interstate movement of livestock caused the federal government to fix a quarantine line along the south borders of Cochran, Hockley, Lubbock, Crosby, and Dickens counties in Texas.

[31] Mackenzie to Mackay, March 30, 1894. Mackenzie traveled on passes on the Fort Worth and Denver system in Texas and on the Santa Fe lines.

Cattle from south of this limit—fixed and enforced by the Department of Agriculture—were prohibited from crossing the line during the "ticky" season, February 15 to December 1. Since the Matador range lay entirely north of the boundary and since it was in the company's interest to keep its herds and land free from infection, Mackenzie proposed "to use all legal means to prevent cattle from being driven from the south to the north of the line" and instructed Ligertwood to "send a man you can depend on down to the southern part of our range with instructions to use all lawful means in keeping cattle back."[32] At the same time he succeeded in getting a deputy United States marshal appointed to patrol the "fever line." But the disadvantage of an intrastate line soon became apparent. Cattlemen from below the quarantine resented the advantage held by their fellow Texans north of the line, and ranchmen of the Panhandle were opposed to southern cattle's being brought into the cleared zone. Among both elements were those who derided the need for a quarantine until late in 1891, when a herd from the Gulf Coast was brought to Childress. During a storm these cattle were loosed from their pens to prevent injuries and before they could be recovered had scattered for miles in every direction. Within a short time nearly all the settlers' cattle near Childress died, and the scoffers became believers.[33]

To secure equitable regulations and their enforcement and protection other than that afforded by the federal government, Mackenzie and other Texas cattlemen called on Governor James Hogg "to get him to embrace in his special message, calling a session of the Legislature, a clause asking the Legislature to pass a law creating a Sanitary Board in the State, whose duty it would be . . . ascertain if possible where the quarantine line should be put to prevent the spread of Texas fever." The Governor told the delegation that he could not bring up the matter in his message,

[32] Mackenzie to Ligertwood, April 11, 1891.
[33] Mackenzie, "The Matador Ranch," 99.

but did agree to have a bill prepared to present to the legislature and promised to uphold the federal line.[34]

Realizing that Hogg had given no satisfactory reply to their request, the members of the committee next visited Washington, where the Secretary of Agriculture, J. M. Rusk, heard the complaints of those who felt themselves handicapped by the federal government's action in establishing the line so far to the north. Mackenzie later admitted that he went along on this trip not so much to get the line moved south as to see that it was not moved further north; he reported that Rusk "impressed on the Committee the necessity of recognizing his rulings" and that "the members of the delegation from south of the line left the Secretary fully convinced that he could not be trifled with."[35] Thereafter the grumbling subsided as a majority of southern cattlemen reluctantly accepted the restrictions.

With the variety and scope of the company's business operations increasing during the 1890's, Murdo Mackenzie found his own activities growing apace. The demands on his time and energy—exactions which would have drained the resources of a less sturdy man—were continuous; and while he would have preferred the quiet enjoyment of his family and home, the manager never avoided a journey or a meeting when he felt his presence at a place or with people would prove beneficial to the company's welfare. A "log" of his travels in 1897 indicates something of the nature and frequency of his trips:

> January 3. Left Trinidad for the ranch; spent a week with Ligertwood going over portions of the range; returned home January 12.
>
> January 19. Left Trinidad for Strong City, Kansas, to obtain pasturage for 1,000 steers. Returned home January 26.
>
> February 20. Left Trinidad for the ranch; went on to Fort Worth to attend a meeting of the Executive Committee of the

---

[34] Mackenzie to Mackay, January 12, 1892.
[35] Mackenzie to Mackay, February 11, 1892.

Stock Growers Association of Texas, March 4–8; went on to the Association's annual convention in San Antonio, stopping in Austin to confer with the Land Commissioner regarding the leasing of state school land. Returned home March 15.

March 19. Went to Estelline, Hall County, Texas, to witness loading of cattle bound for Strong City. Accompanied herd to Kansas, saw cattle unloaded and went on to Kansas City. Returned to Strong City March 28 to inspect cattle and returned home March 29.

April 4. Went to Childress, Texas, to attend court, the Company having filed suit to recover the amount of a note due by a Mr. Brown. Returned home April 11.

April 12. Went to Denver to see the railroad officials about rates for shipping steers from Estelline to Orin, Wyoming. Saw John Clay in Denver.

April 27. Left Trinidad for the ranch; returned home May 2.

May 10. Went to the ranch; saw steers bound for the Western Ranches range entrained; returned home May 15.

May 31. Went to the ranch and remained two weeks during spring roundup; returned to Trinidad on June 16.

June 20. Went to Strong City to inspect herd and to Hope, Kansas, to negotiate for the purchase of 21 purebred heifers. Returned to Trinidad on July 1.

July 9. Went to Hope, Kansas, to take delivery of the heifers; shipped these to the ranch and went to Strong City to inspect the cattle there. Returned home July 12.

July 17. Left Trinidad for the ranch; remained there until July 24 and returned home.

August 12. Left Trinidad for Strong City; went on to Chicago to witness the sale of several carloads of Matador steers shipped from the Western Ranches range. Returned to Trinidad on August 23.

September 1. Went to the ranch and remained two weeks during fall roundup and branding. Returned home September 16.

September 19. Mackay arrived in Trinidad and went on to the ranch with Mackenzie; returned to Trinidad September 27.

October 1. Mackenzie and Mackay went east, the manager

stopping in Kansas City to market the cattle shipped from Strong City. Mackenzie returned to Trinidad October 10.

October 28. Went to Topeka, Kansas, to receive and ship a carload of bulls to the ranch. Returned home on October 30.

November 1. Went to Denver to arrange sale of 1,000 heifers to a Mr. Harrison.

November 19. Left Trinidad for the ranch. Went on to Seymour, Texas, to attend court on November 28. Returned to Trinidad December 6 and remained there for the rest of the year since Johnstone had gone to Scotland for a visit.

A visit to the ranch was invariably followed by a complete report on range conditions:

I went to the ranch on the 10th inst. returning home on Saturday; while there I went over all the range. I am sorry I have to report that the range is in anything but satisfactory condition, though on the whole the cattle look fairly well. I first went out on the plains and there is not much grass but it is green and if we get rain soon we will have good grass there. I next went over to the Mott and spent two days going over the range there and North Pease. The grass in the shinnery all through that country is pretty good and cattle look well. There is plenty of water yet.

When you come down towards the ranch below where Boone lived, on the White Flats, there is really no grass at all, and it will take considerable rain to make grass start there again. This applied I may say to all the White Flats north and east of the ranch. I next went over Dutchman Creek and found the grass all right but needing rain pretty badly. The cattle are looking fairly well. In fact all the cattle look as well as I ever saw them at this time of the year, which is really a surprise to me, considering the condition of both cattle and range going into the winter. I next went south to Croton and visited the Hanna pasture on my way down going to Croton by Wichita tank. This country is of course dry, there being no water south of Tongue River except what we saved by tanking and windmills till we reach Croton pasture. In the Hanna pasture we have water in the northeast corner. We have kept the water open at the mouth of Saunders Hollow by scraping, and we have two windmills, one at the lake where we had lunch, (you will remember the place) and another at Matt Johns' old place. We have a tank in Beef Hollow about 5 miles south of Matt Johns' where there is still some water, but it cannot stand out much longer if the dry weather continues. Wichita tank is dry and we had to move all the cattle from that section to Patton Springs. The grass in Croton was wonderful considering the number of cattle there, but on account of the dry weather the water is very strong [gyp-like], and consequently the cattle did not do much good for ten days. We moved about 4000 head from this pasture north to Patton Springs where at least they can get plenty of good water. I was at Croton during the time they were rounding up and had a good opportunity of seeing the cattle. We had some trying weather while down at Croton. We had a dreadful windstorm from the north accompanied by a very unusual frost. We had ice one morning at least ¼ inch thick. From Croton I returned by Croton Point; on this route we came by the new tank called Boggy which is located about half way between Croton and Dutchman, and Hanna Pastures and Spur fence. This tank has considerable water yet but will not hold out long if the dry weather continues. We came home by the south end of Dutchman and Patton Springs. Patton Springs has as much water as it had when you saw it, and there is no danger of its going dry, but while the range is green round here there is little or no grass but weeds. After I came back to the ranch headquarters we visited Harnica Pasture and northeast portion of the range. Harnica and Turtle Hole look pretty green, but upon examination there is not much grass, and unless we get an abundance of rain this spring, I am afraid we are not going to be much better off than last year. I am glad to see, however, that the grass is not all dead, but will come if we get sufficient rain. The season so far has been everything but encouraging for grass. We had a fair good rain in March, but since then it has been very dry from parching winds, and prevents the grass from making much progress and just at this time things do not look any more encouraging than they did at this time last year. There was one thing which struck me very forcibly in going over the southern portion of the range and that is the want of living water outside of what we saved artificially by tanking.

Ligertwood has just sent in his tallies of losses. I am satisfied they have taken great pains to find out the losses as near as possible, but as we do not know what loss we had on the outside yet, we can scarcely do more than guess. I am inclined to think we cannot count on less than 5000 head but I will be able to give a more definite figure when we work the outside and Panhandle pasture.[36]

In his annual report to the board, customarily prepared in December, Mackenzie dealt with all matters which he felt were of interest to the stockholders; in time these summaries came to be presented in a form and with a cogency which obviated the need for hurried, last-minute exchanges between the secretary and the manager. A typical report was addressed to Alexander Mackay, Esquire, Secretary, Matador Land and Cattle Company, Limited, on December 24, 1896:

DEAR SIR: I beg to submit my report on the Company's business in America for the year ending 15th inst. and in doing so will deal particularly with the following subjects:

1. Cattle brand
2. Sales of cattle
3. American expenses
4. Lands owned by the Company
5. Condition of cattle and range
6. Condition of improvements

1. Calf Crop. The total number of calves branded up to 15th inst. was 14,492 as against 13,165 up to same date last year; or 1,327 more this year. We are still hunting the range and before the end of this month we may possibly get from 100 to 160 more calves. I expected during the summer that our tally would exceed last year's, but I did not think it would to the extent it did. During the months of October and November a great many young calves dropped, but the very small ones we did not brand; these will follow all right till Spring and we will then tally them with the 7 mark [for 1897]. I think the Board should be well

36 Mackenzie to Mackay, April 25, 1893.

satisfied with the result of this year's branding and while talking on this I think it right to mention that we should not allow our branding to get much above this year's figure, or 15,000 at the outside. The reason is we would not have sufficient range for the herd if we allowed our tally to get larger. Even as it is, I don't think we could safely count on 15,000 calves without taking our two-year old steers away as we now are doing.

To keep down the branding we should take every year a certain number of cows to Kansas and sell them there fast during the summer. These cows should be gathered the fall before and held in some pasture till spring where they could be got handy. Another reason for gathering them in the fall is that the most undesirable cows could then be got. We have gathered some of this kind this fall and we are now holding them in Croton ready to send to Kansas if the Board so desires.

2. Sales of Cattle. We sold during the year 6,099 cattle of all classes. The number of different classes and the prices realized are as follows:

Dakota steers	2114	$66,387.84
Dakota heifers	54	1,249.82
Three- and four-year steers (Matador)	205	5,535.00
Three- and four-year tailings	47	927.93
Two-year-old steers	605	14,520.00
Two-year-old steers, tailings	10	198.00
Yearling steers	205	4,100.00
Cows	2654	41,464.71
Old bulls	205	3,799.18
	6099	$138,182.58

This shows an average of $22.65 or something over one dollar less than last year. It is to be regretted that our average shows less but considering the year, we think we came out well in even making the above average. The 2,168 steers etc. sold from Dakota class as follows:

Single wintered cows	54
Single wintered steers	81
Four-year-old steers	1,657

Five-year-old steers	356
Six-year-old steers	20
	2,168

In our last accounts we took credit for 300 five-year olds but we got 376 over that age. The steers from the North were again disappointing in weight although somewhat better than last year's. Steers from Dakota did not come to market in anything like the condition of steers from Montana, but ours had to contend with the fact that they were small when sent North caused by the drought when they were calves.

The market for cows before the election was very depressed and we in common with others had to accept smaller prices than we got for the same class of cows last year. There were some cows shipped from which we weaned large calves and yearlings, which were rather thin in flesh, but as they were undesirable to keep we thought it best to ship them. This reduced to some extent the average of our sales, our cows averaging $15.62 against $16.40 last year.

We sent to Dakota 3,324 steers in the Spring, vizt. 1,158 yearlings and 2,166 twos. The steers looked well and we got them North in good time to get the benefit of all the season's grass. The cost of shipping and delivering the steers on the range was $1.95 per head. This we think very reasonable.

3. American Expenses. Our expenses on this side for the past year are very similar to our expenses for the previous year. It makes a little difference that we have 12½ months in our accounts this year while last year we had only 12 months, but even with the half-month extra included we show some saving in our expenses. Our expenses as shown by our books are as follows, vizt.:

Wages	$14,024.40
Salaries	9,699.87
Stores	6,955.20
Taxes	12,549.58
Protection	1,997.40
Repairs	1,817.04
Genl. charges	2,434.90

Wolf bounty	895.00
Texas pasturage	7,078.76
Dakota pasturage	4,181.00
	$61,633.15

@ $4.87/£=12,655.13.6 as against £13,489.14.8 or a difference of £834.1.2 in favor of this year. If we add to this difference the wages and salaries for the half month of Decr. it will amount in all to a reduction of something over £1,000. I cannot see how we are going to get below this figure and have the property looked after as it should be; I think on the whole the Board should now be satisfied with our expenses on this side.

4. Lands Owned by the Company. Since my last report we purchased 6,400 acres of land at 50 cts. per acre. I consider this land well worth the money. These lands as you are aware all lie within the Turtle Hole pasture and are first class grazing lands.

5. Condition of cattle and Range. Our cattle on the whole are looking well considering that we had a very dry season. The only place where we have thin cows is at the head of TeePee Creek, but we have weaned the calves in this district from the thinnest cows, removing the cows to Croton where the grass is fine. Over the balance of the range the cattle are in good condition and should go through the winter all right. Our purebred Herefords near the ranch are looking fine and with a fair winter they should come through in good shape. We had in all this year 36 purebred calves, 18 bulls and 18 heifers. In a short time we will have a nice herd which will help us very much in raising our own bulls.

Our range during the year had a sufficient amount of grass, but water was very scarce and we had considerable trouble in supplying our stock with water to drink. We managed by scraping for water and moving stock to keep them from suffering to any extent. Since the weather got cooler water is coming to the surface again in creeks, and I think we will get through the winter all right. Our tanks helped us out very much; none of them went dry except Wichita, but the Wichita has troubled us very much by the bottom falling out when it got full; this happened twice during the summer, and now we have decided to abandon the old site and build a new one half a mile further up.

6. Condition of Improvements. Our improvements are all in good preservation. We expended about $500 more in repairing them than we did in the previous year, but this extra work was all required to keep things in order. During the year we sunk a well three miles north of headquarters and erected a windmill on it. We found we were losing a lot of grass in this district for want of water. This well has been a great success; it will water all the cattle that can graze in that vicinity. We built a large dam on the head of Bear Creek in Turtle Hole pasture, but since it was built in Septr. there has been no water to fill it up. When we do get water to fill it up it will help us very much in that locality.

You will note that in charging the rent for the Dakota steers, I charged $1.00 per head for single wintered cattle and $2.00 for the others.[37]

Only through an intimate knowledge of the range and the ranch activities could the manager have developed such a report; and only by having the contents of such reports at hand could the directors have reached the decisions and established the policy which sustained the company through bonanzas and breaks.

By 1896 the value of Mackenzie's program was becoming apparent; his basic concept—that quality be attained regardless of cost—had meant heavy expenditures for purebred bulls and through the culling of inferior cows.[38] But despite these and the additional costs for pasturage at White Deer and in Dakota, the directors recommended the payment of a modest dividend—the first since 1889—on February 16, 1897.[39]

[37] Mackenzie to Mackay, December 24, 1896.

[38] "If we can obtain a bull that will add ten cents a head to the price of Matadors over a period of years, there is no price too great for us to pay in order to buy that bull. It isn't a question of whether we should pay $5,000 or $50,000 for him. It isn't a question of money at all. If he will improve our herd, we cannot afford NOT to own him." Mackenzie, quoted in M. Riordan's "Murdo Mackenzie, Range King," *The Westerner* (Denver), Vol. 6, No. 10 (October, 1943), 71.

[39] Fourteenth Annual Report, 5. This dividend of 2.5 per cent on the paid-up capital absorbed £5,000 of the £7,005 balance at the credit of the year's Profit and Loss Account.

The table below shows the balance of the Profit and Loss Account and the dividend declared for each year during the period 1891–1901; and while these figures do not reveal the complete story of the company's financial status—the value of land and herds, inventories of stores, debentures, and other assets and liabilities—the dividends in particular furnish evidence of the organization's fiscal health at the time indicated.

TABLE 1*

YEAR	BALANCE		DIVIDEND
1891	£ 254	(credit)	none
1892	1,888	(debit)	,,
1893	3,380	,,	,,
1894	171	(credit)	,,
1895	2,581	,,	,,
1896	7,007	,,	2½%
1897	14,339	,,	3¾
1898	21,365	,,	6¼
1899	25,708	,,	,,
1900	21,149	,,	,,
1901	18,005	,,	,,

* From the annual reports for the years listed.

Here are mirrored the results of the drought of 1892 and the panic of 1893, the increase in income from the sale of improved stock wintered on northern pastures, the high livestock market quotations accompanying the outbreak of the Spanish-American War and their subsequent decline, and the adverse effect upon cattle prices exercised by the failure of the middle-western corn crop in 1901.

During this eleven-year period the herd strength dropped from 70,200 in 1892 to 58,000 in 1893, then climbed slowly so that in 1901 it was rated at 69,200 head, very near the limit which Mackenzie believed the ranges could safely hold. The two principal factors accounting for variations in the herd count were cattle sales and the calf crop. The first was affected by market prices and the company's annual monetary requirements, and ranged from 4,827 head in 1895 to 9,812 in 1901. The calf brand, determined in large measure by the weather, varied from 5,309 in 1893 to 17,335 in 1901; the low tally in 1893 was due to the drought of the previous year, which left cattle in poor condition and caused many cows to slip their calves.

Experience gained during his first ten years as Matador manager convinced Mackenzie that the Hereford breed could not be equaled as range stock. Moreover, he challenged the accepted notion that highly bred cattle would become unproductive; with a marked predilection for Anxiety blood, he developed a small purebred herd and recorded, year after year, a calf crop of over 90 per cent in this select group. Moreover, the directors had come to expect among range cows a calf tally of 50 per cent—one calf for every two cows—but by providing a minimum of fifteen acres per range animal, running four bulls to every hundred cows, and furnishing "a plentiful supply of water at a distance not greater than four miles between watering places," Mackenzie increased the productivity of the range herd so that by the opening of the twentieth century a calf crop of 80 per cent was not unexpected.[40]

At the turn of the century two developments, both indicative of the westward surge of America's population, forced the Matador company into new lines of endeavor. The first of these, the threatened dissolution of its contract with the Western Ranches, led to a search for a more permanent footing in the north; the second, the expiration of the White Deer lease, led to the purchase of additional land in Texas.

Even though Murdo Mackenzie had objected to two features of the Matador's arrangement with the Western Ranches—the company's inability to control its cattle on the Belle Fourche and the absence of clauses fixing responsibility in the event of loss or damage to the stock—he had endorsed the contract, since the prospect for gains outweighed the risks; too, sustained criticism of the terms might have caused the board to drop the whole

[40] Alvin H. Sanders, *The Story of the Herefords*, 774–78.

venture, and that would have been disastrous to the manager's program. Fortunately profits from the enterprise were substantial, and there were few occasions for complaint on the treatment given Matador cattle; losses among the Dakota steers were seldom as high as anticipated, and when beeves scheduled for shipment escaped the roundup and spent an additional year on the range, there was no protest from Mackenzie.

. Until 1898 no serious dispute marred relations between Mackenzie and John Clay, but in that year there arose a situation which, while not important in itself, involved a principle and provided an occasion for the manager to renew his criticism of the contract. On a large open range such as that controlled by the Western Ranches, it was inevitable that there should be some mixing and straying of cattle; in fact, when the first Matador steers reached Dakota in 1892, some were mistakenly gathered with other brands and shipped to market. This occurred time and again during the next six years and was recognized as being unavoidable. In such a case the seller—the person who gathered the cattle—would remit to the company the proceeds from the sale of Matador steers after deducting freight charges from the range to market. This procedure worked very well until June, 1898, when the Dundee office received the proceeds from the sale of two stray steers; deducted from the sale price of each were charges for "freight and yardage," and in addition "there were deductions in one case of $19.55 and in the other of $25.20 for 'feed and freight.' " Upon inquiry, Mackenzie found that the Standard Cattle Company of Ames, Nebraska, had shipped the two steers along with its own cattle from the Western Ranches range in the fall of 1897, had fed them corn all winter, and had sold them in Chicago in the spring of 1898. To Mackenzie, the question was not one of paying the Standard people for the feed, but of placing responsibility on the Western Ranches for allowing Matador steers to leave the Dakota range for unauthorized feeding. His position was made clear to Clay: "If these steers are some of those we gave the Western Ranches to pasture, and I have no reason to think otherwise, we must look to you to deliver the steers to us at the railroad as provided in our contract."[41]

Clay's reply revealed that his views were opposite to those of Mackenzie:

> In regard to the cattle shipped by Mr. Allen [Standard manager] we cannot take the responsibility for him for having taken some of your cattle off the range. Everyone gets a very large number of strays into their herd every season and an old experienced ranchman like yourself should certainly know this, and doubtless you have shipped many, many strays to market yourself. . . . In referring to your contract I do not think it says anything about people shipping strays with your brand upon them.[42]

Realizing little could be gained by continuing the exchange, the manager notified Clay of his intention to refer the matter to Mackay and warned Clay that should larger sums be involved in similar cases, the company would hold the Western Ranches liable. In sending to the secretary copies of the correspondence between himself and Clay, Mackenzie suggested that there were other flaws in the contract which might provide the bases for future difficulties:

> You will notice in Mr. Clay's letter that he shirks the main issue. Our contract is distinct and clear that we deliver to the Western Ranches so many cattle, free of charge to them, on their own range, that we pay them for the full number delivered, for the first year, and that they deliver back to us at the railroad nearest their range for the consideration of an additional dollar, the cattle, either as threes, fours or fives. If Western Ranches takes no liability in the matter I would like to know what we are getting in return for our money. It might be possible that some farmer would take up twenty or thirty of our steers, feed them for six months, send them to market, deduct feed charges, and give us whatever is left. . . . It is quite possible that Mr. Clay will write you on this subject, and it is for you to say what we should

[41] Mackenzie to Clay, July 7, 1898.
[42] Clay to Mackenzie, July 20, 1898.

do. . . . There are several questions which have arisen in connection with the contract . . . which have no direct bearing on this particular point at issue. We find all through that their object is to take no responsibility whatever, at the same time they insist upon getting their pound of flesh.[43]

In August, Mackenzie received word that the board supported his position completely and that when the secretary made the annual trip to inspect the ranch, he would "take occasion in going through Chicago to emphasize this view to Clay."

Whatever its immediate result, this episode marked the beginning of a breakdown in relations between the Matador company and the Western Ranches; and when in 1900 the latter organization's managing director refused to enter into a long-term contract with Mackay and informed the secretary that the annual rental would be increased to $1.125 per head, Mackay advised Mackenzie to consider what course the company might follow should it "finally determine to part company with the Western Ranches." The secretary realized that the Edinburgh corporation, unlike the Matador, had acquired title to very little land within its range and that as settlers pre-empted choice sites along streams and around ponds in the Belle Fourche country, the Western Ranches would find itself with oceans of grass and no water, its pastures worthless for grazing.

Although Mackenzie did "look around some" in the Dakotas and Montana, four years passed before he could give proper attention to locating a suitable range in the north; a more urgent matter had arisen in Texas. In 1901, when the company attempted to renew its lease on the pastures in Carson and Gray counties, the White Deer Lands people were unwilling to accept the terms proposed by Mackay. According to Mackenzie's information, the refusal to re-lease was due to the owners' decision "to start a town at Pampa . . . and to reserve all the land around Pampa to sell to settlers."[44]

[43] Mackenzie to Mackay, July 27, 1898.

At the beginning of 1902 the company realized it had only six months in which to obtain pasturage for its yearlings; and since no suitable tracts were available for lease and "a separate pasture for holding young steers was counted indispensable to the Company if the business of maturing steers was to thrive," the board resolved "with reluctance but entire unanimity to purchase a pasture capable of carrying about twelve thousand head."[45] The implementation of this decision, providing as it did a second permanent base from which to operate, permitted the company to widen the scope of its activities in the north and to attain, within a decade, a prosperity rare in the range cattle industry.

[44] Mackenzie to Mackay, November 23, 1901. Cf. L. F. Sheffy, *The Life and Times of Timothy Dwight Hobart*, 174–95.
[45] Nineteenth Annual Report, 5.

～3～

Cattlemen, Politics,
and the "Beef Ring"

THE POSSIBILITY that the Matador officials might be persuaded
to purchase rather than lease land for their yearling steers occurred to Murdo Mackenzie during the summer of 1901. At a
cattle raisers' meeting in Fort Worth on August 26, Mackenzie
told Colonel A. G. Boyce, the general manager of the XIT Ranch,
that the Matador lease on the White Deer would expire in 1902
and asked Boyce if any of the XIT lands would be for rent. Boyce
replied that there were no pastures for lease but that the Capitol
Freehold Land and Investment Company, Limited, had begun
to divest itself of some of its holdings and that there was a possibility one tract of the syndicate's property in the Panhandle
could be purchased.[1] If Mackenzie was interested, he did not
indicate it at the time; but two weeks later he wrote Boyce that
while the Matador company was negotiating for a renewal of
the White Deer lease, "some things connected with this pasture
were not entirely satisfactory, especially the water question,"
and asked Boyce to send information regarding the provisions
which the XIT made for watering its cattle on the plains. After
inquiring about the distance between wells and acknowledging
that "you have had a great deal more experience in this matter
than I have," the manager got to the real point of the letter:

[1] In July, 1901, the Capitol syndicate, owner of the XIT, sold over 235,000
acres of its Yellow Houses Division to George W. Littlefield and over 49,500
acres in the Bovina Division to J. E. and J. W. Rhea. Haley, *The XIT Ranch of
Texas* (1953), 218.

In the event of our not making arrangements for the White
Deer pasture, it is possible that we might talk with you about
buying the pasture you spoke to me about when I was at Ft.
Worth, and I shall feel obliged if you will write me full particulars, giving me the size of the pasture, the nature of the ground,
and how it is watered.

You might state as near as you can what shelter there is in the
pasture. If you have a map showing the location . . . with all the
fences marked on it and the windmills and watering places, it
would help me very considerable.[2]

Since Mackay was due to arrive in New York on September 25
to negotiate with Frederick de P. Foster, one of the White Deer
Lands owners, Mackenzie wanted to have at hand as much information as possible about the XIT property if the negotiations
should fail. The XIT manager's prompt reply contained the information needed:

As to the pasture I was talking of selling you, it lies just south
of the Canadian River, is on the east boundary of our possessions,
and is known as the Alamositas pasture. It is about twenty miles
from Tascosa and about twenty-five miles from Channing. This
pasture is well watered with running creeks, springs and dams.
There are no windmills. It has good protection, and I think it is
as fine a pasture as can be found in Texas, and contains about
150,000 acres. It has good corrals, a little horse pasture or two
and a few small hay vegas [meadows]. If you are at all inclined
to buy and will come and look at this pasture I am satisfied you
will take it. It is going to sell before long and I would much prefer getting a good neighbor like yourself than someone of whom
I know nothing.[3]

Acknowledging receipt of the map, Mackenzie promised
Boyce that "if we do not arrange about our lease at White Deer

[2] Mackenzie to Boyce, September 12, 1901.
[3] Boyce to Mackenzie, September 13, 1901. A map accompanied the letter;
the pasture lay in the center of Oldham County, Texas where the Canadian
River, cutting a groove across the High Plains, produced the rough country
which characterized the Alamositas division of the XIT.

it is possible I may get our people to consider the purchase of this pasture of yours." However, he made no mention of the matter during Mackay's month-long visit in America, for he had no statement from the XIT people concerning the price of the land; too, he was plagued by a doubt that the pasture was large enough for the company's purposes. A letter to Boyce asking for terms and suggesting that the Matador needed more land went unanswered until Mackay departed for Scotland; even then, though he indicated that an additional fifty thousand acres could be bought out of the Rito Blanco pasture, which lay north of the river, or from the Escarbada division south of Alamositas, Boyce gave only the terms—"one tenth cash, balance in nine notes at six per cent annually." Mackenzie had to write once more to get the price.

On November 21 the Dundee office received its first knowledge of the activities:

> Since you left here I have put myself in communication with Mr. Boyce of the Capitol Syndicate Co. and I have now heard from him, stating he will sell us the Alamositas pasture of 150,000 and a sufficient number of acres of the Rito Blanco pasture to make up the number of acres we require. Their price is $2.00 per acre, one-tenth down and the balance in nine deferred payments of equal amount, bearing 6% interest. From all I can hear of this pasture, I think it is the best proposition we have yet before us, and if we cannot make some satisfactory arrangement with the White Deer people, my own idea would be that we should try and secure this pasture from the Capitol Syndicate people. When you take into consideration the losses we have had at White Deer and the amount of money it takes for feed to keep the cattle alive, it is a question with me whether this extra outlay at White Deer would not be sufficient to meet nearly the yearly payments we would be out in paying for this new pasture.[4]

Mackay's reply was encouraging, though he warned that the purchase scheme might prove too large for the company's re-

[4] Mackenzie to Mackay, November 8, 1901.

sources. He asked for "all particulars" so that the board would
"have time to weigh carefully the consideration and come to a
mature judgment in the matter."

In support of his own views, Mackenzie drafted the outline of
a plan which he sent to Mackay for the directors' consideration.
Admitting that financing the operation "might be a little hard to
begin with," he reckoned that "on the whole it would be better
to buy than to take chances of renting another pasture" inasmuch
as negotiations with the White Deer owners were leading nowhere:

> Supposing that we sent 6000 cattle a year to Dakota, we could
> sell from this number at least 5000 every year; take this number
> at $35.00 per head, which is a very safe estimate, and it will give
> us $175,000 a year from this place [Dakota]; besides we could
> sell $60,000 worth of steers from Texas and $60,000 worth of
> cows, making a grand total of $295,000. Supposing also we pur-
> chased 250,000 acres of land, the total purchase price would be
> $500,000 and the down payment each year would be $50,000; if
> we deduct $50,000 from $295,000 we have $245,000 left which is
> practically what we now have. I consider that the rent we would
> have to pay for the White Deer pasture or any other pastureland
> enough to carry our cattle would cost us about as much as the
> interest due annually on this sum would amount to; besides this
> interest would be reducing every year by about $3000 so that in
> a few years it would be a small item comparatively speaking. Of
> course we would have the taxes on the land to consider, but I
> think, taking it over the ten years, that the rent we are now pay-
> ing at White Deer would much more than pay for both interest
> and taxes.[5]

On both sides of the Atlantic the inclination to buy grew
stronger. Early in December, Mackay cabled the Trinidad office
to arrange a thorough inspection of the Capitol company's pasture, and in his letter confirming the cable disclosed his dissatisfaction with the terms of the White Deer Lands lease as proposed

[5] Mackenzie to Mackay, November 23, 1901.

by agents Russell Benedict and George Tyng. Concerning the purchase, he said, "The Board will recommend buying with some reluctance as it means laying down a very large sum of money; at the same time if there is no other alternative they will, I think, be prepared to recommend such a course if the terms are not too onerous." Instructions for the inspection were somewhat detailed:

> As preliminary to any consideration of the scheme, the Board want a thorough inspection made. . . . You will make this inspection just as complete as it is in your power to undertake and you will, of course, employ any additional assistance which you think will be necessary. . . . If we have to face the shareholders with a scheme involving a large purchase we must be prepared to show that the purchase is made only after the most exhaustive inquiry. We should like you to send us at once a map of the pasture showing the broken country and the water supply.
>
> We would like you to work out an estimate of the number of steers which you could run on 200,000 or 250,000 acres, showing what the cost per head would be, and working charges. You will be careful also to ascertain that there is not the drawback in this pasture which we discovered in the White Deer with reference to feeding qualities in the grass during winter.
>
> There will be time enough to consider the financial aspects of the transaction when we are satisfied about the desirability of the purchase. We would like you to sound Mr. Boyce when you meet him as to whether better terms could not be got considering the magnitude of the transaction. We might possibly manage to pay down at once a much larger sum than what is stipulated for, and we should certainly not be willing to pay 6% upon the deferred payments. Try him with $1.50 per acre and hold up ready money in front of them. Of course the final settlement will rest with Farwell [John V. Farwell, managing director] in Chicago, or possibly with the Trustees for the debenture holders in London. The money goes to them. If you can find out from Mr. Boyce just who will finally settle the transaction we might manage in London to do a little negotiating.[6]

6 Mackay to Mackenzie, December 6, 1901.

With this display of interest from the board, Mackenzie hastened preparations for an inspection. When a report was circulated that the price of all XIT lands would go up after the first of the year, he drew a promise from Boyce that the two dollars an acre price for Alamositas would stand and proceeded with the calculations requested by the secretary.

During the last five days of December the inspecting party—Mackenzie, Johnstone, Dave Somerville, Jack Lucket, and Frank Mitchell—rode over the Alamositas and Rito Blanco pastures, and on December 31, Mackenzie wrote his report:

> During our inspection we were well satisfied with everything we saw; there was an abundance of water everywhere and with the exception of one place I do not think that a cow has to travel over two miles to get water. . . .
>
> The Alamositas Creek runs very nearly from the Canadian River to the edge of the breaks, and runs a strong stream of water and is everlasting. . . .
>
> On the whole I do not think I ever saw a pasture that is better watered and the quality of the water is first class; it reminds me of the springs we see breaking out around the foot of the plains in our Matador pasture. In going over this range I was much impressed by the splendid shelter for cattle; it reminded me of that country coming down the head of Turtle Hole; also that country south and west of the Mott. . . .
>
> We are unanimous in feeling that the Company could not get a better steer pasture in the Panhandle than this one. The Alamositas pasture extends to about 150,000 acres; I think this would be entirely too small for our purpose and we proposed taking in a part of the range north of the Alamositas pasture between that and the Canadian River; we also proposed at the east end of the range to cross the Canadian and take in a strip of about two miles wide to give us an outlet to the railroad [the Fort Worth and Denver], as a pasture there would be handy for shipping. This additional piece of Rito Blanco pasture would amount to about 60,000 acres, making a total of about 210,000. . . . Before going to the pasture neither Mr. Johnstone nor myself felt that anything short of 240,000 would be sufficient for us, but

after seeing the range and quality and quantity of the grass, we came to the conclusion that the Alamositas pasture would carry what cattle we would want to send up there. . . .

I tried Mr. Boyce with a proposition to pay all cash and asked him the lowest price on this basis, but he told me that this [$2.00] was their lowest price that would buy it, either cash or on deferred payments. Mr. Boyce is the sole agent for selling this land and I do not think it would be advisable to attempt to go past him with a view of getting a lower price. . . . We have to decide within a month or five weeks what we are to do.[7]

During January, 1902, when negotiations with the White Deer people were broken off, the board sent for Mackenzie, and on January 18 he sailed from New York on the Cunard liner *Etruria*. He arrived in Dundee in time to appear at the annual meeting of the shareholders on February 7, and there made such an effective presentation in support of the Alamositas purchase that those present voted unanimously to approve the proposal. Mackay immediately cabled Johnstone and Boyce that the Matador company would take an option on 210,000 acres of the XIT property and lost no time in setting forth the terms under which Mackenzie could act in closing the contract with the Capitol agent.

Shortly after his return to America, Mackenzie met Boyce in Fort Worth and handed him a synopsis of the points which the Dundee company wanted covered in the contract. On March 27 the two managers met again in Amarillo and, acting as agents for their respective companies, signed a memorandum of agreement. According to this document, the Capitol Freehold Land and Investment Company, Limited, agreed to sell to the Matador Land and Cattle Company, Limited, "two hundred and ten thousand (210,000) acres of land more or less, situated in the

[7] Mackenzie to Mackay, December 31, 1901. Later in the day the manager wrote that taxes would be "less than $5.00 per section, about one-third of what we pay . . . at Matador" and added that "the Capitol Syndicate and LS [Ranch] control this county and it is entirely in their hands, and we would of course do our part to keep taxes down."

County of Oldham, in the State of Texas . . . in what is known as the Alamositas pasture" plus certain lands described as a part of the Rito Blanco pasture and some lands then belonging to the Reynolds Land and Cattle Company; the Reynolds lands were to be procured by the XIT prior to the date of transfer of all the properties, May 15, 1902. The buyer agreed to pay two dollars an acre. It was stipulated in the agreement that the Capitol syndicate would survey the lands to be transferred and that the Matador would erect a fence along the bounds of the property where no fence existed at the time of the transfer.

At a called meeting of the Matador shareholders on April 18, a resolution was approved to amend the company's Articles of Association so that the directors could borrow sufficient money, estimated at £25,000, to permit paying the Capitol company in full.[8] Mackenzie was authorized to sign the contract for the company.

On September 28, 1902, the deed transferring 198,732.1 acres to the Matador company was filed for record at Tascosa, then the county seat of Oldham County; for this land the vendors received $397,464.20. Later in the year title to an additional 15,229 acres was conveyed to the buyers, so that at the end of 1902 the Matador claimed 213,961 acres in its Alamositas Division.

While it had been anticipated that the transfer of property would be completed in May, the delay until September did not deny to the Matador the use of its new pasture in the summer. On June 12 the first steers from White Deer were turned loose on Alamositas grass, and by the end of the year seventeen thousand head bearing the "V" brand were grazing along the Canadi-

---

[8] The lenders were:

Scottish American Mortgage Company	£10,000 at 5%
George Halley	5,000 at 4½%
John Robertson	5,000 at 4½%
David Wilkie	5,000 at 4½%

Halley, Robertson, and Wilkie were Matador directors. The loans were secured by a vendor's lien.

an. Mackenzie had planned that not more than twelve thousand steers would be placed at Alamositas, but a severe drought in Motley County during the summer and fall made it necessary to move cattle from that area and pasture them elsewhere. The move was temporary, however, and when the drought was broken in 1903, the herd at Alamositas was reduced.

With the acquisition of the Oldham County lands, a permanent change in the company's organization was effected in America. The original range—the "home ranch" in Motley County—became the "Matador Division," and its superintendent, Arthur Ligertwood, continued to report directly to the manager. On the Canadian the "Alamositas Division" was created, with Dave Somerville as superintendent. Like Ligertwood, Somerville was responsible to Mackenzie. Each division kept its own set of books, accounts, payrolls, and correspondence files; and the operations of each were reflected in records kept in Trinidad and Dundee.[9]

Alamositas became, in Mackenzie's words, "the half-way house for young cattle between the main ranch and the range in Dakota." Annually it received the yearling stock from the Matador Division and shipped to the northern ranges the two-year-olds for double-wintering. The Fort Worth and Denver Railroad, extending along the northeast edge of the range, provided convenient transportation facilities from the southern ranch and to the northern pastures; in addition, the railroad installed cattle pens and a loading chute at a switch, appropriately called Murdo, where the line ran next to the company's property.

Hardly was the ink dry on the deed transferring the Alamositas land to the Matador when Mackay began to explore possibilities that the company might secure long-term leases on grasslands in Canada. In fact, during his annual visit to America in September, 1902, he spoke to Mackenzie about Dominion lands, and before sailing from New York in October visited in Ottawa,

[9] Subsequently, divisions were created in Canada, South Dakota, and Montana.

where he "had two interviews with the Land Commissioner and one with the Minister of Interior" and learned that a maximum lease of 100,000 acres of public land might be obtained in the western provinces. Since Mackay's brother-in-law, W. A. Burns, was the manager of the Bank of Nova Scotia in Ottawa and was a personal friend of the land commissioner, the secretary felt that the Land Department would "afford all the information and the best treatment" to the company in its inquiries. First it had to be determined "if the raising of steers were profitable under the conditions—a 20% duty, the cost of carriage north, and a suitable market." Mackay promised "to find out the likely outcome to the steer if sold for the eastern market" and instructed Mackenzie to inquire about railroad rates.[10]

In Montreal, Mackay was disappointed to find that "an average of $45 net" could be expected for cattle sold on the range and that charges for freight and insurance from the western provinces to England would amount to thirty dollars a head. The profit thus obtainable was no inducement to enter upon a venture in Canada, but the fact that the Western Ranches pastures were in danger and that cattle from the Belle Fourche were reported to be light in weight in 1902 led Mackay to the conclusion that it might be "most necessary" to have a try at the Canadian lease.[11]

Mackenzie, though not particularly enthusiastic about the "Canadian proposal," informed Mackay that he could "find out most of the particulars . . . for shipping to Canada and from there to the seaboard by writing," but that he would recommend no part of the country as a range "without first going over the ground and making a thorough inspection."

[10] Mackay to Mackenzie, October 16, 1902.

[11] "I am very much afraid that the watering places in Dakota are taken up by small holders to such an extent that cattle have to travel too far for water." Mackenzie to Mackay, November 18, 1902. Neither Mackay nor Mackenzie would subscribe to Clay's theory that Panhandle ranchmen were "breeding their cattle too fine," which resulted in a smaller bone structure and, consequently, a reduction in weight.

The directors looked with favor on the matter from the outset and directed Mackay to write the government at Ottawa concerning the possibilities of a lease. The secretary's letter, addressed to the Honourable Clifford Sifton, minister of the interior, included a statement of the terms under which the board would apply for a lease:

> The Board contemplate sending next Spring some of their officials to inspect the lands in Alberta and Assiniboia, if a lease can be secured from the Canadian government for a long term of years at the usual rate of ⨍2 per acre, and if the lease can be made on such terms that exclusive rights are secured for the land leased. A lease granted with the right of settlement to squatters and others would be of little or no use for the purpose of this Company, as the business, if gone into at all, would be prosecuted on a considerable scale; and if the Company were exposed to vexatious annoyances and blackmailing at the instance of squatters and others their business would not be worth pursuing under these conditions. My Board would therefore be obliged if you would see your way to grant in their case a lease which would exclude the right of settlement. We should like, if possible, to secure 100,000 acres under the lease, but if the law does not permit of any single lessee holding direct from the Government so much land we should like a lease for the maximum amount permitted.[12]

The letter found its way to the office of J. W. Turriff, commissioner of Dominion Lands, who replied that he was prepared to "grant a lease for 21 years on the most favourable terms, namely, not subject to homestead entry or withdrawal of the lease for purpose of sale." Upon receipt of this encouraging information, the board authorized Mackenzie to arrange for an examination of the country with whatever assistance he might need and urged him to keep the Dundee office informed of developments.

In anticipation of the authorization, the manager had made contact with several cattlemen who had had experience in Ca-

12 Mackay to Sifton, November 19, 1902.

nadian ranching and with others who contemplated action similar to that of the Matador, and was prepared to go into the western provinces in January, 1903. However, the resignation of Henry Johnstone at the end of 1902 created a vacancy which had to be filled before Mackenzie could leave, and the new accountant, Mackenzie's nephew, John MacBain, became ill shortly after moving to Trinidad, so the inspection was delayed until the summer.[13] An exceptionally severe winter and a late spring in the Panhandle so retarded branding and shipping at the Texas ranches that it was July 14 before the manager could leave.

On July 20, Mackenzie arrived in Medicine Hat, province of Assiniboia (now Alberta). After spending a day in the Land Office, he went on to Lethbridge and Calgary, where he had the good fortune to meet an old acquaintance, Henry Smith. Persuading Smith to accompany him on his tour of the ranges, Mackenzie soon discovered that the good grasslands in Assiniboia were already in the hands of the railroads and that those lands not granted to the Canadian Pacific Lines had been ceded to sheepmen, a situation which made it "out of the question for us to think of going into that country." He found that "to go further north than Calgary would bring us within the radius of the deep snow in winter and outside the radius of chinook winds," and decided to go elsewhere. Upon receiving information that there were vacant lands in Saskatchewan, he and Smith turned eastward to Swift Current; what they saw from their point of view as cattlemen was reported to Dundee in August:

> We had to have a team at Swift Current to inspect this country, which took us four days. The Saskatchewan River is 25 miles north of Swift Current Station, and our objective was immediately north of this river. We got to the river in the evening and were lucky to find a half-breed named LaPlant, to whom we were referred at Swift Current to act as our guide. We crossed on a ferry at this place, which is operated by the government, and

13 MacBain entered the company's service in 1898 and spent four years at the Ballard Springs headquarters, where he did the clerical work for Ligertwood.

drove due north over thirty-five miles of the finest piece of country I ever saw in my life. We spent three days going over the range, and during all that time we did not see a living animal except ducks and geese, and I think three antelope. The grass is better than anything I have ever seen and there is an abundance of water. There is one place of, I should say, thirty to fifty miles, and you can never at any time get out of sight of water; lakes everywhere, and the best kind of blue-stem and grama grass up to the very tops of the mountains. We decided if any place would be suitable for a good cattle range, this was the place, and it has the further advantage of being unoccupied. True, there are a few settlers along the north side of the Saskatchewan River at this place, but they have only a few cattle, and at least three-fourths of the river front is still open for a distance of 120 miles. We are very much impressed with this place as a cattle range. It has an abundance of shelter and has the further advantage of the Saskatchewan River being on the southeast and east boundaries, which is really a very necessary thing in this country to keep your cattle at home. A place there which we were particularly well struck with was a bend of the river, which is sixty miles across from where the river begins to bend, to where it comes back on the same line again. In other words, the river makes the shape of a half-moon, and right across the base of the half-moon the distance is sixty miles.

I cabled you immediately upon my return that I was very much impressed with the range in the Canadian country and that something should be done immediately if the Board intends sending cattle into that country. My reason for this was that thousands of people are now looking for a suitable location for ranging purposes, and it is only a matter of a short time when all this country will be taken up. If we could get the Canadian government to give us the land on the river front, as they have been doing with other people, I do not anticipate any encroachments at this particular place for a long time to come. It is true there are disadvantages, the worst being having to cross the Saskatchewan River, which is 400 yards wide at the ferry, and I think where the ferry is, is about the narrowest place I saw. While it has this disadvantage, it would be a great advantage to have the river on three sides of us, as this would act as a boundary to keep our cattle at home.

We did not investigate any country farther east than this because we were informed by people who knew that this was as far east as we should risk going. . . . The half-breed who acted as our guide is a man forty to forty-five years of age and he was born and raised in this district. He told us that the snow falls to a depth of six to ten inches, and sometimes a foot, but the snow never stays on the ground long on account of the chinook winds. There is another very material advantage in connection with this part of the country; it is hilly and rolling, and affords a great deal of good shelter for cattle during storms.

The breaks of the Saskatchewan River do not extend very far out, but there are several deep canyons running out from the river four to six miles and these afford good shelter for cattle. Another benefit derived from being in a broken country is that on the southern side of the hill the snow always melts from the heat of the sun, and it would afford grass for the cattle after a storm as well as shelter. . . .

Before deciding to do anything in this matter, the board should fully consider the pros and cons. I would have no hesitation in recommending the board to send cattle to Canada if our only object was to get them fat. I do not think I ever saw a better grass country, and from all the information I could gather, the losses there are not any heavier than we have in the range country in the States. In getting the cattle into Canada we have to pay a duty of 20%, but I am told the Canadian government is very lenient in the valuations. If we decided to bring our cattle back from Canada and sell them in Chicago, we would have to pay a duty of 27%, and this I am afraid would put a bar to ever thinking of disposing of our cattle in this way. The only other alternatives would be to sell to traders there who come to the range to buy cattle or ship direct to Liverpool, to be sold there on behalf of the Company. I had several talks with cattle men in Canada on this point, and they assured me that there would be no difficulty in making arrangements to get space to ship our cattle to Liverpool if we failed to get a fair price for them at home. The buyers were coming around to see the cattle men when I was in

Canada, and they were offering three and a-half cents per pound for cattle on board cars. . . .

Supposing we decided to send our cattle to Canada, and pay the Canadian Government 20% duty. We could get our two-year olds in there at a valuation of from fifteen to sixteen dollars, and the duty on this would be about $3.00 per head. The cost of taking them up there would be between $3.50 and $4.00, so that we would have a fixed charge of from $6.50 to $7.00 per head on all the cattle sent. A great many people take in yearlings so as to get them in on less valuation but then they have to feed a great number of them during the first winter, which more than gets away with the difference they would have to pay between year-lings and two-year olds. I asked several people there if they did not think, in their opinions, two-year olds would do as well in that country as they did in Montana or Dakota, and the answers they gave me were that they had no hesitation in saying that two-year olds would do fully as well in that part of Canada as they ever did in either Montana or Dakota.[14]

Reports that the range along the Belle Fourche was excessively dry, rumors that John Clay was getting ready "to wind up the Western Ranches any year," and a belief that a reciprocity treaty between the United States and Canada would soon be arranged led the board to apply for a lease in Saskatchewan. Mackay and Mackenzie presented the company's request to the government officials in Ottawa in the fall of 1903; but as weeks passed into months without action, it became apparent that the land com-missioner and the Minister of the Interior were in no hurry to approve the Matador request. Mackay was inclined to think that the delay was due to "natural timidity" on the part of Turriff, the land commissioner, who had promised full co-operation in 1902, when the lease question was first raised. It seems more likely that Sifton, who was promoting the settlement of the west-ern provinces through immigration, was reluctant to deny to settlers the pre-emption of so much good land, at least until after the elections of 1904.[15]

[14] Mackenzie to Mackay, August 14, 1903.

By the spring of 1904, Mackenzie was "thoroughly disgusted" with the situation and was becoming suspicious of the Canadian officials and their motives in prolonging negotiations. As other and more urgent problems presented themselves, he became content "to let the Canadian proposition . . . lie in abeyance" until he had time to take it up again; but Mackay, realizing that the manager would be busy shipping and marketing cattle during the spring and summer, began to push the Ottawa officials to action through a series of letters to the Department of the Interior. As a result of his efforts, the Department "decided that the application would be considered for an area not to exceed 50,000 acres" and requested the company to designate the tract it wanted.[16]

Despite their disappointment at being offered only a fraction of the land needed, the directors instructed Mackenzie to proceed to Ottawa at his earliest convenience and select the desired acreage. Again the manager was balked, for he found that the Canadian Pacific Railroad had laid claim to a section of land on the north bank of the Saskatchewan in the very center of the range applied for by the Matador. Government officials, seemingly unaware of the necessity for a solid block of land, suggested that other sections were available, but Mackenzie was insistent that the lease conform to the terms set forth by the board and refused to accept substitute proposals. He went again to Ottawa in November "to explain . . . the true reason why we wanted the land in one block" and this time "had no difficulty whatever" in getting the desired tract.[17]

In February, 1905, Mackenzie went to the Saskatchewan country with Dave Somerville, who had indicated his willingness to superintend the Canadian Division. After a look at the

15 To speed settlement of the Canadian West, Sifton had established immigration offices in the United States, the British Isles, and in continental Europe. *Cambridge History of the British Empire*, VI, 515–16.

16 Perley G. Keyes, secretary, Timber and Mines Branch, Department of the Interior, to Mackay, May 4, 1904.

17 Mackenzie to Mackay, December 5, 1904.

region "during the season of hard weather," Mackenzie returned to Colorado, leaving Somerville at Swift Current to become acquainted with the land and the people and to determine the cost of fencing the lease.

In March the contract was signed by the Canadian officials and the company; under its terms the Matador obtained a "closed lease" on fifty thousand acres along the left bank of the Saskatchewan River due north of Swift Current for an annual rental of approximately £200. A reserve clause in the contract provided that the lease would be given up upon two years' notice by the government.

On June 1, 1905, the first Matador cattle bound for Canada went on board fifty-five cattle cars at Murdo, the loading station at the Alamositas Division. This shipment, consisting of 1,842 steers and 180 spayed heifers, was unloaded ten days later at Waldeck, just east of Swift Current on the Canadian Pacific Railroad, with a loss of twenty-eight head. The herd was driven north and, since the Saskatchewan was in flood, was held on the south bank until June 18, when the waters subsided. The cattle were crowded into the stream for the quarter-mile swim to the company's range. Here the "Drag V" brand, as it was called in Canada, was to remain for seventeen years. In the autumn of 1905, Somerville was able to report that a headquarters house had been constructed, a fence erected across the northern boundary of the lease, and sufficient hay cut and stored to carry the stock through the winter.[18]

Concurrent with negotiations for the Canadian land, the Matador company undertook to rent additional pasturage in the north, looking forward to the time when it would have to move its cattle from the Belle Fourche. Information that a bill before Congress in 1903 would allot grazing leases on the public domain in proportion to the land owned by cattlemen meant to Mackay

[18] Somerville to Mackenzie, October 9, 1905. Subsequent leases from the government and from the Hudson's Bay Company increased the Canadian Division to 150,000 acres.

that the Western Ranches could no longer maintain its position on the open range, since the Edinburgh syndicate (on whose board Mackay was serving) owned very little land and therefore would not be entitled to much in the way of a lease.

Mackenzie had already been disturbed by a letter from Clay in which notice was served that after 1903 no Matador cattle would be received by the Western Ranches, and although this was later amended to permit a maximum of six thousand head to graze along the Belle Fourche, he was so irritated by the tone of Clay's letters that he suggested to the board that "we establish a branch of our own up there and run our cattle ourselves. We have not been paying the Western Ranches for the grass; we have been paying them for looking out after our cattle and the grass is as much ours as it is theirs." Mackay conceded that the Western Ranches had "no exclusive legal right to the range," but pointed out that it did have a "better moral right" than the Matador, since it had been the Western Ranches' business to run cattle on the Belle Fourche for twenty years and on this basis it "had naturally a preferential claim to the grass."

The increasing losses suffered by Matador herds in the Dakota pastures—7 per cent in 1899, 11 per cent in 1900, and 27 per cent in 1901—strengthened Mackenzie's resolve to sever connections with Clay's company at the first opportunity. This was not long in coming, for in March, 1904, at a meeting of the Texas Cattle Raisers Association in Fort Worth, he learned that the Hansford Land and Cattle Company was negotiating for a lease of several hundred thousand acres lying within the Cheyenne River Indian Reservation near Pierre, South Dakota, and cabled Mackay to obtain full details from the Hansford home office in Scotland.

The Sioux Indians, who occupied the Cheyenne River reservation, proposed to offer for grazing a pasture containing 700,000 acres lying within Dewey and Armstrong counties west of the Missouri River and south of the Moreau River. It was expected that the rental would run to about three and one-half cents an acre. Mackenzie learned that while no railway ran across the

95

reservation, the Chicago, Milwaukee and St. Paul line extended to a point just across the Missouri River east of the prospective lease and that the railroad would undertake to deliver cattle to the west side of the river by means of a pontoon bridge. He found that the freight rate from Texas to the reservation would be the same as the one from the Belle Fourche country and that an additional advantage would be gained in shipping to market since the charge from the Missouri to Chicago was twelve dollars a car less than the charge from the Western Ranches range. In offering to inspect the range, Mackenzie admitted that he was "rather taken" with the prospects, an attitude that may be attributed in part to the unsatisfactory progress then being made with Canadian negotiations and to his desire to break off relations with the Western Ranches.[19]

Upon receiving instructions from the board, Mackenzie traveled over the reservation ranges during the first week in April, 1904. The report sent to Dundee contained a description of the region and some of the conditions under which the leaseholder would be required to operate:

> I must say this pasture pleased me exceedingly. It is very similar to the part of the Canadian country where we found so many lakes, only the shelter is considerably better. The country is rolling, with deep depressions without any stretch of country being high and level. The grass is what they call gumbo grass and buffalo with grama mixed. The grass is very fine and the sod is as good as anything we ever saw in Canada. The reason for this is that the country has been kept clear of cattle from the outside and has never been tramped out. . . .
>
> I was so pleased with the appearance of the country that I had no hesitation whatever in cabling you recommending the Company lease this place. The range as a whole is, in my opinion, everything that could be desired; as the grass has never been eaten out or trodden down, it will stand a great deal of eating. We must, however, not overstock this place as we are restricted to one head for every thirty acres.

[19] Mackenzie to Mackay, March 13, 1904.

There is one condition attached to the leasing . . . and that is that every Indian who is head of a family is allowed to graze one hundred head on the reservation, but unless he owns the stock himself he is not allowed to borrow the money to buy stock to put in or to accept cattle from outsiders for this purpose. Before going to see this place I was rather skeptical about the use the Indian might make of this allotment. In many cases the Indians choose their allotments along the river bank and I was much afraid they might take it into their heads to fence this up. Upon investigation, however, and seeing the character of the people, I am satisfied we need have no fear of anything of this kind. In the first place they are too lazy to put up a fence if you gave them the material, and in the second place an Indian is not allowed to fence any land until he first proves up on his allotment.[20]

In connection with the report, Mackenzie pointed out that he and Burton C. "Cap" Mossman, the Hansford representative, were in accord on the subject of the land each company would bid for; similarly, since the Dundee office had kept the Edinburgh office of the Hansford company informed of its intentions, both companies "acted with each other's knowledge, and harmoniously." The Matador took the position that the Hansford claims should be met first and that Mackenzie should make his offer on what remained.

With power of attorney to act for the company, Mackenzie went to Washington early in May and submitted to the Department of the Interior an offer to lease 530,000 acres of the Cheyenne River Indian Reservation for a period of five years at an annual rental of three and one-half cents an acre. Notice that the bid had been accepted was received on May 17, and he immediately made preparations to post the necessary bond with the Indian agent at the reservation.[21]

The "Dakota Division" of the company lay in the northeastern corner of the Cheyenne River Reservation, a Sioux preserve

[20] Mackenzie to Mackay, April 9, 1904. Cf. Frazier Hunt, *Cap Mossman, Last of the Great Cowmen*, 234–38.
[21] Mackenzie to Major Ira Hatch, May 26, 1904.

which covered approximately three million acres. The range selected by Mackenzie was bounded on the east by the Missouri River and on the north by the Moreau River, though the division headquarters was built north of the latter stream. To the south the "Turkey Track" brand of the Hansford Company moved into the region selected by Mossman, and on the west the "Three V's" —VVV—of the Western Ranches could be found. The Milwaukee Railroad, with its terminus at Evarts on the east side of the Missouri, had been instrumental in fencing a six-mile-wide strip extending due westward from the river for a distance of eighty miles. This lane, with watering places spaced about twelve miles apart, provided a trail for herds on their way to or from the railhead and was regularly used by cattle operators who stocked the Cheyenne River and Standing Rock reservations.

Early in June the Matador directors concurred in Mackenzie's recommendation that the annual shipments of steers which had previously been sent to the Western Ranches would henceforth be sent to the "Soo" reservation until the Dakota lease was stocked with at least sixteen thousand head. The cattle already on the upper Belle Fourche were to remain until the fall sales began, at which time all would be gathered, the four- and five-year-olds sent to market, and the three-year-olds shipped to the reservation. Until the new division could be stocked to the desired limit with the company's cattle, the manager was authorized to load the ranges with other brands; and in keeping with this plan, over two thousand steers belonging to the Chiricahua Cattle Company of Los Angeles were placed on the Cheyenne River lease in 1905 at a charge of $2.50 a head a year.[22]

Dave Somerville, who had been at the Alamositas Division since 1902, went north to take charge of the Dakota range and was on hand when the first cattle arrived at Evarts in July, 1904. By the end of the summer 7,500 Matador steers and spayed

[22] For some unknown reason the Western Ranches did not gather the Matador three-year-olds in the fall, 1904, and it was not until the following year that the last of the company's steers left the Belle Fourche.

heifers were on Sioux grass; here the brand was to remain for ten years.[23]

Concurrent with the transactions in land designed to give the company a substantial base of operations in Texas and to permit the carrying out of its northern range program were a multitude of other activities bearing on the welfare of the Matador establishment and the well-being of the cattle industry as a whole. Of special significance were the efforts of the company officials, led by Mackenzie, to reduce the control which a few packers exercised over the livestock market and to enlarge the regulatory powers of the Interstate Commerce Commission.

The Matador's awareness of the "Beef Ring's manipulations" dated from 1886, when William F. Sommerville wrote that "Chicago packers have absorbed almost the entire butchering business of the country"; however, if the combine's operation had brought any hardship to the company during the first twelve years of Mackenzie's management, no mention was made of it, and only when the packing industry became a target of Theodore Roosevelt's trust-busting activities did Mackay raise the subject with Mackenzie:

> There has been a great deal of writing in the home papers regarding the American Beef Trust. We should like to hear what view you take of the dangers arising from the control of the markets by Armour and Swift and others. American papers are so apt to extravagance that it is difficult for us to make due allowance.[24]

The Dundee office was apparently much more concerned at

[23] Somerville remained in Dakota for a year; as noted earlier, he went to the Canadian Division in 1905 (See Appendix A). An excellent account of the life of a Matador cowboy on the Cheyenne River range is found in Ike Blasingame's *Dakota Cowboy* (New York, G. P. Putnam's Sons, 1958). Ernest (Ike) Blasingame's name first appeared on the payroll of the Dakota Division in May, 1905; off and on for a number of years he worked for the company in Dakota, Canada, and Texas.

[24] Mackay to Mackenzie, May 27, 1902.

the time than was Mackenzie, who discounted the trust's ability to control the market:

> Regarding the Beef Trust I am at a loss to see what the American people are howling about. The packers have to pay from 6¢ to 8¢ per pound for the beef on foot and it is ridiculous to suppose they can supply the consumer with beef at the same price that they could when they were paying 4¢ to 5¢ for live cattle. In a time of this kind it is next to impossible for the packers to control the price of beef as it is so scarce on the market that each of them is fighting to get it. If there was a glut of livestock on the market then the buyers could put their heads together and press down prices, but as long as there is a scarcity as we now have, you need not be afraid of their being able to do anything. I think the government is chasing after a night mare when they are taking any steps in the meantime to keep down the price of beef.[25]

This opinion, which Mackay accepted at face value, was revised within twenty-four months, for in the spring of 1904, Mackenzie was providing information to the federal authorities who were investigating the packers' trust. His new view, the peculiar position in which he found himself, and his caution in involving the company were clearly revealed in a letter to the secretary of the Colorado Cattle and Horse Growers Association:

> I notice in the letter which you have written to several of the cow-men . . . that you have set forth that Mr. S. H. Cowan and myself went to Washington and had . . . an interview with the Department of Commerce and Labor regarding their investigations of the beef trust. In the future, I think it would be well not to mention any names but simply state that members of the committee had interviews. . . . You are aware that we have a great many cattle to sell, and if the packers should find out that I personally went to Washington to look into the affairs of their beef trust, you cannot for one minute suppose that they are too good to hold our cattle up when they go to the market. I do not object to taking my fair share of this work, but I do not propose to be

[25] Mackenzie to Mackay, June 11, 1902.

made the butt of such a strong combination as the packers of this country now are. I simply mention this so that you may be more careful in the future. If the packers should make a set on our company on account of me interfering in this matter, I would have to quit the committee entirely because my company would find fault with me if I were to do anything which would react on their interests. I am satisfied that upon reconsideration you will see the necessity of being circumspect. Personally I want no glory out of this at all; I am merely doing what I can for the interests of the business, but you have no idea how far-reaching such men can be if we push them to the bitter end.[26]

Indicative of his revised opinion was his statement in his annual report to the company in December, 1904, that ". . . I am convinced that they have a combine and that the whole policy of the packers is controlled by two or three men." The board, relying on Mackenzie's appraisal, reported to the shareholders on February 7, 1905, that ". . . there is a widespread belief in the West that the principal markets have become too much under the control of a few buyers. . . . The President of the United States . . . entered upon an enquiry last year to ascertain the truth of these allegations . . . and has followed up by actions which are now pending in the law courts. . . . It is believed these actions will have a favourable influence upon the future of the cattle industry."

Whatever "favourable influence" was forthcoming was several years in arriving, for suits against the National Packing Company—the merger of Armour, Swift, and Morris—in 1905 resulted in defeat for the government. The Department of Justice's prosecution of other cases likewise met with failure during the period 1902–10; and although the National Packing Company was dissolved by action of its directors in 1911, the net effect of the prosecutions was merely to limit monopoly power, not to destroy it.

Throughout the period of agitation and rebellion against the

[26] Mackenzie to Fred P. Johnson, June 3, 1904.

beef trusts Mackenzie remained neutral, at least in deed. As an entrepreneur, he had no desire to destroy the business structure within which he and his company operated, though he deplored the packers' ability to control prices and felt that federal action was necessary. His attitude was set forth in a letter to J. Ogden Armour in April, 1910:

> I am very anxious that the country should know how the stockmen of the West feel toward the packers. Personally I feel that our business is a mutual one; without the cattlemen the packers could not keep on their business and without the packers we would have a hard job to dispose of our product, and I therefore feel we must stand or fall together.

Whatever contributions the Matador made toward curbing the packers' monopoly, they were negligible when compared to the services rendered in securing for western shippers a more equitable schedule of railroad rates and in pressing for enlargement of the Interstate Commerce Commission's powers. Mackenzie's activities in the direction of rate reductions were begun in 1896 and were carried on, in general, through representations made to the railroads and to the government by the various cattlemen's associations in which the Matador company held memberships. In these endeavors the manager displayed one of his greatest talents—his ability to harmonize the conflicting opinions held by the cattlemen he represented.

At the annual convention of the Texas Cattle Raisers Association in 1896, a committee was appointed to confer with the officials of rail lines which connected Texas with Kansas City and Chicago. In explaining to Mackay why he would be away from the Trinidad office for a time, Mackenzie wrote:

> The reason we have to go to Chicago is they have raised our rates from Texas. . . . The difference in rate this year, if we do not get it reduced, will mean about forty cents per head more than we paid last year, and we are going to Chicago hoping that we may be able to induce these gentlemen to not only reduce

the rate to what it formerly was but . . . somewhat lower. I am sorry at having to go at this time but it is very important that the matter should be attended to and it takes people who have a good many cattle to ship to get a hearing from these gentlemen.[27]

Actually, the railroads had not increased the rate as such but had changed the method of computing the cost of using a cattle car. Until 1896, a fixed charge was made for the use of a car from one point to another. The new charge was based on weight—a fixed rate for each one hundred pounds of cargo. This meant an increase of about thirteen dollars a car over the old cost for a shipment from Estelline to Kansas City. The cattlemen had no particular objection to paying freight costs based on weight, but felt that the rate per hundred pounds was high.

As a result of the meetings with the railroad officials, the old system of reckoning freight charges was restored late in 1896; and during the next eight years the Matador manager participated in no moves aimed at reducing shipping rates, though he did object to the railroads' charging him the same amount for a short haul as for a longer one:

> As you are aware, we have always paid Kansas City rates to all points in Kansas, and I don't believe that even the railroads would feel that it was fair to the cattlemen to still continue to pay Kansas City rates to points in Kansas then charge full local rates from these points in Kansas to the market.[28]

In 1904 the first sustained effort to secure redress for the cattlemen's grievances against the railroads was opened when a committee from the National Live Stock Association met with traffic managers of several lines serving the West "to complain of the slow time made by the roads in moving cattle . . . and of the discrimination in freight rates." Rail officials, admitting that the stockmen had good grounds for complaint, promised better serv-

[27] Mackenzie to Mackay, June 7, 1896.

[28] Mackenzie to W. F. Biddle, traffic manager, Atchison, Topeka and Santa Fe Railroad, March 18, 1898.

ice in the future but made no commitment on rates at the time. The Association was prepared, if no satisfactory answer was forthcoming, to carry the rate question to Congress "to get a bill passed regulating the freight on livestock." Mackenzie summarized the cattlemen's plan in writing to Mackay on March 1, 1904: "Our Interstate [Commerce] Commission . . . has certain powers but they do not go far enough, and we expect to get the necessary powers vested in this commission to enable them to regulate freight on all commodities."

When it became apparent that no relief in the matter of rates would be granted by the railroads, the Association began an all-out effort to bring before Congress the facts upon which its pleas for regulation were based and to obtain the support of key members of both houses. Before success could be anticipated, however, the livestock shippers had to be brought into accord, for the various local and regional associations were jealous of one another, personality clashes were frequent, and individual ambitions threatened unanimity of action. During the period of turbulence and discord when the movement was getting under way, the Matador's Mackenzie served as whip and mediator, and with adroitness and force worked constantly to achieve the major goal. Illustrative of this diplomacy and tact was his handling of a situation which developed early in 1904, when the Texas Cattle Raisers Association invited representatives from all the major cattlemen's associations to meet in Denver "to see if some means could be devised by which rates on the railroads could be properly adjusted." As soon as the overture was made, some officials in the National Live Stock Association announced that the meeting was nothing more than an attempt on the part of disaffected persons to break away from the National and found another organization. Mackenzie's denial of such an intent was immediate and to the point:

> I am sorry to see that some people are trying to make out that this is simply a plan to get people together to start a new cattle association, but I want to assure you that there never was any-

thing farther from the minds of the people who suggested this meeting in Denver. . . . The sole object is to meet together and see if we cannot devise some plan by which the existing evils can be remedied, and if we meet as business men, I have no doubt in the world but what some good will come out of our meeting.

There are certain parties who are very jealous of all meetings except in their own associations, but we, as cattle men, should not listen to anything of this kind, but meet together and see if something cannot be done to help out a business which has a hard job now to exist.[29]

To strike directly at the source of unwelcome rumors and to correct whatever misapprehensions might have existed in the minds of those who were circulating them, Mackenzie wrote to Charles F. Martin, the secretary of the National Live Stock Association in Denver—in addition to fomenting strife among the cattlemen, Martin had taken it upon himself to invite sheepmen to the Denver meeting, though he had nothing to do with the original idea or plan for the gathering:

I had intended writing you some time ago regarding a paragraph which I noticed in the Denver *Republican.* This paragraph was headed "Sheep and Cattle Men United in Rate Fight" and went on to say that the Secretary of the National Live Stock Association had received quite a number of letters from sheep men inquiring if they would be allowed to take part in the meeting of 3rd May, and that the Secretary had replied to as many of these as possible, advising them that they would be and urging them to be present.

I trust this is merely the talk of a newspaper correspondent and that he was drawing on his imagination. Our object in calling this meeting was to have as many cattle men present as possible, and you were invited, as I understand, as Secretary of the National Livestock Association, to send a committee of three, and if anything has been done beyond this, I am sure it was not

[29] Mackenzie to a Mr. Stewart, secretary, South Dakota Cattle Raisers Association, April 8, 1904.

in accordance with our understanding. I'm afraid if the sheepmen come to Denver in any force that they will feel aggrieved
if they are not allowed to take part in the proceedings, and from
what I have heard on the outside, the chances are there will be
great opposition to their doing so. The sheepmen, as I understand it, have an organization of their own and there is no reason
in the world why they should not help us in this matter, but it is
not the intention to form any new association at this meeting; it
is merely a meeting of the cattle men to devise some plan by
which they can be relieved of the grievances now existing, and
I am afraid if the sheep men are brought there they will do more
harm than good. . . .

I want to be frank with you in this, and I trust that you will
accept what I have said in the spirit that it is given. . . .[30]

When Martin explained that he had been misquoted, Mackenzie relented somewhat but insisted that both Martin and
Fred P. Johnson of the Colorado Cattle and Horse Growers Association had said too much on the subject of the meeting, re-
minding Martin that the railroads were "more anxious than ever
that we should fight among ourselves."

At the Denver meeting in May a majority of those present
favored a vigorous campaign to put more power into the hands
of the Interstate Commerce Commission, and within two weeks
Mackenzie and Judge S. H. Cowan of Fort Worth were in Washington to lay before the commission evidence in support of the
cattlemen's cause.

In the capital the interviews and conferences produced little,
since 1904 was an election year and many congressmen and senators, as well as the President, were preparing for the summer
and fall campaigns. The trip was not without value, however, for
late in May the manager wrote to Henry C. Wallace, manager
and associate editor of the influential *Wallace's Farmer*, published in Des Moines:

Upon investigating matters at the capitol city, we found that

[30] Mackenzie to Martin, April 22, 1904.

your representative, [Peter] Hepburn ... was largely responsible for the holding back of the bill introduced last year to put greater power in the hands of the Interstate Commerce Commission. I think this is a matter you people in Iowa should thoroughly investigate, and if you find that this is true, something should be done, either to get Mr. Hepburn pledged to support this bill at the next session, or do something to oust him from his position. It is very important that we should have all members of this committee [House Committee on Interstate Commerce] with us, for if some of the members from the western states oppose us and fight against what we want, then how can we expect to succeed?[31]

Wallace's reply explained why, in time, Hepburn developed an interest in rate regulation:

You probably do not remember that 15 years ago Mr. Hepburn was in Congress and in opposition to measures intended to help the farmers of this state from unjust, unreasonable railroad rates. Mr. Hepburn opposed us then as now and we carried the matter into his district and after a fight so bitter that the district has ever since been known as the "Bloody Eighth" we downed him for re-election. The trouble, however, is that the railroad people never sleep while it is hard to keep the people awake to their interests. As a consequence six years afterward Mr. Hepburn came up again and was re-elected. I think, however, that he has not forgotten his experience of 15 years ago and if we can get the right kind of evidence we may be able to make him see the light.[32]

During the next two years Mackenzie was occasionally subpoenaed to appear before Congressional committees and the Interstate Commerce Commission, and twice presented evidence to Theodore Roosevelt in an effort to secure the President's support of the cattlemen's demands. That Roosevelt's

[31] Mackenzie to Wallace, May 26, 1904. Henry Cantwell Wallace was appointed Secretary of Agriculture by Harding in 1921; he was the father of Henry Agard Wallace.

[32] Wallace to Mackenzie, May 31, 1904.

views underwent a change during the period 1904–1905 is indicated in the manager's reports to Dundee. The first was written after the President's message to Congress in December, 1904:

> I am glad to see that the President of the United States has come to our way of thinking about the Interstate Commerce Commission. When I was in Washington in May [1904] he would not agree to our proposition at all, but instead wanted to put all powers in the hands of the Department of Labor and Commerce. . . . I think however we put him to thinking and . . . he came out boldly in his message demanding of Congress all that we had asked for.[33]

Six weeks later Mackenzie wrote that while in Washington in January, 1905, he had "the pleasure of an audience of three-quarters of an hour with President Roosevelt and he expressed himself as highly pleased with our demands and the conservative manner in which we had gone about it and promised me that unless Congress passed a bill such as indicated in his message . . . he would call a special session for this purpose and keep on calling special sessions until they would pass a bill to suit him."[34]

In his appearance before the Senate Committee on Interstate Commerce in January, 1905, Mackenzie was questioned in detail about the increase in shipping rates during the period 1898–1904. It was his claim that not only had rates been raised to unreasonable figures, but service during the same period had become poorer.[35] So effective was his presentation of the evidence supporting his contention that Senator Stephen B. Elkins, chairman of the Senate Committee on Interstate and Foreign Commerce, invited him to a private conference and expressed his pleasure at hearing testimony that "threw light on the subject which he never saw before."

[33] Mackenzie to Mackay, December 22, 1904.
[34] Mackenzie to Mackay, February 4, 1905.
[35] U.S. Congress, Senate, *Regulation of Railway Rates*, Hearings before the Committee on Interstate Commerce, 59 Cong., 1 sess., *Sen. Doc. 243*, XVI, 119–26.

By the end of May it was clear that the success of the cattle-men's program hinged on the action of the Senate in regard to a bill which the western shippers were promoting. Cognizant of this fact, Mackenzie asked Judge Cowan to go to Washington to appear again before Elkins' committee and requested the Senator to give consideration to the information which Cowan would present. Sending Cowan alone was a mistake, for the op-posing interests overwhelmed the committee by sheer force of numbers and for a time it appeared that a compromise measure might wreck the westerners' cause. Cowan's report, written three days after the hearing, colorfully described the situation as the fiery attorney saw it:

> The Senate Committee has been overrun, overtrained and overfed by RR witnesses, henchmen, favored shippers, poli-ticians, statisticians, traffic men, RR presidents, attorneys, liars, trust magnates, and other forms and kinds of criminals who have by sheer numbers and oft told stories made the committee think they are legion. The committee was looking for an excuse to do nothing so they think they have it in this voluminous record of incongruities, falsehoods, false reasoning and false tale-telling. They adjourn today and "repair" to their respective homes to di-gest their trust food, etc., etc., and to return with a digested scheme against the interest of the people. . . .[36]

The "digested scheme"—the Senate's compromise—would have given the commission power to fix rates which would not have become operative until confirmed by a court of competent jurisdiction. In short, the plan would have placed on the com-mission the burden of applying rates to a particular line or por-tion thereof, and each individual case brought before a court might have gone on indefinitely.

Throughout 1905 and into 1906 the cattlemen continued their efforts to arouse the American public through the circulation of pamphlets and letters and the publication of editorials. In his annual report to the board in December, 1905, Mackenzie wrote:

[36] Cowan to Mackenzie, May 24, 1905.

"Public sentiment has been aroused to such an extent that Congress feel something must be done." Acknowledging that the critical stage of the fight was still ahead, he reported that a measure "which sets forth exactly what we want" had been prepared and that Roosevelt and Elihu Root had approved this bill.

The turning point in the struggle came when the so-called "Hepburn Bill" was reported to the Senate by the upper chamber's Interstate Commerce Committee late in February, 1906. Since all declarations, both for and against the measure, were made of record, few senators dared show their opposition in open session. After nearly twelve weeks of debate the "rate bill," slightly amended, was passed and returned to the House. In June, 1906, the lower chamber accepted the Senate's amendments and sent the bill to the President, who signed it late in the month.[37]

The board and Mackay had reason to be doubly grateful that the long fight had been won, for not only would the company be spared the uncertainties of arbitrarily assessed and excessive shipping charges, but it would receive greater benefit from Mackenzie's services and attention to company affairs and travel expenses would be reduced. When the company auditor called attention to the increased expenditures in Mackenzie's travel account for 1904, the manager made a sincere effort to withdraw from the executive board of the Texas association, but gave in to the demands of his friends and agreed to remain on con-

---

[37] While there is little indication that Peter Hepburn actively pushed the measure which bears his name, he certainly did nothing to obstruct its passage after Wallace made him "see the light." The Hepburn Act of 1906 was in the form of an amendment to the original Interstate Commerce Act of 1887; in addition to increasing the number of commissioners from five to seven, the act gave to the Commission the power to fix maximum rates upon complaint and after a hearing; an aggrieved carrier could appeal to the courts for an injunction against rates so fixed; an appeal from the circuit courts went directly to the Supreme Court. The power to fix maximum rates was the most important feature of the act and represented a radical change from the old concepts and functions of the Commission. Joseph H. Beale and Bruce Wyman, *Railroad Rate Regulation* (2d ed.), 56–60.

dition that the Matador directors approve his continued participation. Before the Dundee officials could act, however, Mackenzie's associates in the western cattle industry were insisting that
he accept the presidency of the newly formed American Stock
Growers Association. The matter was laid before Mackay:

> There has been an association formed called the American
> Stock Growers Association. . . . Cattlemen from all parts of the
> country have come to me and have written asking that I accept
> the presidency and I have told them positively that I would not
> do so. In case such pressure might be brought to bear on me that
> I cannot refuse without giving some good excuse I submit this to
> you and I shall act in accordance with what you wish me to do.
> The contention of the cattlemen is that I am more familiar with
> the present situation than most anyone in the business. I do not
> say this in the way of egotism, but I merely state the case to you
> exactly as it is, and I am giving the opinion of others and not my
> own. . . . I can assure you that taking a position of this kind is
> entirely against my inclination, but then sometimes you can
> scarcely avoid making a sacrifice for the sake of the general
> business.[38]

Since Mackay was on a vacation in Rome when the letter
reached Dundee early in April, 1905, his assistant, W. L. Pattullo,
summoned the board and presented the question. On April 15,
Mackenzie received the cabled decision: "Accept presidency.
Matador incur no expense." On the same day Mackay wrote:

> The willing horse will always get the burden to draw and the
> time comes when the load gets beyond him. Now, we want you
> to be a long time with us, and all this work is not wise in your
> interest. At the same time I recognize the difficulty in which you
> are placed. The board will fall in with your own suggestions,
> believing that you will take care that the new duties don't clash
> with your duty to the Company, but I think you should stipulate
> alike in your interest and Mrs. Mackenzie's, that your accept-
> ance of office is limited to one year; and further that the Associa-

[38] Mackenzie to Mackay, April 1, 1905.

tion must give you a paid VP or some equivalent officer to do 9/10 of the work.[39]

With the company's attitude established and recorded, Mackenzie allowed his name to be placed on the ballot, and at the American Association's first meeting in Denver he was elected president. He secured authorization to appoint a secretary and an attorney, and named T. W. Tomlinson to fill the post of "secretary and manager" and Sam H. Cowan as the Association's attorney.[40]

With its cattle grazing on well over one million acres of grass during the first decade of the twentieth century, it is little wonder that the Matador name came to symbolize the range cattle industry in America and its herds to represent the best in beef throughout the West. The worth of its breeding program, initiated by Hank Campbell and refined by Murdo Mackenzie, was given formal recognition in 1902, when a carload lot of Matador steers won the grand champion prize as best yearlings at the International Live Stock Show in Chicago. In the years that followed other blue ribbons were won by Matador steers at Chicago, at the American Royal shows in Kansas City, and in Denver, but of greater satisfaction to the Dundee Scots were the receipts from the sale of cattle matured on the Dakota and Canadian ranges; here was concrete evidence of the herd's superior quality, and here was proof of the directors' wisdom in sanctioning the northern range ventures. Indeed, had not its four- and five-year-olds from the Dakota and Canadian divisions brought top prices during the period from 1902 to 1910, the company might have had to sell its lands and herds and close its books, for its commitments were heavy and the market was unstable.

Notwithstanding the large disbursements for land and grass outside its home range and the multitude of activities in which

[39] Mackay to Mackenzie, April 15, 1905.

[40] In 1906 the National and American associations joined to form the American National Live Stock Association; Mackenzie was elected president and served in that office for two terms, until January, 1908.

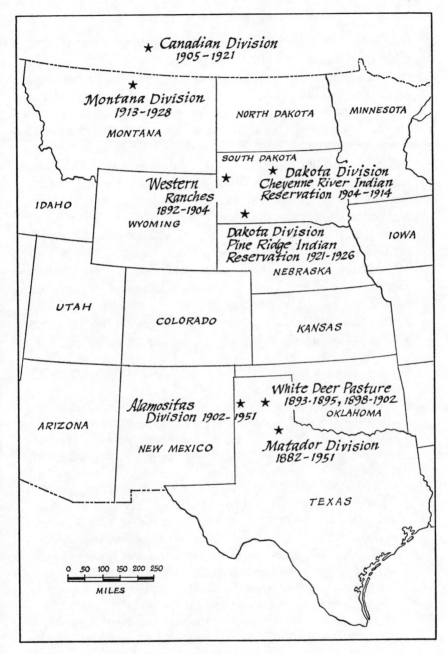

Approximate Locations of Major Ranges

its officials were engaged, the company never lost sight of its main investment, the Matador Division. Here lay the bulk of the land held in fee, and here was the source of its wealth in cattle, the breeding herd. From the ranch headquarters at Ballard Springs, Arthur Ligertwood supervised the activities of all employees on the division. In number the hands varied with the seasons from some three dozen in the winter months to twice that many in the summer; the variety of chores performed was reflected by the payroll positions—wagon boss, line rider, cook, gardener, farmer, milkman, freighter, windmill man, rider, clerk, blacksmith, ranchman, nighthawk, bronc breaker, and teamster.

In 1902, John Clay arranged, through Mackenzie, for Professor John A. Craig of Iowa to visit the Matador Division. Published in the *Weekly Live Stock Report*, Craig's account of his visit contained a valuable description of the ranch's operations, its soil, stock, and vegetation as seen through the eyes of a trained observer, and a pertinent commentary on the utilization of semiarid lands:

It was one Saturday morning last July when the writer left Childress, Texas for the Matador Ranch, in the care of a driver sent from headquarters. Nothing unusual marked the journey, unless the occurrence of a heavy rainstorm could be so termed. As a matter of fact, it was unusual, for this section of Texas has been suffering from the drought, especially that portion of it west of us. The storm passed through a course of development very unlike that usual in the north, but none the less very typical of a Texas storm. A large black cloud suddenly rises over the horizon on our right. This to the weather-wise native never means anything, but the forecast changes as soon as another appears on our left. Even this is not considered an augury of rain, but when they move towards each other then it is "sure suspicious." . . . In this instance the clouds united and for some time it rained heavily all around us, and then a central movement towards us began and we were in the midst of the deluge. The unusual feature generally associated with a Texan storm is that

John MacBain

Matador Division Headquarters, Motley County, Texas

Trail herd, Canada, 1921

Remuda, Saskatchewan, 1921

Murdo Mackenzie

Alexander Mackay

Raising dust: a Hereford bull on the Matador Division range

The branding chute

it comes steadily towards you while the wind current about you blows in the opposite direction. . . .

As you see the rain sweeping like a moving transparent sheet over the hills and valleys for an hour before it reaches you it cannot but be impressed on you that the eye is but a weak instrument to measure distances in this immense country with its vast prairie panoramas. . . .

After a short drive we leave the sandy and comparatively level and low section of country to ascend gradually to the "gyp" hills and descend rapidly through the torrent-torn and rugged ravines which scar their sides and upper levels without the least indication of regularity. . . . These hills grow good mesquite grass and the draws and ravines afford shelter to cattle, consequently they are considered specially adapted for winter pasturage. . . .

It is thirty miles from Childress to the ranch gate so it is well on towards evening when we reach the first camp at Turtle Hole. A short distance from the gate we have our first view of the camp with its neat new buildings sheltered by the hill and a valley stretching before it. The night is spent here and next morning with a fresh team we start for headquarters. The "driveway" from the gate leading up to headquarters is in proportion to the vastness of this immense domain, for it is twenty-five miles long. The most of it is over "gyp" country but as soon as the bank of the Middle Pease river is reached there is a change in the character of the soil and the nature of the growth upon it. . . . Close around you everything is a deep red, the road in front and the sides of the ravines. . . . The wide bed of the river is in front shimmering white in the heat. . . . It has been so dry that it has been necessary to scoop out water holes in the river bed so that the cattle might not be required to travel too far in search of water. . . . The opposite bank rises less abruptly and the eye is quick to catch the new tint—the grayish green of the sage bush in fresh growth. . . . This rolling country again brings up a reference to distance, for that point to the right, standing out prominently but apparently near, is at the foothills of the Llano Estacado or Staked Plains at least twenty-five miles away. . . . This sage-bush country continues until we near the small town of Matador, a couple of miles from headquarters. The surrounding country here lies in a long valley and when we reach the head of it we are at the ranch headquarters where we are greeted at the gate by Mr. A. G. Ligertwood, the superintendent.

The rest of the day we spent around headquarters resting in the cultured and comfortable home presided over by Mrs. Ligertwood. Incidentally we were also learning what we could of the operations of the ranch and their scope. One of the chief objects of interest at the headquarters is the water supply. Eleven springs have their origin just back of the residence. A dam was built a little below their outlet and a beautiful lake of small dimensions was formed, which is stocked with black bass. A pipe gives a drop of about ten feet to a hydraulic ram and this forces the water into a tank about fifty feet above. From this tank, eight feet in diameter, the water is piped to the residence and mess house; the overflow goes to the stables and irrigates the small garden of peaches and vegetables a short distance below. Grouped near the residence are the ranch office, the commissary, the mess house and stables, making quite a substantial looking colony. We early availed ourselves of the opportunity of scanning a map of the ranch to get a true conception of its location and arrangement of pastures. The ranch consists of 800,000 acres, not unlike in general shape the lower portion of South America. . . . It embraces all kinds of soil and country which we shall attempt to describe as we pass over typical portions on our trip later on. In reaching headquarters we find that we entered it at the northeast corner and came southwest toward the center. We have in view going to the most southerly point to see the round-up, about forty miles away. Last year [1901] 17,674 calves were branded. . . . There were, as near as may be estimated, 69,213 head of stock on the ranch, including six hundred horses. . . . The Matador is really a stupendous breeding ranch with its herd of purebred Herefords and its high grades of both Shorthorn and Hereford descent. The home herd of Herefords produce the most of the sires used for the improvement of the grade herds. . . . From Mr. John MacBain who attends to the bookkeeping connected with Matador affairs we learned that there were seventy-five men on the Matador pay-roll at that time and most of these were engaged in the roundup which was just beginning at the time of our visit.

The next morning in company with Mr. Ligertwood we start for the roundup forty miles distant behind an active and durable pair of horses. For some time we travel over sandy land with its thinning growth of sage brush and gradually reach the hills with their red gypsum soil. . . . We cross the Tongue River [the South Pease] and the outlook is a succession of red draws and green hills with the river a band of bleached white sand. There is a good sod of buffalo grass and green mesquite, but none of the cactus of the more southern plains. About noon we see in the distance Sanders [Saunders] Hollow, our first camp, surrounded by high and sweeping hills at the head of a valley where hackberry displaces the mesquite. . . . After dinner we again take up our journey and soon are in a country of new character—prairie glade—where there is no growth of shrubbery and the land lies very level with only a few smooth rises and drops in many miles. The cattle here are getting fresh grass and are loath to quit grazing because of our presence. . . . Leaving here we reach John's Well where a number of cattle are drinking from a miniature lake formed by the overflow.

Right here [at Matt John's place] is an illustration of real life bearing on a leading question in range circles at this time and as the light it throws on the question is clear I wish to make a brief reference to it. In the mid-summer number of the *Century* an able writer on topics of the south and west discusses peculiar ranch conditions under the title "The Tragedy of the Range," and his information covers a wide scope but it is evident he has not seen the feature that is here so clear. In the article referred to the large ranches are universally condemned and the position of the "nester" or small settler universally sustained without mention of a single mitigating circumstance. In the article there is no reference to the possibility of some land being valuable only when used for range purposes. It can hardly be possible that the writer of this article in his journeyings over the west has not seen large tracts of land admirably suited for a cattle range, and yet it is sheer foolishness to think of all of it furnishing a living to nesters, much less to think that any one hundred and sixty acres of it could do so. Without sufficient water supply, far from the railroad, and on land suited only for grazing, what can the nester do but starve? He cannot run his own cow outfit for the expense in proportion to the cattle he could keep would be too great. As a matter of fact, he rarely has capital to put up his own windmill, but uses that of the large ranch owner. Not infrequently the nester fences in his own holdings then turns his cattle on the range of the larger ranch and calls for them after the ranch has rounded them up and sent him word. Sometimes, too, the use of the best bulls of the ranch is secured. . . . But worst of all there is a class of nesters or "flitters" as they are dubbed that use every means to harass large ranchmen so that the latter will buy them off and then they will move on to other localities and operate the same way, while incidentally inviting the sympathy of the reformer and the vote-fed interest of the professional politician. From the article referred to it would seem that the cattle companies of Texas were all giant dogs in the manger without a single redeeming feature. . . . At John's Well there is a section that was homesteaded in 1889, the first section taken up in that part of the country. It is apparently good land but there is not enough rainfall for farming. . . . The best farmer in the world could not make a living off it without grazing cattle. Now the Matador, in the line of business, is making a profit from 800,000 such acres because it is engaged in an industry for which the conditions are favorable, and it is very doubtful if there is any other vocation which could make the land nearly as productive. . . .

In the pasture which we pass through there is much of what is called "shinery," that is, largely covered with very small "shin" or scrub oak. It is hardly large enough to shelter the cattle. The land is not rough, the soil being a sandy loam. On the edge of the shinery is generally the most productive soil, for the sand mixes with the heavier soil of the lower land and makes a fertile blend. . . .

We again reach rougher country and wend our way among hills and draws. We are in country of this kind when Duncan's Tank is reached. Some of the cattle are about the pool of water.

... The calves are all of lusty and robust type with thickly meated backs and without any of the coarseness which used to characterize range-bred stock. We are on the heights again and soon come within view of the head of the Wichita River. From the right the land slopes down to the miniature lake, a streak of leaden color in the distance. Back of it the hills rise, white with the dried needle grass which the cattle do not touch until it has matured and whitened and the needles blow away. . . . We finally reach the "little horse pasture" which is so named because it has only 640 acres, then we know we are nearing camp. As we pass down the slope of a valley we catch a glimpse of a level stretch of newly cut Johnson grass. This lies surrounded by bluffs of weathered red and gray gypsum. We make a turn or two and then are at Croton Creek Camp.

In this pocket on the banks of Croton Creek we come upon one of the three outfits engaged in the roundup. It seems an ideal camping spot because it is sheltered and on the high bank of a running stream. . . . We have a hearty meal from the chuck wagon. The cook is the only one in camp; at three in the morning the cowboys had left camp and were, up to this time, still working at the roundup. Soon the horse wrangler comes in with his charge, a band of horses needed by the cowboys in their work. Then the cowboys come loping in, at first singly or in pairs, then together a crowd at a quick lope. From before daybreak until twilight, almost continuously in the saddle rushing cattle out of ravines or over dusty plains tires a man out. . . . Supper over, their work is not yet done for six are told off in pairs to act as guards over the herd during the night. The foreman, W. J. Drace, and the cook, with the writer and one or two others rest on tarpaulins while the foreman reports to the manager. . . .

We leave camp soon after breakfast starting for the roundup and this drive includes the roughest part of our journey. . . . The position chosen for the roundup is a level piece of table land free from shrubs of any kind; there are few prairie-dog holes, consequently the footing seems good for the horses. About ten o'clock the cattle begin to gather, coming in bands from all directions. . . . Dust rises, calves bawl, cows low and there is a spasmodic poltering of horses' feet and a few shouts, and while everything is alive and moving yet it is all under control and really stationary. When three or four riders start after a steer that breaks out you momentarily expect the whole shifting mass to scatter over the adjacent hills. Now is the time to take a general view of the scene—four thousand cattle of all colors, on a high plain, with a score of cowboys on the edges of this shifting mass. . . . On the left is the dry herd of six hundred head moving contentedly among the mesquite in charge of three cowboys. Two bands of horses with only ropes about their necks are nearby and the cowboys begin to change horses. Behind us is the "hoodlum" wagon with the branding apparatus. . . . At 11:30 the decks are cleared for action for the "cutting out" begins. The cowboys work in relays, taking turns at cutting out and bunching the cattle. Mr. John Jackson, the senior foreman of the three outfits, directs operations; the horses and men know their parts but the cows and calves make as much trouble as they can though this is reduced to a minimum by the keen work of the horses—chasing, dodging and turning with surprising agility. . . . The dust rises like a funnel from the center of the mass and falls like spray over all. . . .[41]

Professor Craig's comments directed against the use of semi-arid lands for farming represent one view on an issue that had become increasingly critical in the dry lands of the West. Certainly the interests of the farmer and the rancher were antagonistic; and while the farmer usually won out in a humid region, the natural conditions—soil, rainfall, and terrain—in the Matador country favored the cattleman and enabled the company to hold on and even to gain ground despite advances in dry-farming techniques and plant adaptation. The acquisition of "suitable sections" in the Matador Division continued until the outbreak of World War I and in almost every case represented the "purchase of lands offered for sale at bargain prices" by homesteaders. The problem of consolidation was peculiar to the home range, for Alamositas, unlike the Matador Division, was a solid block completely controlled by the owners.

[41] John A. Craig, "Among the Matadors," 3-15.

That there were difficulties with settlers and other landowners is a matter of record; legal expenses constituted a significant item in the company's "American charges," and out of its Protection Account the board paid range detectives—usually Pinkerton men —for securing evidence on trespassers, thieves, and vandals.[42] When difficulties arose, the company customarily took action through the courts; it was large enough and had the resources to do so.

As long as land prices remained moderate, the manager did not hesitate to contract for the purchase of desired tracts; but in 1903, when five sections of grazing land were offered at three dollars an acre, he hesitated and sought the directors' approval:

> The price of land is getting to the point where I do not feel justified in acting without special instructions from the board, and I would like you to give me a limit as to the price. . . . I would like to have your instructions as to the amount of money the board would like to invest in any one year. . . .[43]

Mackay's reply returned the responsibility to Mackenzie with emphasis that whatever lands were bought must be paid for out of the proceeds of each year's land and cattle sales, and reminded the manager that he was in a better position than the board to estimate what the revenue for each year would be. This guidance was of little comfort, for less than three years later in his annual report to the company, Mackenzie called for a new statement of policy:

> Lands in Motley and adjoining counties are now held at such a high figure that it would not be profitable for the Company to buy them, even if we wanted to. I feel that the time has come

---

[42]Early in 1909 some "bad characters" cut six miles of new fence in the vicinity of Saunders Hollow and burned several sections of grass; at the same time Ligertwood received threatening letters from people who had "some imaginary grievance" against the ranch. Mackenzie hired a Pinkerton detective, who went into the area as an Ohio farmer looking for land, became acquainted with the suspects, and "got the goods on them." Mackenzie to Mackay, March 3, 1909.

[43]Mackenzie to Mackay, February 9, 1903.

when we should give up all hope of buying land, except in very exceptional cases.

Values of land are now so high that in the near future the Company should decide what it should do regarding its future policy. It is past the stage of experiment—the growing of cotton in the counties below the plains. During the past two years cotton has been grown successfully on our range, and if this should continue to be a success (and I have no doubt it will) it certainly will be more profitable for the Company to break up their ranch at this place and sell the land to farmers. . . . I would not advise doing this for a short time, but I have information which leads me to believe that in the near future a railroad will be built through that country and then lands will boom to a price hitherto unknown in that locality. When this time arrives the company should consider seriously what it should do and I bring it before your notice in this manner so you might be considering it for future action.[44]

The board noted with satisfaction that feature of the report which dealt with the probable upsurge in land values at its Matador Division, but advised that no special mention of the subject would be made to the shareholders until the manager's views could be "confirmed from cash receipts." As a result of this "wait and see" policy, the company continued to expand territorially at its southern ranch for ten years after Mackenzie felt it should "give up all hope of buying land." In 1907, when the Swenson interests purchased the Espuela ranch with the reported intent of dividing it into farms and pastures, the Matador board stated to the shareholders that "the Company's lands ought to command good prices within a few years when settlement has further advanced,"[45] and during the year sold nearly six thousand acres "at the very satisfactory average price of $7.79 per acre."[46] But 1907 was the only year during 1901–11 in which land sales exceeded purchases; in 1908 the depression slowed all business

[44] Mackenzie to Mackay, December 27, 1905.
[45] Twenty-fourth Annual Report, 5.
[46] Twenty-fifth Annual Report, 4.

transactions, and in 1909 "the dry weather in the summer injured cotton growing in the Company's district and checked the demand for land for agricultural operations."[47] The demand remained in check until the opening of World War I.

Even after the acquisition of Alamositas and the leasing of pastures in South Dakota and Canada, the company continued to base its cattle sales policy on what became known as the "board's requirements"—an estimate of the income necessary to pay the American expenses, provide for a dividend, and place a small sum in the reserve account. However, regulating the number of cattle sent to market each year became increasingly difficult since the herd was divided and dispersed among the four divisions. Lost was the choice to throw on or withhold from the market sizable numbers of cattle as prices fluctuated. For example, some five thousand two-year-old steers were placed on the Cheyenne River lease in 1904; all these, minus losses, were due to be marketed in 1906 to make room for the two-year-olds from Alamositas; in turn, the number of two-year-olds scheduled for shipment from Alamositas had been determined by the number of yearlings received there in 1905. To hold over any appreciable number at any one division would have meant overstocking that range. Such flexibility as remained under these circumstances was used in adjusting the size of herds as range conditions changed on the different divisions.

The average annual loss amounted to 7.5 per cent of the total herd but varied with the classes and location of the cattle; for the cows it was relatively low, for calves slightly higher, and for northern steers as high as 15.0 per cent.

Until 1910 practically all Matador stock shipped from the northern ranges was sold through commission houses in Chicago. Direct rail connections from the Dakota and Canadian pastures plus the fact that the best prices could be obtained at the Chicago stockyards accounted for this fact. Small lots of feeders and the Texas steers and cows were most frequently sent to Kansas

[47] Twenty-seventh Annual Report, 5.

City because of that market's proximity to Kansas feeding pens and southwestern pastures.

In 1909 the United States tariff was so revised that in the following year the company was unable to return its Canadian cattle for marketing in Chicago. The new regulations subjected stock originally exported for feeding purposes to the same duty, on reimportation, as was imposed on cattle bred outside the United States.[48] Since the duty and freight costs would have amounted to $26.00 a head, all thought of sending mature steers to Clay's commission house was abandoned, and Mackenzie made inquiries regarding shipping costs from Swift Current to Liverpool. Here expenses would have reached $27.00 a head. Thus, when he was offered $58.00 at the ranch, Mackenzie sold over two thousand four-year-old steers to a Winnipeg buyer. In 1911 the same class of cattle brought $62.50 "sold direct from the pasture."

The credit balances and dividends for each year during 1902–11 were determined in part by the weather, in part by general business conditions. When consideration is given to all factors—the purchase of Alamositas, expenses attendant upon getting established in South Dakota and Canada, and the addition of lands at the main ranch—it is apparent that the company prospered during the decade.

TABLE 2*

YEAR	CREDIT BALANCE	DIVIDEND
1902	£20,520	6¼%
1903	6,105	2½
1904	5,920	2½
1905	7,034	2½
1906	11,685	3¾

[48] "Under the Act of 1909 the specific rates on cattle amounted to about 20 per cent ad valorem on animals under one year and 28 per cent on animals over one year." Lynn Ramsay Edminster, *The Cattle Industry and the Tariff*, 116. Until the passage of the Act of 1909, Matador cattle were allowed to re-enter the United States duty free.

1907	12,549	3¾
1908	9,541	3¾
1909	8,504	3¾
1910	12,508	5
1911	38,767	5 plus 5% bonus

* From the annual reports for the years listed.

The downward break in 1903 and 1904 was attributed by Mackenzie to a drought along the Belle Fourche and to a combination of the beef trust's manipulations and a strike by the packing-house workers in 1904. The depression following the panic of 1907 accounted for the low returns in 1908 and 1909.

The manager's occasional trips to Scotland were scheduled so that he could be present at the company's annual general meeting in Dundee. Upon such visits—in 1902, 1907, and 1910—he reported to the shareholders and answered questions asked by those present. Customarily the meetings ran smoothly, but in 1907, James C. Robertson, the company's auditor, made a long speech in which he criticized the costs of management, Mackenzie's traveling expenses, and his connection with the American Stock Growers Association. He added that he was about to travel on business and pleasure in Mexico, the United States, and Canada and that he would visit two of the company's ranches and would report thereon "without any cost to the company."

In replying to Robertson's criticisms the manager stated:

I am perfectly satisfied that the cost per head of running the Matador cattle is as low, if not lower, than any other Company, with probably the exception of one, and the cost per head is the only way we can calculate the cost of running cattle. With reference to the American Stock Growers Association we contributed our share like other people toward the upkeep of that Association. I devoted some attention, with the consent of the Board, to that work. We contributed only our proportion to its upkeep. If I had time to go into the benefits derived by cattle companies from such an association I could convince everyone in the room that it is the best money we ever invested. We have put railroads in the position where we are not under their control in the matter of rates as hitherto but in the hands of a committee whose duty it is to see that we are not charged extravagant rates. With regard to my expenses it is as easy to stop them as it is to stop a clock. The Board has power to tell me that I am not to travel. If the Directors say, "You cannot go from home and cannot visit the property of the Company," I will say to the Company, "I am obliged to you for paying me a salary for doing nothing." I also say that if you refuse me permission to visit and supervise the property for which I am responsible, I cease to be your manager. Your properties are separated a distance of over 2,000 miles and I cannot go from one to the other without paying expenses. I cannot do it out of my pocket.[49]

Within a few weeks Robertson visited the Matador and Alamositas ranches and reported to the board from Trinidad on June 3, 1907, that he had received every courtesy at the hands of the manager and the superintendents, that Mackenzie's views on land sales appeared to be sound, and that operating costs were "kept down to the lowest level consistent with efficiency." When the report was read to the shareholders on February 11, 1908, the secretary noted that it was a "satisfaction to the directors to have Mr. Robertson withdraw the charges made the previous year," and the auditor rose to state:

I would add to the letter which has been read by Mr. Mackay that it was a pleasure to find myself able to write home to him in those terms. . . . Mr. Mackenzie and I did not agree on policy, but I would repeat what I have said in the letter—that Mr. Mackenzie undoubtedly is doing what he believes to be the best in the interest of the Company. We must leave these matters in his hands, believing that he, on the spot, is best informed as to what course should be adopted. Of course you understand that the

[49] Report of Proceedings, Twenty-fifth Annual General Meeting of Shareholders, 10–11. John Robertson, one of the directors and a brother of James C. Robertson, had died some months earlier. The auditor was obviously upset at this meeting, for he directed a number of critical remarks at the company in general and at Mackay in particular.

spreading out of the business to ranches so far removed from each other adds greatly to the expenses. Mr. Mackenzie thinks that is warranted and there we must leave the matter.[50]

As a result of the visit to America, Robertson's health, disposition, and understanding of the company's operations were improved; he remained as auditor for the organization until 1930 and never again spoke critically of the management's expenses at a shareholders' meeting.

Early in 1909, Arthur G. Ligertwood resigned as superintendent of the Matador Division and was succeeded by John M. Jackson, the senior foreman at the home ranch. Ligertwood had been associated with Mackenzie for over twenty years, and his departure was keenly felt.

Deep and personal tragedy entered Mackenzie's life later in the same year when Dode Mackenzie was shot to death on December 11 at LeBeau, South Dakota.[51] Young Mackenzie had been superintendent of the Dakota Division since 1906, when he had moved from Alamositas in an exchange of positions with H. F. Mitchell, and had been responsible for the Matador steers, numbering some sixteen thousand head, on the Cheyenne River Reservation. If his own grief caused Murdo Mackenzie to falter, there was no indication of it; he promoted James R. Burr, the bookkeeper at the Dakota ranch, to the superintendent's position and carried on the numerous activities in which he was then engaged without a break.[52] In January, 1910, he went to Scot-

[50] Report of Proceedings, Twenty-sixth Annual General Meeting of Shareholders, 8–9.

[51] New York *Times*, December 12, 1909. Also, cable, Mackenzie to Mackay, December 13, 1909. According to the *Times* the killer was Bud Stephenson, a former Matador hand. The names "Bud Stevens" and "Bud Stephens" appeared on the Dakota division payrolls in 1906. Stevens (or Stephens) was acquitted in March, 1910. Accounts of the shooting are in Blasingame's *Dakota Cowboy*, 288–89, and Mari Sandoz' *The Cattlemen* (New York, Hastings House, 1958), 468–69.

[52] In Mackenzie's estimation Burr was the model cowman. "I would like very much to get hold of two or three good boys from the old country whom we could hold in reserve in case of emergency. I do not care to get town-raised boys be-

land to be present at the annual meeting of the shareholders and
there gave a full report on the company's operations, including
the negotiations for construction of a railroad through the Matador Division.

It is not known whether the loss of Dode Mackenzie and the
departure of Arthur Ligertwood were factors influencing Murdo
Mackenzie's decision to leave the company's service. Early in
1911, Percival Farquhar, an international financier of Paris and
New York, met the Matador manager in Denver and told him
that he believed meat could be produced cheaply in the unde-
veloped sections of South America and exported to European
markets. In the same year, Farquhar organized the Brazil Land,
Cattle and Packing Company and asked Mackenzie to become
manager of the new enterprise. Mackenzie hesitated. He was
sixty-one years old, and his business interests were well established. His property at Stonewall, thirty miles west of Trinidad
on the upper Purgatoire, provided a place of rest and opportunity to exercise his skill as a fisherman. The Mackenzie home in
Trinidad was the center of social life for friends of the family.
But the lure of a new adventure was strong, and the decision was
announced to Mackay in August, 1911:

> The offer these people made me was so flattering and so much
> beyond anything that I ever expected to receive that it about
> knocked me off my feet, but upon thinking the matter over I felt
> if climatic and other conditions would suit that I would not be
> doing justice to my family and myself if I did not accept it. . . .
> The name of the town in which we would have to live is Sao
> Paulo. . . . The name of the company is the Brazil Land, Cattle,
> and Packing Company. It owns about 2,500,000 acres of land

---

cause in a majority of cases they are not a success in our business. What I would
like to get are boys like James Burr, who have been raised on a farm and who
have had a little knowledge of stock. Town boys are hard to handle and they are
not as a rule willing to wait until the opportunity arises to be promoted. They
expect too much right from the start." Mackenzie to Mackay, June 7, 1906.

. . . about 6,000 miles of railroad and proposes to build three packing houses.[53]

When the Dundee board indicated it would not stand in the way of such an opportunity, Mackenzie recommended the appointment of John MacBain to the managership and spent the last four months of the year placing his own and the company's affairs in order. Early in January, 1912, he took his family to Scotland for a brief visit before moving to São Paulo and left the managerial reins in the hands of MacBain.

[53] Mackenzie to Mackay, August 26, 1911. Mackenzie received a five-year contract at a salary of $50,000 a year.

~~4~~
Railroads and Oil

THE FOURTH MANAGER of the Matador Interests in America, John MacBain, was born in Tain, Scotland, on August 18, 1867. He had entered the company's service in 1898 and for four years worked as bookkeeper on the ranch at Ballard Springs. Following Henry H. Johnstone's resignation as accountant in December, 1902, MacBain succeeded him and moved to Trinidad early in 1903.[1] His experience at the Motley County ranch and in the manager's office gave him a thorough knowledge of the company's affairs and made him the logical successor to Mackenzie. He was a member of the executive boards of both the Texas Cattle Raisers Association and the American National Live Stock Growers Association and had earned a reputation for meticulous attention to detail, a characteristic which was reflected in his reports to the board and in instructions to his subordinates. A tall man, well over six feet in height, MacBain lacked something of his predecessor's bluntness, but was nevertheless a person of determination and vigor, completely dedicated to the company's service.

No changes in policy or procedures followed the new manager's appointment, but some adjustments in personnel were required, since James Burr went to Brazil with Mackenzie and Dave Somerville followed in 1913.[2] To head the Dakota Division

---

[1] MacBain was a nephew of Mrs. Murdo (Isabella Stronach MacBain) Mackenzie. Shortly after moving to Trinidad he married Minne Lenhart of that city.

[2] Within weeks after his acceptance of the position in South America, Murdo

MacBain sent James M. (Mat) Walker, a wagon boss at the Ballard Springs ranch, and to handle the clerical work and serve as his own assistant, he moved William W. Kerr to Trinidad from Motley County. J. R. Lair, also an employee on the Matador Division, was sent to Canada to replace Somerville.

A test of MacBain's ability to deal with the superintendents occurred before Mackenzie had climbed the gangplank on his voyage to Brazil. When Mat Walker, anxious to go into the winter with a full crew at the Dakota Division, attempted to hire some of the hands away from the Matador Division, Jackson protested to MacBain and wrote a sharp note to Walker: "I have always taken you to be one of my friends till recently but of late your actions do not point that way; in the future if you have any desire to have any of the men that are working under me, I think the least you can do would be to consult with me in the first place."[3] Fortunately a snowstorm delayed delivery of Jackson's letter, so that MacBain could send definite instructions to Walker before the Dakota superintendent could reply to Jackson:

> Jackson is feeling badly about your writing to some men that he had at work for the winter. It seems that you wrote the men and they in turn wrote Jackson saying that you had offered them better wages to work for you. I explained to Jackson that Burr had offered several of the men that you had hired to work all winter a better job in Brazil and that on the 15th of last month several of the men had left your employment which left you in a pretty bad plight. For the future, if you want any men from Texas who are working for Jackson you should first write to Jackson asking him if he can spare the men and if so for him to send them on. If, however, you want any of the men who are working for Jackson during the summer but not during the win-

Mackenzie received over five hundred letters asking for positions in Brazil. In addition to Burr and Somerville, other Matador employees who went to work for the Brazil Land, Cattle, and Packing Company included Murdo's sons John and Alex Mackenzie, Homer and Roy Vivian, and Emmett Roberds, who later became superintendent at Alamositas.

[3] Jackson to Walker, January 1, 1912.

ter you are at liberty then to write the men direct; I think it would be better for all concerned if things were arranged this way.[4]

Walker received the two letters on January 25, and while he could "not see that Jackson had been wronged to the extent of getting so badly swelled" about the matter, he assured both Mac-Bain and Jackson that he would not bother the latter any more.

The first major problem—and certainly the most involved—which confronted MacBain had to do with the laying of a rail line across the Matador Division range. While the possibility of a railroad's entry into Motley County had been mentioned by William F. Sommerville as early as 1886 and an inquiry had been made about what support the company would give to a proposed line from Vernon to Matador in 1906, it was not until 1910 that a firm approach was made to the board regarding concessions and a bonus in return for the construction of a railroad from Quanah westward through Paducah and to the High Plains.

Sam Lazarus of St. Louis, president of the Acme Cement Plaster Company, had been instrumental in forming the Acme, Red River and Northern Railway, a short line originally projected to extend from Acme in Hardeman County to the Red River and thence to a connection with the Frisco system—the St. Louis, San Francisco Railway—for the purpose of tapping the large gypsum deposits at Acme. In 1909 the charter of the short line was amended to give the road a new name—the Quanah, Acme and Pacific—and to permit a revision of its route. The plan to connect with the Frisco was abandoned; and when construction from Quanah to Acme—a distance of six miles—was completed, Lazarus decided to build westward by way of Roswell, New Mexico, to El Paso.[5] By 1910 thirty-seven miles of track were laid to Paducah, and Lazarus, as president and principal stockholder of the railroad, began looking for a right of way

[4] MacBain to Walker, January 4, 1912.

[5] Carl Harper, "Movements toward Railroad Building on the South Plains of Texas," MS, 178.

through Motley County; naturally he sought to obtain as many concessions as possible from the large ranches through which his road would extend. In order to draw out the Matador, he pointed out that there were several open routes in the country west of Paducah: one of these ran through the center of the company's range, another crossed a portion of it, and the third missed it entirely. If Lazarus thought the Scots would betray any strong desire to secure a road through their range and would offer a generous bonus, he was disappointed. The board knew that the best grade to the High Plains lay within its property—Sommerville had pointed out this in 1886—and refused to be drawn into any agreement which would give Lazarus one foot of ground without securing for the company a voice in prescribing the route.[6]

Mackenzie wanted the proposed road to go through the town of Matador, since he had been informed "on good authority" that another railroad company planned to build from Dallas through Seymour to Plainview and believed that this line would cross the southern part of the range; the company then "would have two roads instead of one and that would enable the disposal of . . . property to the best advantage."[7]

Lazarus' initial proposal called for the Matador to pay to the railroad a bonus of $1.00 an acre for all land belonging to the company lying within three miles of the line; this would have amounted to $640 a section, or $3,840 a mile. In addition, the railroad president wanted a right of way, water privileges, and land for depots and sidings and proposed that two sections of the Matador property be set aside for townsites, with the company and the railroad to share equally in the proceeds from the sale of lots in these townsites. Because Lazarus was willing to

[6] The ascent, from east to west, lay along the ridge between the South Pease and TeePee Creek and followed the small tributaries of the former stream to their sources along the cap rock. Sommerville stated that this was "the best grade within a hundred miles."

[7] Mackenzie to Mackay, April 15, 1910.

take his bonus in land at a fair value, the manager recommended that his terms be met, but since the matter was one of great importance—"the turning point in the history of the company"— he insisted that Mackay come to America and deal personally with Lazarus. In keeping with the board's instructions, the secretary sailed for the United States in May, 1910—some three months earlier than his annual trip was customarily made—and in a series of conferences with Lazarus assured the latter that the bonus in land would be given. On the basis of this commitment, the railroad president went about the business of raising money with which to continue his project.

During the last half of 1910 few exchanges occurred in connection with the railroad; the Dundee people did not want to appear anxious lest Lazarus take advantage of their concern and make heavier demands, and the promoter was having difficulty in obtaining financial support, but early in 1911 he announced that he had succeeded in interesting a New York financier in the proposed road and asked the company for a written statement that a bonus of one dollar an acre would be granted him on all Matador land lying within three miles of the track. Mackay furnished the statement that the company would pay the bonus with certain reservations having to do with the route and instructed the manager to go over the possible courses which the road could take. Traveling in buggies, Mackenzie, Lazarus, and a group of surveyors spent several days inspecting the country between the South Pease and TeePee Creek, then traveled over the northern portion of Motley County; here the engineers pointed out the disadvantages of routes north of Ballard Springs and convinced Mackenzie that the idea of building the line through the town of Matador should be abandoned.

During Lazarus' stay at the ranch a group of citizens from the town visited the promoter and insisted that the railroad should be built through Matador. When Lazarus expressed the doubt that such a route would be feasible, the delegation declared its belief "that if the road did not come to Matador it would be the fault of the company," and next pleaded with Mackenzie to intervene on behalf of the town and stated that, in the people's opinion, he could see to it that the line ran through Matador if he were so inclined. Mackenzie told the committee that he had advocated the building of the road through the town but that the construction costs for any route north of the ranch headquarters would be higher than for one along the South Pease, and suggested that if the citizens wanted to get the road through Matador, they would have to raise the money to take care of the difference in cost between the northern and southern grades.[8]

During the summer surveyors laid out the right of way. It crossed the South Pease at about the Motley-Cottle county line and followed the divide between the South Pease and TeePee Creek to a point eight miles south of the ranch headquarters; here the town of Roaring Springs was laid out, and from this place the road was projected along a westward course to the High Plains in Floyd County.

In September, 1911, Mackay and David Wilkie, a director, entered into two agreements with Lazarus in Chicago; both were conditional understandings. One obligated the company to pay to the Quanah, Acme and Pacific Railway Company one dollar for each acre of Matador land "lying within three miles of each side of the railroad measured from the center of said railroad" and to grant a right of way one hundred feet wide through its property, plus additional tracts for sidings and stations. The second called for the formation of a townsite development company, to which the Matador would convey 640 acres at each of three townsites in Motley County; the stock in this organization was to be held equally by the Dundee and the St. Louis people.[9]

Later in the year Lazarus proposed to create an agricultural development company which would purchase land and place it on sale to farmers. The Matador agreed to sell to the development company sixty thousand acres in the southwest portion of

[8] Mackenzie to Mackay, April 20, 1911.
[9] Board Minute Book, VII, 330–37.

its range at a price of ten dollars an acre; in payment, the cattle company would receive $600,000 of the preferred stock of the proposed land company and $600,000 of the common stock, while $600,000 of the common stock would be issued to the Quanah, Acme and Pacific.

Thus matters stood when MacBain became manager. No steel had been laid on Matador property, and Lazarus was still trying to raise the cash to begin construction. When the Quanah, Acme and Pacific's option on the right of way across Motley County expired early in 1912, the board asked MacBain to remind Lazarus of that fact but to let the promoter know that he still had opportunity to submit evidence of his financial ability to build the railroad. In May, 1912, MacBain met the railroad president in St. Louis, and on this occasion Lazarus assured him that he could build the line if the company would agree to give him a lump sum of $125,000 when the first train ran over the road, to enlarge the townsite acreage, and to permit him to lay used rails rated at not less than sixty pounds. The manager explained that the $125,000 figure was high—equal to $1.05 an acre—and that the board probably would not agree to pay a higher bonus than that originally agreed upon. In reporting to the secretary, Mac-Bain expressed doubt that the company owned as much land within the three-mile limit as Lazarus claimed, but acknowledged that "if he zigzagged close to all our lands," he might be correct.[10]

While the directors agreed to meet some of Lazarus' requests, they would not go above the bonus of one dollar an acre; and when Mackay figured that the company-owned land within the six-mile-wide strip amounted to 78,680 acres in contrast to the 119,047 acres claimed by the railroad, it appeared that the whole project would be abandoned. But Lazarus was not one to quit. On June 5 he cabled the Dundee board:

If you will give lump sum eighty-five thousand dollars bonus

[10] MacBain to Mackay, May 18, 1912.

payable after construction of first forty miles in lieu of one dollar per acre, will arrange to close matters with your representative and start work. This would cover all bonuses on land beyond forty miles you own on plains and am personally underwriting other fifteen thousand to make this trade go.

When the directors agreed to these terms, Lazarus told Mac-Bain, "You tell your people that I am going through with this thing and for them to be getting their money ready to turn over to me about the first of May next year."[11]

In December, 1912, the board affixed the company seal to a contract which had been signed in November by Mackay and Lazarus. It bound the Matador to pay to the railway the sum of $85,000 "upon the construction and operation for thirty days of both passenger and freight trains on the first forty miles of the railroad." The Quanah, Acme and Pacific was allowed "to re-lay rails of sixty-five pounds weight approved of by a competent authority as good and suitable," and received a guarantee of a right of way one hundred feet wide through the company lands in Floyd County at such time as the railroad would be extended onto the cap rock.[12]

Track-laying operations began before the year was ended, and in June, 1913, the rails reached MacBain Switch, forty miles west of Paducah and six miles west of Roaring Springs.[13] On June 19 a special train carrying prospective settlers ran from Quanah to Roaring Springs, heralding the formal opening of the latter town, and on the next day regular train service between the two towns began. The company's payment of $85,000 was not mailed to Lazarus until September 23—the railroad president had kindly permitted deferment until the Matador could make payment out of its receipts from fall cattle sales.

The Roaring Springs Townsite Company did a brisk business

11 MacBain to Mackay, June 26, 1912.
12 Board Minute Book, VII, 432–35.
13 In 1928 the Q., A., and P. was extended to Floydada, where it connected with a branch line of the Panhandle and Santa Fe system.

in disposing of town lots following the completion of the railroad. This organization, formed at Fort Worth in December, 1912, was headed by Lazarus and had as its officers two vice-presidents—Charles H. Sommer, a railway official, and Arthur G. Ligertwood, who had returned to Texas—a secretary-treasurer, MacBain, and an assistant secretary-treasurer, J. D. Harkey. The townsite company had a modest capitalization of $50,000 made up by $20,000 in promissory notes signed by MacBain and Lazarus, and by title to 960 acres of land—the townsite—valued at $30,000 and deeded to the development agency by the Dundee corporation.

The sale of lots valued at $24,000 within five weeks of the town's opening caused high hopes that the Roaring Springs community would soon become a thriving metropolis. The optimism characteristic of its promoters—and of land developers throughout the West—was reflected in a report given by J. Nicoll Smith, a director who accompanied Mackay to America in 1913, to the shareholders in Dundee:

> Mr. Mackay and I travelled over the new railroad both going to and returning from the Matador property. . . . Near the terminus of the line the new town of Roaring Springs is being built. . . . On our visit there was great activity in the little settlement where some fifty buildings of various kinds were being erected. The station buildings are very neat and attractive and the streets are laid out on a wide scale for a western town. A cotton gin has been built and was in operation when we were there. A large lumber shed has also been erected and a big stock of lumber accumulated to meet the wants of settlers. A small bank building was also under way and a church nearly finished; altogether, the little town is full of bustle and showed signs of having a promising future.[14]

The new community might have enjoyed greater prosperity had there been an exodus from the county seat to the railroad

[14] Report of Proceedings, Thirty-Second Annual General Meeting of Shareholders, 6–7.

town. Early in 1913 some twenty citizens from Matador peti-
tioned the company for aid in building a railroad to connect
their town with the Quanah, Acme, and Pacific line. Mackay rejected the terms outlined in the original proposal, since the company was asked to bear the burden of costs—a request which
MacBain labeled as "purely the work of Socialists in that part of
the country"—but after the railroad reached Roaring Springs,
the Scots consented to give a bonus to the citizens of Matador
for constructing the Motley County Railroad. The townspeople
immediately secured a charter, and in 1914 the short line was
completed; its eight miles of track connected with the Quanah,
Acme and Pacific at Matador Junction, three miles east of Roaring Springs. In explaining the company's payment of the $10,000
bonus when the road went into operation, Mackay stated, "Apart
from the value to the Company of this additional means of transportation, we felt justified in making the payment as an evidence
of our willingness to help the townspeople of Matador in a
scheme upon which they had set their hearts and toward which
they had subscribed very liberally."[15]

The agricultural development company which Lazarus had
proposed in 1911 ran into difficulties and never received title to
any portion of the sixty thousand acres offered by the Matador;
the chief obstacle to completing the formation of the agency was
Lazarus' refusal to accept the lands which the ranch offered. The
properties assigned by the Scots were either too far from the
railroad or too unproductive to attract farmers; on the other
hand, the company felt it could not permit Lazarus to pick
choice lands, either in small or large tracts, lest it lose its watering points or the contiguity of its pastures. As a result of this
stalemate the cattle company and the railroad entered into a
contract which granted to the latter a portion of the proceeds
from those land sales which the promoter and his associates ar-

[15] Report of Proceedings, Thirty-third Annual General Meeting of Shareholders, 8. In 1926 the Motley County Railroad became the property of the Q.,
A., and P., and in 1936 it was abandoned.

ranged, and reserved to the Dundee office the right to approve such sales. Titles to lands sold under this arrangement were transferred directly from the company to the buyers, while receipts from sales were deposited in the townsite company's account in a St. Louis bank.

Despite a drought which held down land sales in the vicinity of Roaring Springs, the Matador directors reported that during the thirty months following the opening of the railroad, 6,693 acres of company property were purchased by "home seekers and farmers"; and in 1916, when sales recommenced on a considerable scale, the directors announced that 9,812 acres were sold. The wartime boom accounted for the disposal of over 27,500 acres in 1917—the peak year—but the demand for land continued to such a degree that in 1923 the sale of 60,000 acres under the "Lazarus contract" was completed.

The drought of 1913, which sent powder-dry dust swirling along the South Pease to discourage settlers there, struck the Matador at another division—Dakota. Light winter snows and high winds on the Cheyenne River range left little moisture in the ground; and when Mat Walker reported that the Indians were developing a strong disinclination to renew the company's lease along the Missouri, MacBain went to South Dakota to inspect the range and to make arrangements either to retain the Sioux grass or to secure a lease elsewhere. His findings were reported to the secretary:

> Nearly every one that I talked to in South Dakota seems to be of the opinion that the Indians themselves do not want to give another lease on the land but want to stock the pastures with their own cattle. It is pretty hard to tell when this question will come up for settlement but the first thing that will have to be done by the Department of the Interior is to find out the will of the Indians and this can only be ascertained through their usual Indian councils. The half-breeds were always against the leasing of this land and they will be the ones that we will have to fight in order to get a new lease. . . . It is impossible for a Matador

man to go to one of the councils and be heard, and it occurred to me that the best thing we can do is see Mr. King [Thomas J. King, a former agent at the reservation] who is now no longer connected with the government, with a view of getting him to appear before the Indians' council and advise them as to giving us a new lease on the lands.[16]

King gave little encouragement regarding the company's chances to stay in Dakota; and when he suggested that a portion of the Fort Belknap Indian Reservation in northern Montana might be leased from the Gros Ventre and Assiniboine tribes, he was asked by MacBain to investigate. MacBain notified the Dundee office of developments and began a study of railroad timetables to determine what effect a move from South Dakota to Montana would have on the company's schedules and shipping costs. He learned that the distance from Roaring Springs to the Montana shipping point, Harlem, was seventy miles longer than the distance from Roaring Springs to Evarts, South Dakota, but that the Montana "run" to the Chicago market was 470 miles longer than the trip from the Dakota Division to the same market. To MacBain this meant "a day and a-half longer on the road from the Belknap reservation than from Dakota to Chicago and consequently a greater shrinkage in the weight of cattle going to market." Despite this disadvantage he felt that the company "would sacrifice a golden opportunity if it failed to look into the Montana range."

On the basis of this recommendation the board authorized MacBain to take Walker and Mitchell to Montana and to "make an exhaustive report" on his findings at the Fort Belknap Reservation. In compliance with these directions, the manager and the Alamositas superintendent met Walker at Cushman, Montana, and went on to Harlem, arriving at the agency on April 19. The report to Mackay on April 28 was a complete one:

[16] MacBain to Mackay, Irons and Co., March 11, 1913. When the company's first lease on the Cheyenne River range expired in 1909, a second five-year lease was obtained.

141

The headquarters of the Belknap Reservation are located about four miles south of the town of Harlem on the south side of the Milk River. Harlem is on the main line of the Great Northern Railway. . . . The reservation begins at a point about seven miles west of the town and on the south side of Milk River and runs about due south forty-two miles, thence east about twenty-eight miles, thence north about thirty-five miles to the northeast corner of the reservation where it again touches Milk River. The reservation has never been surveyed except by running outside boundary lines. . . . It is estimated to contain about 500,000 acres. The agent in charge thought that after deducting all the land that will be set aside for irrigation purposes that there will be about 400,000 acres for lease as a grazing proposition. We spent three days going over the reservation and made a general inspection of same from a range point of view. We started from the agency . . . and went south in a zig-zag course until we came to St. Paul's Mission. This place is located at the foot of what is called "The Little Rocky Mountains" and about forty miles from the agency. All the way down we crossed a number of small creeks and saw several lakes. Water was running in nearly all the creeks and ravines but of course the melting snow might have caused this. However, we secured the services of a guide who spent twenty years on the reservation and he assured us that all the creeks named on the map have water running in them the year round. . . . The character of the country from the agency south for the first fifteen miles is long, rolling prairie on both sides as far as we could see. We could see on our right going south, some distance away, very high, sharp-pointed hills and that the country was much broken up by deep ravines, all of which our guide assured us contained living water. The old grass now on the ground can hardly be described. It is the best that Mitchell or Walker has seen in a long time. The old grass is actually knee deep on the flats. It appears to be in excellent condition. We counted five different kinds of grasses, three of which are blue stem, grama and buffalo. Of course there is no stock of any kind to speak of on the reservation and hasn't been for two years, except what the Indians own and the agent says that one thousand head will cover the entire number on the range. There are very few cattle in that part of the country, the bulk of the stock being horses. We found that the reservation had been leased to sheep men up until two years ago but that the government decided to turn them out on account of their having destroyed the range.

From St. Paul's Mission we had to double back over the same road we went in on for about six miles on account of the hilly nature of the country. Then we struck off in an easterly direction until we came to a sub-agency called "Lodgepole." At this point we were about the center of the pasture on the south and about two miles from the mountains. The entire south end of the reservation is bounded by a high range of mountains which rise to an altitude of about 4,800 feet and there is naturally a large area of broken land and some deep canyons all of which afford excellent shelter. The guide and several others that we met told us that the snow never gets deep enough in the south end of the reservation to hurt the stock or cover up the grass for long periods and that the canyons never hold snow deep enough to prevent stock from taking shelter in them. Of course we did not see why the snow should not drift into those canyons just the same as any other part of the range. We were told that for a distance of about ten miles from the south end of the reservation the snow did not lie on the ground as long or as deep as in the northern part of the pasture on account of that particular section of the country being subject to chinook winds all through the winter which has the effect of melting the snows on the west and south sides of the hills. All the people on the south side of the reservation say that it is impossible to use sleds for hauling in winter as is done farther south in the same state and this is pretty good indication that the snow does not lie very long on the ground. All the heavy storms in this country come from the northwest which would drift the cattle to the southeast where the best shelter is. From St. Paul's Mission to Lodgepole we found grass and water abundant, even the tops of the hills are well sodded and grassed. There are hundreds of deep depressions all over the country but unlike our Dakota range there is very little brush or willows or shrubbery of any kind to be seen on the range except around the Indian villages and these are all fenced.

There are about 1200 Indians [Gros Ventres and Assiniboine] on the reservation and they are located on the banks of the Milk River on the north and at St. Paul's Mission and Lodgepole in the south. They are all together in small villages on the outskirts of the reservation. . . . From the cowman's point of view this reservation cannot be surpassed. The north half could be used as summer pasture and the south half as winter pasture. Hay can be cut on almost any of the flats on the north. . . . The agent told us that he has the authority to lease the pasture for two years, from first of May next, at $1.60 per head for cattle and $2.00 per head for horses. We told him that it would not be worth our while to move into the country for two years but that if he could give some assurance of getting a lease for five years that we would submit the proposition to our Board of Directors. . . . He stated that if we placed ten thousand head on the range at $1.50 per head per annum that he would give us absolute control for five years if the Department [of the Interior] at Washington would agree to the extension of time from two years to five. The Department now regulates the grazing on all reservations to one animal (cow or horse) for every thirty acres of land. . . . If we could make some satisfactory arrangements to pay on the basis of a dollar fifty per head per annum with a liberal allowance for losses on the second year, it would perhaps be the best plan to lease the land on that basis. For example, if we could arrange to pay $1.50 per head for the first twelve months, then for the second sixteen months we would pay on the actual number shipped out on the $1.50 per head basis. . . . This is the cheapest grazing in this country at the present time and grazing, like everything else, is now advancing in price. . . .

Both Mitchell and Walker say that the Belknap country is far ahead of Canada from a grass, water and shelter point of view, and also a good deal better than the Dakota range as it now stands. . . . In the event of your agreeing to a lease of the Belknap, provided same can be had for five years, we then could ship there all the cattle intended for Dakota this spring, and at the same time we could also ship three or four thousand cows from Matador to make up the required number of ten thousand head and this would, to a large extent, relieve the situation at the Matador division. These cows could be shipped to Chicago next fall when fat. From Dakota we can ship all the three- and four-year-old steers and heifers that are fat and any balance we have in Dakota can be sent to the Belknap. The Dakota lease can be cancelled after the semiannual lease is paid next July and that would give us possession of the Dakota range until December and then we can get a permit to graze there for as long as we want in 1914. Our Dakota lease expires the first of July, 1914. We have no hesitation in recommending that an application be made for the Belknap Reservation for a five-year absolute lease, based on five cents per acre or $1.50 per head per annum, because it is the only available tract of grazing land left in the north. The whole country is settling up very fast.[17]

Prior to preparing the report, MacBain had gone to the Canadian Division and had cabled Mackay from Swift Current recommending that the company apply for a lease on the Belknap reservation. Upon his return to Trinidad, he found the board's authorization to proceed with the necessary steps and promptly notified the reservation superintendent, Major H. H. Miller, that a formal application was being filed and requested permission to cut and stack hay at different points on the reservation to tide the cattle over in a hard winter. The changing nature of range stock was recognized by the manager: "The days of the survival of the fittest are past and as cattle are now expensive it is absolutely necessary that provision be made for them during hard weather."[18]

Early in May, MacBain went to Washington and succeeded in getting the permit approved and forwarded to the Secretary of the Interior for final action. Although formal sanction of the lease did not take place until July, the company received notice late in May to move its cattle to the Milk River range, and on June 7 trains carrying Matador stock left Murdo and Paducah bound for Montana. Since both Texas divisions were in "deplorable

17 MacBain to Mackay, April 28, 1913.
18 MacBain to Miller, April 29, 1913.

condition" because of the drought, these and subsequent shipments lightened the loads on their pastures. By July 16, Mat
Walker had received over sixteen thousand head at Harlem.

According to the terms of the contract between the company
and the United States government, the former received grazing
rights on the Fort Belknap Indian Reservation for a period of
five years from July 1, 1913. For these rights the Matador paid
$1.50 a head per year on a minimum of ten thousand head. The
government agreed to put the fence around the reservation in
first-class condition, and the lessees were obligated to maintain it.

Mat Walker was made superintendent of the Montana Division and divided his time from the middle of 1913 through 1914
between the Dakota and Belknap pastures. Because of the exceptionally large shipments of cattle from Texas to Montana
during 1913, the Dakota herds remained at the Cheyenne River
Reservation; and while efforts were made to clear this division
when the company's lease expired in 1914, some strays were not
recovered until the following year, although the books were
closed at the end of 1914.

So severe was the 1913 drought on the Texas ranges that even
with the addition of the Belknap pasture and the retention of the
Dakota Division, MacBain was forced to seek more grass. Efforts to lease the Prairie company's Romero pasture adjacent to
Alamositas failed, but early in June, MacBain arranged with
E. H. Wheeler of Wilson, Colorado, to lease for one year a pasture of eighty thousand acres on the Butler Ranch near Walsen-
burg. For the lease and for looking after the cattle, Wheeler was
to be paid $5.25 for each head of Matador stock placed on the
Butler pasture; and while this was the highest rate paid for grass
to that time by the company, MacBain felt that a heavy expenditure would be better than to keep the cattle at home and lose
them. In August, after the stronger cattle had been sent to Canada, Dakota, and Montana, the Colorado pasture was filled with

5,339 dry cows and yearling heifers from Alamositas and Matador. These cattle did well during the fall, but an early snowfall
of thirty-seven inches followed by alternate thaws and freezes
so decimated the herd that only 3,181 head were alive in May,
1914. Of the survivors, over 2,000 were shipped back to the
Matador Division and 1,164 were sold.

When rains began to fall on the Texas ranges late in 1913, it
appeared that the drought was broken. Snows during the winter at Alamositas and Matador provided the moisture to give
plants a good start in the spring, but with the growing season
weeds soon outstripped the grass, and a new search was begun
for space on which yearling stock could be placed while the
ranges recovered. Inquiries were made throughout the state, but
the best prospect was found adjacent to Alamositas when Arthur
Ligertwood located a "possible vacancy" on the Romero pasture
of the Prairie Cattle Company. This tract of some 200,000 acres
lay north and west of the Alamositas in Oldham and Hartley
counties, and at the time Ligertwood first hinted at its use
(March, 1914), it was fully stocked with Prairie cattle. However, John M. Shelton of Amarillo had an option to buy the
Romero lands after May 1, 1915, and told Ligertwood that he
would lease the grass to the Matador for two years at a price of
three dollars a head per year. Before Ligertwood, the company's
agent in the negotiations, could act, Shelton underwent a change
of mind and made a substitute proposal, offering the south half
of Romero—a pasture of over 100,000 acres—for two years on
condition that the company put no more than one yearling to
every fifteen acres; the Matador would have sole use and full
charge of the pasture and be responsible for the improvements
found on the land.[19]

Since Mackay wanted to see the pasture, he and one of the
directors, Sir Francis Webster, sailed for the United States late
in May and, following conferences with Shelton, agreed to lease

[19] Ligertwood to MacBain, May 10, 1914.

for two years, beginning on May 1, 1915, a pasture of about 113,000 acres at a cost of twenty cents an acre per year. The exact size of the Romero pasture was not known since, at the time the agreement was signed, the Prairie company had not transferred to Shelton the deeds for the land.

Matador yearlings had just begun to graze on Romero grass in May, 1915, when Shelton offered to sell to the company the pasture it had under lease. His initial price was $4.50 an acre for 120,067 acres described in the deed which the Prairie company had transferred to him, and his terms were $1.17 an acre cash at the time of sale and the balance in five equal payments bearing interest at the rate of 5 per cent. MacBain believed Shelton wanted to sell that half of the Romero pasture which lay south of the Canadian River to get money with which he could purchase "the Bravo pasture which belonged to Messrs. Fuqua, Herring and the Landergin brothers of Amarillo."[20] Mackay suggested that the Romero might be obtained for less than the owner asked and instructed the manager "to try to get the Bravo owners to come down in their price to Shelton so he in turn might lower the price on the Romero pasture"; but MacBain learned that, while Shelton might take less than $4.50 per acre for Romero, the Bravo price could not be lowered, and so he offered Shelton $4.00. The Romero owner was willing to bargain and after several months agreed to sell at a price of $4.25 per acre. On May 1, 1916, title to 121,622 acres passed to the Matador for a down payment of $123,000; the balance, in four annual payments of $70,000 each at 5 per cent interest, was paid off in 1920.[21]

With the annexation of Romero to the Alamositas Division and the purchase of a small pasture—7,826 acres—near the Bel-

[20] MacBain to Mackay, Irons and Co., May 18, 1915.

[21] Disposal of the south half of the Romero pasture and the subsequent acquisition of the Bravo placed Shelton's property in a block north of the Canadian River.

knap range in Montana, the company's holdings in land rose to 879,735 acres in 1916, a peak year in this regard. Thirty-five years after Thomas Lawson's report, the Matador, with its leased and owned grass, could still claim that its cattle ranged on "a million and a-half acres."

Behind the Dundee Scots' willingness to undertake such ventures as the move to Montana and the purchase of the Romero pasture was "the satisfactory nature of returns from land and cattle sales" prior to and during World War I. Thanks to the quality of its herds and the size and efficiency of its operations, the company enjoyed a brief era of prosperity before general war broke out in Europe in 1914. As the conflict progressed, prices of all commodities rose, and those of foodstuffs reached figures never before known. Indicative of the latter were the average sums received by the Matador for its northern cattle during the period 1913–18: although weights varied annually with weather and grass conditions, average prices (per head) in the various classes increased each year, with the exception of 1915, when an outbreak of hoof-and-mouth disease disturbed the Chicago market.

TABLE 3*

CLASS	1913	1914	1915	1916	1917	1918
Northern Steers	$82.74	$88.21	$86.51	$92.08	$122.40	$146.37
Northern Heifers	73.45	76.47	68.17	71.09	94.94	120.13

* From the annual reports for the years listed.

While tax payments—British and American—and feed costs climbed during the years of war and drought, prices such as those listed in Table 3 and receipts from land sales at the Matador Division enabled the company to keep its shareholders happy; even auditor Robertson was prompted to exclaim, after thanking Mackay for presiding at the annual meeting in 1917, "Long may he preside and declare a dividend of 20 per cent!"

TABLE 4*

YEAR	PROFIT	DIVIDEND
1912	£66,813	10% plus 5% bonus
1913	37,593	10 plus 5 "
1914	61,932	15 plus 5 "
1915	62,735	15 plus 5 "
1916	52,826	15 plus 5 "
1917	40,067	20
1918	40,603	20
1919	44,050	20
1920	67,913	20

* From the annual reports for the years listed.

The comparatively low profit shown for 1913 was due to heavy expenditures in leasing and shipping necessitated by the drought of that year. At the other end of the table, though prices dropped in 1919 from the previous year, expenses were kept to a minimum; a further decline of prices in 1920 was somewhat offset by a substantial increase in the number of Matador steers sent to market.

Until 1912 the best livestock prices obtained by the company were those brought by its steers from Canada, and the operation along the Saskatchewan was rated as the most profitable of the Matador activities in the north; costs were relatively low—seldom were there more than a dozen hands employed—and there were few expenses for improvements. However, during Dave Somerville's last year in Canada a decline in weight of the cattle was observed; and when he visited Scotland on his way to join Mackenzie in Brazil early in 1913, he attended a meeting of the board of directors and made certain recommendations regarding the company's future in the provinces. It was Somerville's opinion that Matador cattle had been infected with mange through contact with settlers' stock. Since the company's herds were kept together on prairie grasslands during the summer but were allowed to range in the breaks and canyons where they mixed with infected cattle during the winter, the superintendent felt that provision should be made to feed all Matador steers for one hundred days during the winter. He recommended that four or five "camps" be established where feed—principally oats in sheaf—could be stacked and fed twice a day on the ground; he reckoned that two sheaves a head each day would actually put weight on the cattle, and that two men at each camp could feed twelve hundred head and cut ice on the river so that watering places would be available. Somerville believed that the steers, if handled in this way, would be heavier by 150 pounds and would escape the risk of infection. The feed could be obtained by purchase and by extending the company's farming operations.[22]

For a variety of reasons these recommendations were not adopted in full. In April, 1913, Lair was advised that the Canadian government was preparing to inspect the Matador lease to ascertain what portion of the land might be suitable for agriculture; the superintendent was naturally reluctant to demonstrate, at company expense, that any part of the range was useful for farming. In addition, the United States tariff on the importation of livestock was abolished late in the same year, and Matador four-year-olds could once again be marketed at Chicago. When prices rose with the outbreak of war, the company sought to avoid the Canadian tariff by applying for the free import of its two-year-old steers into Saskatchewan—a privilege enjoyed by Canadian nationals—on the grounds that meat was important to the diet of Canada. To the government's inquiry as to whether the imported cattle were for Canadian consumption or consumption elsewhere, the company replied that because of market fluctuations its stock was sold sometimes in the United States, sometimes in Canada. As a result of continued negotiations in Ottawa, the Commissioner of Customs ruled that Matador stock could be taken to Canada duty free in 1918.

22 Board Minute Book, VII, 455–60. In 1911 several hundred acres of the lease had been planted in oats to create an emergency feed supply. Somerville's plan would have meant planting some two thousand acres.

At this point the United States entered the scene when the War Trade Board required the posting of a bond guaranteeing the return of the Canadian shipment after two years. Recognizing the possibility that the government in Ottawa might commandeer the herd, preventing its return to the United States and causing a forfeiture of the bond, the company undertook to get the board's order rescinded, and succeeded, after weeks of endeavor, in substituting its written pledge for the bond money.

The farming operations to which Somerville referred in his conference with the directors in January, 1913, never constituted a major item in the company's activities, though experimental work in crop raising and the production of small amounts of feed for emergency use were carried on from the time the Scots acquired the ranch at Ballard Springs. Mindful that the Articles of Association and the charters authorizing it to do business in the various states called for the company to "engage in cattle raising," the directors avoided agricultural programs except those that provided supplemental feed for selected classes of cattle or were experimental in nature. For example, the Annual Report for 1889 stated:

> The farming experiments begun two years ago [in Motley County] were extended last spring and a satisfactory crop was raised of sorghum, millet, and Johnson grass. Some grain of a promising character was also raised. The success is of moment in establishing the value of the Company's land for farming purposes. A large part of the crop will be applied in feeding a number of cattle of different ages over winter, and the results of this experiment will be watched with interest.

In the years that followed, settlers took over the experimental work in Motley County, but the Matador Division continued to raise feedstuff for its own herds and kept farmers and farm hands on its payroll until the middle of the twentieth century.

At Alamositas a plan was developed in 1908 to pump water from the Canadian River to irrigate some two hundred acres of alfalfa, sorghum, and maize. This was in the nature of an experiment; and when the results proved successful, the irrigated area was increased to five hundred acres and a small canal was constructed in 1911.[23] Through this ditch, several thousand yards in length, the water lifted from the river was distributed to the cultivated lands. In 1914 "preliminary borings" in a section of the Pedrosa pasture indicated the presence of water "at moderate depth and in sufficient quantity" to justify the drilling of two wells and the installation of pumps; from each of these a flow of from eight to twelve hundred gallons a minute was obtained and used for raising feed, primarily alfalfa. With this development the Pedrosa farm came to play a significant role in the Alamositas operations.

Agricultural activities at the divisions in Dakota and Montana involved cutting and stacking native grasses for winter feeding. In general, this work was performed by local labor employed during the haying season only, but riders and other ranch hands were occasionally pressed into what was, to them, a loathsome assignment.

Early in 1913 the company received its first formal inquiry concerning the exploration of its lands for oil when R. Waley Cohen, representing the Shell Transport Company, asked if the Matador would enter into a contract under which Shell would bear the cost of drilling and pay royalty if oil were found; as an alternative, he proposed an arrangement whereby the two companies would share the costs of exploration and the returns equally.[24] After due deliberation, the directors informed Shell that they would "consider favourably a contract upon a royalty

23 In keeping with Texas law (1895), an instrument describing the Alamositas Irrigating Ditch was filed with the county clerk of Oldham County in March, 1911; this document contained a statement of the company's intention to appropriate water from the river, use it for irrigation "for the purpose of stock raising," and return the surplus to the river. Board Minute Book, VII, 286–91. Under the law, as a riparian proprietor, the company had to show beneficial use of the water and return unused portions to the stream.

24 Board Minute Book, VII, 477.

basis," since they were not prepared to make large expenditures for drilling operations. Negotiations were suspended, however, when the two parties could not agree on terms.[25]

In January, 1916, the company employed H. B. Goodrich, a geologist, to examine the Matador and Alamositas divisions "for oil or other minerals at a fee of $2,500 plus personal expenses," and Mackay indicated to Goodrich what the board expected by way of reports:

> You are to have a free hand to make your examination in your own way, but we should like to have from time to time general indications of the area you are dealing with and any conclusions, tentative or final, which you may form.
>
> It occurs to me that you should, in the first place, take in the country of which Roaring Springs is the centre, because in that country a fairly vigorous campaign of selling land is going on. If there are any oil indications which you think should be taken note of, we ought to suspend for a time selling land, or sell it only subject to the reservation of the minerals. About a year ago, our people tried to sell with this reservation, but nobody would buy, and as we had no evidence of there being any minerals, we did not consider it worthwhile to stop our land selling on the chance of oil hereafter being found. If the territory . . . is condemned from an oil point of view our people can go on as they are doing at present. If, on the other hand, you give us encouragement, we might have to take the risk of reducing our land sales by reserving the minerals. . . .
>
> Assuming the Roaring Springs district to be first disposed of, I think you would be better to make yourself fairly familiar with the rest of the Matador range and then make a tour of Alamositas. When this rough inspection of the two ranges has been made you could then settle down to your more careful survey work.
>
> I hope that your stay on the ranches may be pleasant and am sure we can rely upon your giving us a careful and considered judgment upon the question which is a rather important one to a company owning nearly 900,000 acres. I shall be glad to hear

[25] Mackay to Cohen, March 18, 1913.

from you at any time even when you have little of moment to say. I am desirous of being kept informed of the line of your activities.[26]

Goodrich completed his examination late in the spring and sent his report to the Matador board in August, whereupon Mackay immediately sent a copy to the managing director of the Shell Transport Company with a request that the Matador be advised, after an expert had examined the report, whether the document's contents would warrant Shell's making a proposal to the Matador. In January, 1917, the reply was received—"the Shell experts did not think the prospect of finding oil was sufficiently promising to warrant expenditures."[27] In the same month Thomas Carter, vice-president and general manager of the Dundee Petroleum Company of Tulsa, cabled Mackay that the Roxana Petroleum Corporation had concluded that the possibilities of locating oil on the Matador properties were too remote to justify exploration.

Despite the unfavorable nature of the Goodrich report and the lack of interest in drilling on the part of major oil companies, the Matador board persisted in its efforts to secure "a proper test" of its properties. The directors stated in 1918 that if oil existed underneath its ranges, it was not in the best interest of the company to sell its lands at the prices then being obtained, since those prices represented only the value for grazing and agricultural purposes. If a test had revealed the presence of oil, the shareholders would have benefited not only from royalties from production but from a retention of mineral rights in and better prices for lands sold.

Thanks to the interest in leasing and drilling stimulated by the discovery and development of the Ranger field, the company was able to arrange for its properties to be "prospected for petroleum and gas." In March, 1919, an agreement was reached whereby the Dundee Petroleum Company accepted appoint-

[26] Mackay to Goodrich, March 28, 1916.
[27] Board Minute Book, VIII, 241.

ment as the Matador agent "in matters relating to petroleum" and undertook "to procure suitable and responsible parties to sink a well or wells" on the Alamositas and Matador divisions.[28] On March 8, 1920, the shareholders were apprised of the company's position in relation to the oil developments in Texas:

The oil discoveries in the central portion of the state (a long way to the south-east of our property) have been one of the outstanding features of the industry in America. The evidence of the presence of oil from surface indications was meagre, and only a short time ago little belief was held in it except by one or two enterprising and resourceful men. Even two or three years ago the territory was regarded as so speculative that it was dubbed by the experienced operators as pure "wild-cat." Today probably every big oil group in the mid-continent is the holder of oil leases in the central Texas field, and it bids fair to become the leading source of oil production in the U.S. for a number of years. The wells are deep, mostly three to four thousand feet, and in a few cases a depth of 5,000 feet has been exceeded; they are therefore costly wells to drill and capital has to be employed on a lavish scale.

These discoveries have naturally led to much speculating in the leasing of land near to and remote from the central territory. Indeed, the gambling in quite valueless territory has produced so much loss and brought so much ruin upon so many innocent but credulous investors that the State, in association with Chambers of Commerce and other public bodies, has repeatedly issued public warnings. Appeals have also been made to holders of land to discourage, in the national interest, speculators operating in "wild-cat" territory.

Before these discoveries were made in central Texas, the Matador Board had considered the question of the possibility of oil being found on Company ground, and, as you recall, procured a geologist's report on the subject. This report, which did not go beyond the bare possibility of its presence, was submitted at the time to one or two of the big operators to whom we offered what we hoped might be an adequate inducement to put down

[28] Board Minute Book, VIII, 425–26.

one or two test wells. Nothing came of this proposal; even an offer to contribute part of the initial expense was declined because deep drilling was costly, and the prospect of success remote. Nothing further could be done at that time, and the subject was held in abeyance until last year when, with extending interest in the Texas discoveries, the Board determined to employ experienced agents in touch with oil operators and familiar with the technical procedures and pitfalls incident to the highly complex oil business. Our manager is, of course, without experience in such matters, and besides his cattle duties absorb all his time. What decided the Board to make a fresh determined effort to have the land tested for oil was the consideration that before we sell additional land we should know with more certainty that the land which we offer is without oil value. We tried to sell with a reservation of mineral rights, but farmers, at least in our district, refused to buy with this reservation.

In securing a qualified agent to take care of the Company's interest one of the essential requirements was to get an associate whose integrity would be unquestioned, so that in making recommendations and contracts the interests of the Matador would be the primary care. We believe we have secured this through the Dundee Petroleum Company, a corporation formed several years ago under the laws of the State of Delaware. Its operating centre is in Tulsa, Oklahoma, which State adjoins the State of Texas, and is the recognized oil centre of the mid-continent. The shares of the company are chiefly held in Scotland and London, three of the Matador directors are personally interested in the company as shareholders, and the oversight of its financial affairs is undertaken by my firm's [Mackay, Irons and Company] branch office in New York. All this counts for confidence because we have full opportunity to know every important move in the management.

As we have no assurance that the territory in which the Matador and Alamositas Ranches lie contains any oil, being distant from any proved oil field, the Board were naturally desirous to incur as little expense as possible and were at the same time determined that no developments should be allowed which would interfere with the cattle business. An arrangement has therefore been made that no expense beyond the legal costs of agreements entered into will be incurred by our agents except at their own charge, unless such expenditure, being for a special purpose, first receives the sanction of the Board. Two leases, each covering 20,000 acres, have been entered into and as they are made with experienced oil operators of strong financial standing we have every reason to hope that the tests which we have long waited for may in the course of the current year yield at least valuable information as to the strata underlying a large part of the Company's property.

I confess to being not very sanguine of results, but the unexpected often comes in oil discovery and sometimes against the prediction of the wisest geologists. What I regard as our most pressing duty is to determine without delay whether oil is present or not before we alienate more of the Company's land.[29]

The two leases referred to by Mackay were on the Alamositas Division. One test well was drilled to a depth of 3,125 feet in 1920 without an encouraging result and the lease was canceled; the second lease was also surrendered to the company after a test, completed in 1921, failed to show signs of oil. No one offered to drill on the Matador Division, and the company continued to dispose of its lands without mineral reservations during the early 1920's.

Even with high livestock prices, good land sales, and the ability to declare substantial dividends during the war years, the Matador company was confronted with serious problems—increased taxation and droughts—in the same period. The organization was fortunate in that Murdo Mackenzie, having fulfilled the obligations of his contract with Farquhar, returned to the United States in 1917, took up residence in Chicago, and accepted appointment to the board; his experience and counsel were of particular value in taxation matters.

[29] Report of Proceedings, Thirty-eighth Annual General Meeting of Shareholders, 5–6. At the time of the meeting, Mackay, the board chairman, was in America; his report to the directors was read to the shareholders. This was Mackay's first absence from a general meeting.

Director J. Nicoll Smith, presiding at the annual meeting of the shareholders on February 3, 1914, noted that the company's American tax payments for 1913 were some £2,300 higher than for the previous year and, calling attention to the new income tax which would have to be faced in 1914 "by all Americans with an income above a certain sum, and by all corporations whether foreign or domestic," predicted that tax charges "would more likely increase than diminish." The forecast was correct, for while American tax payments in 1914 were £8,029, a slight reduction from the 1913 charge, they soared to £38,910 in 1918. The latter sum included land taxes paid in Canada on the Saskatchewan lease, even though the land was owned by the government, and income and excess profits taxes paid to the United States.

In 1917 and 1918 the company experienced some difficulty with the United States government over interpretations of federal income tax and excess profits laws. When Treasury Department agents challenged the Matador tax returns for 1917 on the grounds that profits reported from the sale of lands were incorrect, the Scots contended that no taxation could apply to the proceeds from land sales until all the land was sold, an argument that was recognized under British law. A second point at issue was the Treasury Department's refusal to give the company the benefit of the £200,000 written off when capital reductions were made in 1893 (from £500,000 to £400,000) and in 1896 (from £400,000 to £300,000). In this instance it was up to the Matador to demonstrate that the £200,000 represented cash paid in when the company was founded.[30] Only after lengthy negotiations with the Washington authorities were Murdo Mackenzie and the company's lawyers able to secure adjustments in the Mata-

---

[30] Mackay to David Elder, September 25, 1918. Each reduction in capital had been accompanied by a corresponding reduction in the value of each share; from 1896 to 1942 the capital, fully subscribed, was £300,000 in fifty thousand shares of £6 each.

dor's tax liability; when a satisfactory settlement was reached in 1919, American tax charges were reduced by £16,840.[31]

Exactly three months after the Armistice was declared on the Western Front, fifteen Matador stockholders assembled at Dundee's Lamb's Hotel to hear Alexander Mackay's report on the company's affairs:

> For the past few years the Directors have been able year by year to present a progressive record of improvement in the Company's business. Market prices of cattle have steadily risen, while our sales of land have been upon a considerable scale and at prices which have enabled us to reduce greatly the capital investment in real estate. The year which has just closed has been not only a record one in respect of cattle values, but has far surpassed its predecessors. The supply of beef cattle in all the American markets was large, but large supplies did not check advancing rates. Cattle were eagerly sought by buyers with the result that cattle owners received a far better return for their offerings than in all previous years. . . .
>
> It is a nice question whether we have reached the top in this ascending scale of prices. The advance cannot continue indefinitely, and a conservative view would incline to a reaction, but cattle opinion, for what it is worth, continues to take a hopeful outlook and what can fairly be said is that for the present there is no sign of a set-back. With open ports and more abundant and cheaper shipping facilities the European demand for American beef must increase for some time. Large as is the productive power for American herds, it cannot be increased except by the slow process of nature, while the demand is urgent and not likely to diminish until the depleted herds in Europe have had time to grow.
>
> Our natural satisfaction in this very favourable report of the market position is somewhat chastened by the less satisfactory account which we give you of the conditions of the herds and pastures in Texas. We have not had to face for many years climate conditions in Texas so trying as those of the past season.

[31] Report of Proceedings, Thirty-eighth Annual General Meeting of Shareholders, 8.

For the third year in succession severe drought has afflicted a considerable area in the western region of Texas and occasioned heavy losses to cattlemen. In the first year [1916] we were entirely outside the damaged area; in the second year we were partially affected; while last year the bad effects were felt over the major part of the Matador range. . . .

The herd at Matador after a prolonged dry season was far from satisfactory. Our calf crop was reduced from 16,280 in 1917 to 14,702; the breeding cows were thin. . . . We looked forward to the winter with not a little trepidation, although we had taken the only protective course left us, namely to purchase heavy stocks of feeding stuffs. It was part of our policy to reduce the number of old cows by sending to market more than the 1,600 head included in our sales for the year, but unfortunately toward the end of the season our cowboys and staff had a visitation of the influenza, and only the most necessary operations could be carried on.

We have experienced the truth of the proverb that troubles do not come singly. Before Christmas winter set in with considerable severity in the Panhandle of Texas. Heavy snow fell and was accompanied by a low temperature which kept the snow in a packed condition for two or three weeks. . . .

Provided we can escape further severe weather in February and March our actual death rate, although above the average, may not be excessive. We have a large amount of feeding stuffs on hand, but the trouble is that when snow falls to great depth you can neither move the feed to the cattle nor the cattle to the feed.

Mackay's anticipation that cattle prices would decline following 1918 was fully realized, for in 1919 the average price of four-year-old steers dropped twenty-four dollars a head and in 1920, ten dollars a head; but these were moderate reductions compared to the decline in 1921, when prices for all classes fell to 50 per cent of their 1920 levels. The sudden drop took the heart out of cattlemen everywhere, shook the livestock industry to its foundations, and rendered bankrupt a large proportion of cattle owners in the United States. Although the credit balance in the

Profit and Loss Account for the year was only £6,993, the Matador company was in a strong financial position at the end of 1921. The last installment on the Romero purchase had been paid in 1920, and the Reserve Account showed a balance of £120,000; the transfer of £10,000 from the Reserve to the Profit and Loss Account permitted the payment of a 10 per cent dividend, an exceptional return in what had been a disastrous year for the industry.

In keeping with its conservative—which is to say prudent—postwar policy, the company gave up its lease in Saskatchewan in 1921, when, in Mackay's words, "the governments of the United States and Canada failed to agree upon a common policy for the import and export of livestock between the two countries" and the Matador found itself "ground between the upper and the nether millstones of this tariff policy."[32] Reflecting the revival of isolationism in the aftermath of World War I, Congress approved a protective tariff program in 1921 which imposed a 30 per cent ad valorem duty on cattle imports and established extremely high rates on agricultural products in general.[33] Accustomed since 1913 to shipping its cattle duty free into the United States, the company realized that the combination of low market prices and a high duty on re-entry would put an end to its operations in Saskatchewan. Also, there was the possibility that Canada, resentful of the United States tariff policy, would impose heavy duties on shipments into the Dominion.

In March, 1921, the government in Ottawa was notified of the company's desire to surrender the lease north of Swift Current, and in May over 2,000 young steers were crowded into and across the Saskatchewan River on a trail drive to the Belknap range; this herd crossed the boundary into Montana on June 8,

[32] Report of Proceedings, Fortieth Annual General Meeting of Shareholders, 5.

[33] Donald M. Marvin, "The Tariff Relationship of the United States and Canada," *Annals of the American Academy of Political and Social Science*, Vol. CXLI (1928), 229.

"before the bars fell."[34] Twelve hundred of the older steers were shipped alive from Swift Current to Liverpool, where they brought better prices than could have been obtained in America. Although the books of the Canadian Division were closed at the end of 1921, the improvements on the range and remnants of the herd, some 250 head, were not sold until the following year.

The withdrawal from Canada marked a turning point in the Matador company's career—the end of one era and the beginning of another, which would see range operations once again confined to the Texas divisions.

[34] Report of Proceedings, Fortieth Annual General Meeting of Shareholders, 5. Mackay's statement was based on MacBain's cable to the board on July 8, 1921: "Canadian cattle crossed international boundary duty free."

5

Back to Texas

SEVERAL MONTHS before the board reached its decision to relinquish the lease in Canada, John MacBain learned that the Newcastle Land and Live Stock Company was seeking to withdraw from its pastures on the Pine Ridge Indian Reservation in South Dakota because of financial difficulties. Realizing that the Matador's pattern of operations—the sending of thousands of steers to northern grasslands annually—could not be altered abruptly, MacBain and Murdo Mackenzie inspected the Newcastle lease during the first week of February, 1921, in company with H. F. Mitchell of Alamositas and Maurice Reilly, the newly appointed superintendent of the Montana Division. The manager's report to Mackay, written in Denver[1] on February 9, described the range:

> The Pine Ridge reservation is located in the southwestern corner of South Dakota and is said to be one of the largest reservations in the West. It is divided into several leaseholds to suit the demands of ranchers for grazing. About two-and-a-half years ago Kinney and McKeon [the Newcastle owners] secured a lease on this reservation covering approximately 330,000 acres at an average rental of sixteen cents per acre, for a period of five years.
>
> The topography of the range is such that there is not a great deal of flat land except the bench land along the streams and in the northwestern and northeastern portion of the lease. It is an ideal cattle range with an abundance of shelter for winter since

[1] MacBain had moved the manager's office to Denver in January, 1920.

the country abounds in depressions and grass covered knolls. At the time we made the inspection there was four to six inches of snow on the ground, and even then the grass could be seen through the snow. There are several streams of good water running through the range the principal of which are White River, Wounded Knee Creek, Porcupine Creek, American Horse Creek, and a part of White Clay Creek. In addition to these there are numerous small rivulets which contain springs and water holes. In parts of the range where no streams are available windmills and earth tanks are provided for furnishing stock water.

Mr. McKeon stated that under normal conditions ten thousand or more tons of hay could be cut on the leasehold. The southern half of the lease has more rough land than the northern half which would permit using the northern part for summer and fall grazing and the southern part for winter feed and shelter. The lease is divided into several pastures by cross fences so as to permit summer and winter grazing in separate pastures. There appears to be an abundance of grass, but personally I do not feel that the grass on the Pine Ridge is equal in nutriment to the grass on the Belknap, but I do feel it is fully as good as the Saskatchewan grass. The grass on the Pine Ridge is more of a wheat grass and very similar to the grass we had on the Cheyenne River reservation in the northern part of South Dakota.

The water supply appears to be adequate and the pasture is equally as well watered as the Alamositas. In addition to the streams and natural water supply there are twenty-two windmills and as many tanks.

McKeon carried on this lease 20,000 head of cattle and about 25,000 sheep during last year. All of the sheep have been removed from the reservation to his sheep ranch in Wyoming, but there are about 7,000 of his cattle still on the lease; these he expects to ship to market in the fall of 1921. If we allow 20 acres per head of cattle this would give us a total of 16,500 head based on 330,000 acres which would cost an average of $3.20 per head for grazing.

We understand that a bill has passed Congress for the alloting of the Fort Belknap reservation to the Indians and when this is done there is a possible chance of our leasehold there being curtailed to a very large extent, and with this in view it might be best for us to assume all of the McKeon lease of 330,000 acres if it can be secured.

As stated, the Kinney and McKeon lease covering about 330,-000 acres has about two and one-half years to run. However, on the first of this year they relinquished about 100,000 acres for the reason that they were not able to finance the proposition. They are anxious to sell out their interest on the Pine Ridge if the government will allow them to transfer the lease.

The method of leasing lands on the Pine Ridge reservation is different from that on the Belknap. On the Belknap we pay a semiannual rate per head to the Indian agent in charge of the reservation and he distributes to the Indians the portion of money alloted to them. On the Pine Ridge each Indian has an allotment of so many acres according to the size of his family and the lessor has to pay the lease money to the Indian personally. The lands held by McKeon comprise about five hundred Indian lessees, and the lease money has to be paid to them in half-yearly installments.

Since McKeon took up the Pine Ridge lease he has expended, according to his improvement account which we saw at his headquarters and a copy of which is enclosed, $65,116.95 which is the cost of 275 miles of fence, 22 windmills, 22 dams and 20 tanks. If we take over the lease he expects to be reimbursed for one half of this expenditure, say $32,558.00. In addition to this he expended for ranch house, barns, corrals, etc. at headquarters the sum of $12,574, but at the time we were there he was not prepared to say how much of a reduction he would be willing to take on these items. There will also be the question of our buying wagons, harness, machinery and hay on hand, and also horses. . . .

The facilities in the way of railroads adjacent to the Pine Ridge are good, with the Chicago and Northwestern on the south and west and the Milwaukee on the north, each within twenty miles of the lease. You will notice that the Pine Ridge is 500 miles nearer to Chicago than is Canada, which we think will save us a shrink of about 25 pounds per head in cattle from Pine Ridge going to market.

The rental of the Pine Ridge lands would be quite heavy,

namely $52,800 per annum, but we might be able to offset this to a certain extent by taking in some outside cattle to pasture at so much per head.[2]

When it became apparent that the Canadian lease could be canceled without difficulty, the board authorized MacBain to proceed with efforts to secure the Pine Ridge pastures. In May the government indicated that the Matador could take up the Newcastle lease, and in the following month shipments to the "new Dakota division" began. Taking advantage of low live-stock prices and the financial stringencies in which other cattle organizations found themselves, the company purchased four thousand steers and by the end of the year had stocked the Pine Ridge range with eight thousand Matador beeves. The superin-tendent's position was offered to J. R. Lair, who had served well and faithfully at the Canadian Division, but Lair decided to leave the company's service, and R. G. Reid, Lair's assistant, was placed in charge at Pine Ridge with headquarters at Porcupine, South Dakota.

The acquisition of the Dakota pasture was, in a sense, a hedge against the possible loss or reduction of the Belknap Division. With both leases scheduled to expire in 1923, and with the col-lapse which overtook business and trade in 1921 fresh in their minds, the directors followed a wait-and-see policy during 1922. It was well that they did so, for on June 12, John MacBain died unexpectedly, and Murdo Mackenzie, who was in Texas at the time, volunteered to take charge of the Denver office until other arrangements could be made.[3] On August 1 the board unani-mously approved Mackenzie's appointment as manager at a sal-ary of $10,000 a year and endorsed an arrangement whereby he would "forego his fee as Advising Director but retain his seat on the Board and be entitled to his fee as Ordinary Director."[4]

[2] MacBain to Mackay, Irons and Co., February 9, 1921.

[3] MacBain's death was attributed to heart failure; he died in Denver and was buried there.

[4] Board Minute Book, IX, 137.

Following this action Mackenzie gave up his apartment in Chicago and moved to Denver.

The year brought other disappointments, for fall sales showed only a slight upturn in prices—to the level of 1911—and the weights of all stock marketed were exceptionally low. The credit balance to American operations was £2,397—the smallest in over two decades—but Mackay's report to the shareholders early in 1923 relieved some of the gloom:

> It is needless to say that our business is conditioned by weather and markets, over which we have no control—we have to accept these as they come. . . . Happily, the cloud is lifting. On the other side of the Atlantic there has been within the past few months a phenomenal recovery in industrial conditions. Most of the big lines of business—iron and steel, copper and nonferrous metals, the textiles, cotton, wool, oil—are all very active and profitable. There is so much demand for labour that non-employment is no longer existent—indeed, there is an agitation to encourage more immigration, by removing the restrictions imposed during and after the war. One may say that all businesses are active and healthy, except those of the farmer and shipowner. The American farmer and cattle owner are doubtless dependent to some extent on foreign markets, and until these improve they cannot get all they are entitled to, but their big market is after all feeding their own people. With so much additional money being thrown into the wage fund of the country, the demand for good food, and more of it, is as certain as the rise of the sun. We may hope, therefore, without undue optimism, to witness healthier conditions in our own business and a gradual return to more prosperous times.[5]

The chairman's hope that an improvement in industrial conditions in the United States would be reflected in a renewed demand for meat at better prices was not fulfilled, for average prices for livestock were eight dollars lower in 1923 than in the previous year; in addition, there was noted a new development—

[5] Report of Proceedings, Forty-first Annual General Meeting of Shareholders, 4.

one which was to affect the company's whole scheme of operations. This was brought to the attention of the shareholders in
March, 1924:

> A change has come over the taste for meat in the U.S.A. For-
> merly, strong four-year-old steers were in prime demand. Now,
> younger meat is preferred, and that change may make a great
> difference to this Company, enabling us to get rid of our . . .
> northern leased ranges . . . and to sell our two-year olds at our
> Texas ranches with the resulting saving of the entire northern
> charges.[6]

Mackay believed that the change in taste for meat on the part
of the American consumer was due to the reduced supply of
beef during the war and to the business recession of the early
1920's, both of which forced people to buy smaller cuts. With
the hope that the American preference for young meat was temporary and in expectation that a revised European economy
would provide once again a market for its four- and five-year-old
steers, the company renewed its leases on the Belknap and Pine
Ridge reservations in 1923. However, tariff walls and unfavorable exchange rates closed off foreign markets; and in 1925, when
it became apparent that baby beef had become a fixture in the
American diet, Murdo Mackenzie informed the shareholders
that the demand for young steers was causing a change in the
cattle business in the West. He made this statement again in
1927 and concluded, "We have to submit to what the people
want, and unless we change to what consumers want, we are
out of the market."[7]

In addition to the reduced demand for mature steers, other
factors were involved in the Matador's decision to effect a gradual withdrawal from the northern ranges. In 1923, when the
Belknap lease was renewed for one year, it was contemplated

[6] Report of Proceedings, Forty-second Annual General Meeting of Shareholders, 4.

[7] Report of Proceedings, Forty-fifth Annual General Meeting of Shareholders,
7.

that the Montana pastures could be cleared of cattle in the fall of 1924 and that the Pine Ridge Reservation could accommodate the three- and four-year-olds until the Dakota lease expired in 1926. This plan was abandoned, however, when the fall sales in 1924 confirmed a suspicion expressed by MacBain in his inspection report in 1921 that the grass on the Pine Ridge was not as nutritious as that on the Belknap. In 1923, when the average weight of the Dakota steers was found to be 150 pounds below that of the Montana cattle, the loss was blamed on heavy rains, intense heat, and swarms of flies which kept the Pine Ridge herds restless and in constant movement; but when the same unsatisfactory weights were reported in the two following years, during which grazing conditions were ideal, Mackay decided that "there must be something lacking in the soil causing the grass, however attractive in appearance, not to be of a nutritious character."[8] The board, realizing that the loss of from 150 to 200 pounds per animal was too great a price to pay for the shipping advantages related to the Pine Ridge Division—its nearness to Texas and to Chicago—negotiated for and secured a two-year renewal of the Belknap lease in December, 1924, and once again shipped its two-year-olds from Alamositas to Montana.

With the expiration of the Pine Ridge contract in April, 1926, the company held its final roundup and tally on the Dakota Division; here another problem was revealed, for after deducting the normal winter losses, the herd strength was found to be some seven hundred head below the expected figure. When the board inquired about the reason for such a shortage in the gather of its cattle, Mackenzie replied that he was convinced that Indians had been stealing and eating Matador beeves for several years. His suspicions seemed well founded, for several Indians had been arrested for stealing cattle on the Pine Ridge range. This trouble also developed on the Belknap reservation, and the manager, feeling that the agent there was "siding with the Indians," complained to the Commissioner of Indian Affairs in Washing-

[8] Mackay to Board of Directors, October 13, 1924.

ton so vigorously that the federal government appointed a detective to guard the company's interests in Montana. This officer, along with a detective employed by Mackenzie, succeeded in catching nine of the thieves, a result which brought some satisfaction to the manager but not an end to his difficulties:

> On the 29th of May [1926] we sent a check for ten thousand dollars to Superintendent [Marshall] Fort Belknap Indian Reservation, being payment in full due June 1 for grazing eight thousand cattle, this being the number on the range and the minimum required by the lease. This check was returned twice with the request that we send twelve thousand, five hundred dollars to cover the minimum demanded by Marshall. With this return Marshall sends a threat that unless this demand is complied with the Indians will take their own way in getting even with us and that he won't be responsible.[9]

Under the terms of the lease the amount sent by the company was correct, since the contract called for a semiannual payment at the rate of $2.50 per head per year on a minimum of eight thousand head. To Mackenzie, the agent's refusal to accept the check was another indication of Marshall's lack of co-operation with the company and a form of harassment designed to force the Matador to cancel its lease. The fact that the Office of Indian Affairs later accepted the payment in the amount originally submitted did little to reduce the manager's anger, and he reported to the commissioner, Charles H. Burke, that "in all our transactions with the Indian Department for the past twenty-five years we never have disputed with the agents of the different reservations as we have with Mr. Marshall." On December 17, 1926, Mackenzie summarized the situation in a letter to Burke:

> Referring to the correspondence which passed between us regarding the cattle killed by the Indians on the Pine Ridge reservation which this company has held under lease from you: we now have closed up our holdings there and find that after writing

[9] Mackenzie to Commissioner of Indian Affairs, Washington, D. C., June 18, 1926.

off a ten per cent loss each year on the cattle we sent to the reservation we are short 1,163 head for the six years and I can only attribute this to the killing of the cattle by the Indians. I am satisfied that the ten per cent allowed by us each year would more than cover any loss we might have from normal causes and that a good many of the ten per cent could be added to the 1,163 additional shortage. In other words, the Indians have killed more than 200 cattle each year since we have been on the reservation and at sixty dollars per head our loss from this cause amounts to $72,000. I am convinced that as things have been going on the Belknap reservation our loss per annum will be more than what we sustained on the Pine Ridge reservation, and I write you this letter to substantiate the complaint that I made to you in my correspondence last summer regarding the Indians being allowed to slaughter our cattle on the [Belknap] reservation.

While the Indian troubles were irritating and costly, they did not constitute the fundamental cause for the company's decision to withdraw from the northern divisions: this was dictated by market conditions and was forecast by Mackay early in 1926:

Perhaps the most significant thing in the Report [for 1925] now submitted is the sale of 1,372 head of young cattle. When Mr. Murdo Mackenzie was present at the last meeting of the shareholders, he made a very interesting speech in which he explained why changes in our methods of selling cattle had become necessary. . . . Formerly we sold the bulk of our four- and five-year-old steers in trainloads of 500 or 600 head to the big packing houses. Last year we failed to sell one trainload to a single buyer. In the future we expect to sell more of our cattle of younger ages to feeders who will finish them off for the market. It may interest you to know that the 1,372 head sold last year have gone into a number of distant states like Iowa, Nebraska, Illinois and Kentucky. We are finding today ready buyers of our young stock because of Mr. Mackenzie's successes in the show ring in years gone by. The feeders are already educated by the results shown in our exhibits, so that feeding steers with a Matador brand does not need advertising.

We have still in Dakota some 5,000 head of old steers and

spayed heifers, and these should all be sold this year when we surrender to the government the lease of the pasture. Our only pasture in the North will thereafter be the government lease in the Fort Belknap Indian Reservation, Montana, together with a few thousand acres of meadow and irrigated hay lands which we purchased many years ago. The period of our stay in Montana will be regulated by the increase in our sales of young cattle from Texas. Probably for a year or two we may continue to send North a number of young steers, thus making the change in our sale methods a gradual one, but our objective is, if possible, to do away with ranching in the North.[10]

Early in 1927 the company notified the government that when the Belknap lease expired in November, no effort would be made to renew the contract. This did not mean that the Matador would vacate Montana completely, for additions to the property purchased in 1916 had given the company title to fourteen thousand acres east of the reservation near Malta; this tract was stocked with sheep in 1926 to obtain maximum use of the grass and to provide an income off the land until the acreage could be sold.

The formal announcement of the Matador's new policy—one it would follow henceforth—was made by Mackay in 1928:

Our main purpose until now has been to raise large crops of calves in Texas and to mature the steers at about four years old on the native grasses of the north. . . . Some four years ago we began to realise that a change in our methods had to be faced. The costs of the northern business were increasing, with a correspondingly less margin of profit, but a more important factor was a growing change in the public taste for what is called baby beef. Big heavy steers were sold at some disadvantage as soon as the consumer set up a demand for smaller joints and early matured beef. The question which we had to decide was whether this change was a passing whim, possibly to be reversed, or a demand which had come to stay. We temporised for a year or two, watching the markets closely, selling a portion of our young

[10] Report of Proceedings, Forty-fourth Annual General Meeting of Shareholders, 4.

stock, but keeping hold of a substantial part of the heavy steer business which has been our anchor sheet for so long a time. A year ago we made up our minds to take the final step, to withdraw from the north and to concentrate all our energies upon the breeding business in Texas and the sale of young cattle. Fortunately for us, this decision was taken in a year when an acute shortage showed itself in all classes of cattle, young and old, in the United States. It was good for us, because we not only managed to sell our heavy cattle from Montana at phenomenal prices, but the younger sales were equally satisfactory.[11]

Although the last group of Montana steers was not sold until 1930, the Matador's cattle operations on the reservation came to an end early in 1928, and J. D. Reid, who had replaced Maurice Reilly as superintendent of the Belknap Division in 1923, took charge of the sheep ranch at Malta.

With its withdrawal from Montana, the company was confronted with the necessity of securing additional ranges in Texas to hold the young cattle intended for sale to feeders; the alternative, a reduction of its cows to effect a smaller calf crop, was considered too drastic, so Mackenzie undertook to lease a pasture of suitable size. In April, 1928, he located a block of land adjacent to Alamositas but failed to obtain a lease, since it was already under rent. The owners, however, offered to sell, and in May and June two tracts lying in Hartley County and separated from Alamositas only by a fence were purchased for eight dollars an acre. On May 18, Francis C. Farwell, Charles F. Harding, and Frederick E. French, representing the Capitol Freehold Land and Investment Company, Limited, deeded 29,822 acres to the Matador, and on June 6 an additional block of 17,754 acres was transferred. Since the Scots "were in the happy position of having a fairly well filled cashbox," they paid for the land without having to issue new capital or assume additional debt obligations.[12]

[11] Report of Proceedings, Forty-sixth Annual General Meeting of Shareholders, 3–4.

174

The contents of Table 5 reflect, in a measure, the ups and downs of the cattle industry during the 1920's, a decade which brought ruin to many livestock owners. The balances in the "Profit" column are indicative of the market prices which prevailed during the years listed, and the dividends declared reveal the state of the company's finances. Particular attention is called to the fact that the payments to shareholders in 1921, 1922, and 1923 were made possible only through the transfer, each year, of £10,000 from the reserve account to the credit balances shown for those years.

TABLE 5*

Year	Profit	Dividend
1921	£ 6,993	10%
1922	2,397	5
1923	530	5
1924	18,704	5
1925	38,700	7½
1926	65,400	10
1927	107,557	10 plus 5% bonus
1928	113,503	10 plus 7½ "
1929	79,135	10 plus 7½ "
1930	70,231	10

* From the annual reports for the years listed.

It has been pointed out that when John MacBain died in 1922, the company was fortunate in that Murdo Mackenzie was able to assume, on a temporary basis, supervision of the Denver office. The board realized that, in view of the depressed economic conditions in America, MacBain's successor should be a person of experience and stability, one who would keep a close watch on the market situation and who, above all, could work in harmony with the division superintendents. When Mackay suggested that Dave Somerville was a good man for the post, Mackenzie agreed

12 Report of Proceedings, Forty-seventh Annual General Meeting of Shareholders, 5.

but disclosed that Somerville had three more years to serve on a five-year contract with the Boston Land, Cattle and Packing Company at a salary of $15,000 a year, a sum which the Matador could not pay "even for a manager."[13] In a personal letter to the board chairman, Mackenzie made a suggestion:

> After giving deep consideration to the subject I have decided to suggest to you that for the time being I take over the management of the Company myself. I do not believe a new man could make the needed corrections without offending our present superintendents and this must be done, for their places would be hard to fill. After a new system is inaugurated the manager we engage could put it on and work in harmony with the superintendents . . . and anything I might suggest in the way of working for the best interests of the Company would be received with good feeling. I also feel that the market this fall must be watched and I know of no one else who can do it.
>
> I know you will understand that I am not writing in a spirit of egotism, but I have studied conditions and realize that it will take an experienced man to keep us out of deeper water. We must be on the alert for a good, capable permanent manager but the man we want will not be found at once and I would feel better satisfied myself in taking charge of the Company until he has been found and trained in our methods.[14]

When the directors approved the appointment of Mackenzie on August 1, they resolved "to ask [him] to keep in view the desirability of selecting a suitable man who might succeed him in the management." In keeping with this resolution, the manager proposed that his son, John Mackenzie, be appointed as his assistant, and in January, 1923, the board approved the recommendation.[15]

One of the "needed corrections" to which Mackenzie referred

[13] Mackenzie, W. Cameron Forbes, and Charles W. Perkins were joint owners of the Boston Land, Cattle, and Packing Company.

[14] Mackenzie to Mackay, July 10, 1922.

[15] John Mackenzie had been in Brazil since 1912. In 1927 the title "Assistant Manager" came into use in connection with his position in the company.

in his letter of July 10, 1922, had to do with paring expenses—a problem which arose with each period of falling prices and declining profits. When wages, supplies, and maintenance costs, which had understandably increased from 1914 through 1918, remained at wartime levels during the recession of 1919–21, the board sent word to MacBain early in 1922 to "do away with unnecessary spending." Upon finding these instructions in the Denver office, Mackenzie ordered Mitchell and Jackson to "cut expenses to the bone" and to reduce wages from fifty dollars a month to forty dollars for those men already on the payroll and to hire new hands at a still lower rate. In examining the records of supplies purchased, the manager found that "luxuries instead of necessities" were being purchased—in one case 100 pounds of seeded raisins had been bought by one of the camp men and in another instance, 125 pounds. Although the men explained that the raisins were being used for pies, Mackenzie had his "own opinion as to the use they were put to and . . . inquiries confirmed . . . that the raisins were used for more than pies and that beverages were used other than water."[16] To prevent the employees from purchasing "such items as extracts, coconut, and canned goods," he established a system whereby all supplies on the Matador Division were drawn from a central commissary located at the Ballard Springs headquarters. As a result of this action the stores account was considerably reduced.

Early in 1923, J. M. Jackson announced his resignation as superintendent of the Matador Division.[17] This move came as a surprise to the board:

> We very greatly regret Jackson's withdrawal. He has been for a long time in our service and he has given us in the past excellent service. He is a man for whom all the members of the Board entertained a very high respect.[18]

[16] Mackenzie to Mackay, May 18, 1923.
[17] Mackenzie to the Board, April 21, 1923.
[18] Mackay to Mackenzie, May 4, 1923.

In April, John Mackenzie was sent to supervise the division's activities until a new superintendent could be selected, and in May, Jackson purchased the hotel in Roaring Springs and moved there with his family.[19]

To fill the vacancy, Murdo Mackenzie first suggested the appointment of James Burr, the former superintendent at the Cheyenne River Reservation lease; the prospect of hiring Burr pleased the board in Dundee:

> Your proposals with regard to filling Jackson's position as superintendent are entirely satisfactory to us. Burr's old association with the Matador coupled with his subsequent experience in Brazil should fit him in a special degree for our work, especially as he is a Scot who understands the cattle business both from the American point of view and from the Scotch investors' point of view. It may be that some Americans regard this Company as being the private property of a few individuals instead of the investment of a great many people. The question of economy is more easily understood by a man who appreciates the difference.[20]

The position was offered to Burr, but he was not free to leave Brazil, and Maurice Reilly was moved from the Montana Division at the Fort Belknap Reservation to the headquarters in Motley County; this shift provided occasion for the appointment of J. D. Reid to the superintendent's post in Montana.

Among the manifestations of the isolationist spirit which characterized American social and political life during the early 1920's was a revival of the movement to break up the large landholdings of aliens. Riding the wave of antiforeign sentiment which swept over the country following World War I, politicians shaped their programs to appeal to the voters' emotions and to capitalize on current public feelings. Judge I. H. Burney of Fort Worth, a lawyer retained by the company, was aware of the

[19] Mackenzie to Mackay, May 18, 1923.
[20] Mackay to Mackenzie, May 4, 1923.

course which might be followed by successful politicians in Texas in 1920:

> It looks to me like Pat Neff will be the next governor and he is a radical. The principal plank in his platform is for a "graduated land tax." If he is elected such a [tax] law may be passed, if not in his administration then I believe it will almost certainly come later. Such a law fixing a normal rate on the first thousand acres and a radically abnormal rate as the acreage increases might make the ownership of above twenty, fifty, or a hundred thousand acres prohibitory, at least for an alien corporation, and such a law would likely be held valid.[21]

While there is little doubt that heavy taxation would effectively serve to break up any large landholding, Burney's apprehensions regarding his client's position were somewhat relieved after he heard Neff speak. The candidate "advocated a law putting a graduated tax on very large holdings of unimproved, uncultivated, agricultural land not used for pasturage or any other purpose in the farming section of the state, but bought or held by speculators for profit only," hence was not meant to apply to the Matador or similar companies. The lawyer did insist that the company use care in its land dealings and reminded MacBain in the fall of 1920 that the Matador could "only conduct the business of raising, buying and selling cattle" and that it had no authority, under Texas statutes, to acquire, own, or hold land for any purpose except to furnish grazing for its cattle or to collect a debt.[22]

In attempting to reassure Burney, Mackay acknowledged that in the process of consolidation some sections of the Matador Division had been isolated, but he contended that it had always been the board's policy to hold no land which was not strictly used for the company's business. In a letter to MacBain, the chairman suggested a course of action:

21 Burney to MacBain, August 4, 1920.
22 Burney to MacBain, October 23, 1920.

In regard to Mr. Burney's letters on the danger to the Company of contravening the spirit of the Texas law which prohibits the retention of any land by a cattle company if the land is not required for stock purposes, I think we have a perfectly clear conscience on this matter. . . . I think we should, at the most convenient early time, make a sale of those scattered sections in Dickens County and on the plains which have disturbed Mr. Burney's mind. He is quite right to press his view upon us but I do not think we are bound to give effect to it immediately if such a step means loss to the Company.[23]

Although Mackay observed that "it is only too evident that there is a [political] party in Texas which advocates the breaking up of large aggregations of land under one control," he felt that no one would advocate "compulsory breaking up" without giving "long notice, say fifteen years," so that the owners could realize a return from their investment.

Whatever security the company might have felt regarding its property was shaken in 1921, when the Texas legislature amended the state's land laws to require corporations to file a complete list of their lands with the county clerks of the counties in which those lands were located. S. H. Cowan, who had replaced Burney when the latter retired, held to the opinion that the new law applied only in the case of lands acquired after 1921 and that the Matador did not have to prepare and file a list of its total holdings, but only those purchased after the amendment became effective. Cowan was wrong, however, and after the United States Supreme Court handed down a decision which served to clarify the Texas law in 1923, the company proceeded to comply with the requirement and, in addition, introduced a land sales program in 1924 to sell acreage not needed in its business.

J. D. Harkey, selected by the manager to locate prospective farmers and to promote land sales, had immediate success; the country was recovering from the depression of the early twen-

[23] Mackay to MacBain, January 4, 1921.

ties, and the demand for land was keeping pace with the nation's industrial revival. During the last two months of 1924, over 4,600 acres were sold at prices which brought an average net return of twenty-five dollars an acre, and in 1925, over 2,200 were sold at a similar price. Sales were made on the basis of a 20 per cent down payment with the balance spread over ten years at 8 per cent interest. In 1926, an average price of $12.74 per acre was received for 5,435 acres, but the overproduction of cotton and the subsequent decline in prices lowered the demand for land, and sales dropped during the early part of 1927.

Until 1924 the Matador board had never considered disposing of the company's lands in large blocks through single transactions, but in that year Alexander Mackay, in America, wrote to the Dundee directors that during his annual visit to the ranches he had had a long conversation with Alexander Smith of Peabody, Houghteling and Company and had told Smith that "if the proper financial group were brought together, [the Matador Board] would be willing to sell one hundred thousand acres at an agreed price, either all in cash, or in cash plus notes endorsed by people whose financial responsibility is unquestioned."[24] On December 1, 1925, the three directors in Dundee—James C. Johnston, George Bonar, and W. D. Macdougall—met to discuss the chairman's letter and the matter of land sales in general, and agreed to authorize Mackay to "use every endeavor in getting in touch with suitable parties who could assist in the sale of the Company's lands."

Following his visit to the divisions in November, Mackay went to his winter home at Lake Alfred, Florida, and from there in February, 1926, wrote to Benjamin Guinness of New York, a Matador stockholder, to whom he had turned in an effort to locate "suitable parties" who might be interested in purchasing all or a portion of the company's lands:

I brought Mackenzie here for two or three days to discuss the

24 Mackay to Mackay, Irons and Co., October 28, 1925.

program for the current year and more especially the land situation.

The point to keep before us is that the values of land in Texas have now risen so high that it will not pay anyone to run these properties as cattle ranches. . . . Between interest and taxes, a buyer could not realize an adequate profit. On the largest part of our land we are assessed for county and state taxes on a valuation of $9.00 per acre. We can carry on and show a profit for two reasons, (1) that the cost to the Company of the land is now reduced to less than $2.00 per acre, and (2) we are not required to return, for federal income tax, the difference between this cost and $13.00 per acre which was the agreed on valuation in March, 1913, when the income tax was first established. You will see, therefore, that we should concentrate upon a scheme of land settlement which, I am sure, if properly carried through would yield to the buyers of the property a handsome profit. . . .

I have no objection to your discussing this matter with your friends and shall heartily join in any scheme, the effect of which would be to return to the shareholders of the Matador the proper profit which they have earned after a lapse of 44 years.[25]

Mackay also wrote to Clarence Dillon of the investment house of Dillon, Reed and Company in New York and asked him to find prospective buyers of Matador lands.

In March, 1926, Murdo Mackenzie received instructions from the New York office of Mackay, Irons and Company to meet in St. Louis with a group of financiers whom Guinness had located and who were prepared "to discuss the particulars regarding the sale of all the Matador ranch." The "interested parties" were Bainbridge Colby, former secretary of state in Woodrow Wilson's cabinet, Albert S. Burleson, postmaster general during the Wilson administration, and Malcolm Hiram Reed of Austin, Texas.

In the series of cablegrams, letters, and conferences which followed, it became apparent that Mackenzie was not fully informed of the Dundee directors' attitude toward the sale of the

[25] Mackay to Guinness, February 15, 1926.

property and that he, personally, was opposed to such action. Prior to the St. Louis meeting he asked Mackay to indicate "the least price per acre the company would accept" and declared that "the purchasers must give time to dispose of the herd unless they purchase the same along with the land." The chairman replied that it was "unnecessary to go below twelve dollars an acre until . . . you have had your meeting and formed an impression of the group" and that the sale of land was conditioned upon the Matador's having the time necessary to dispose of the cattle to the best advantage of the shareholders.

Mackenzie's report to Mackay indicated that some misunderstandings had developed:

> I arrived in St. Louis . . . as per arrangement [and] went to the Jefferson Hotel where Mr. Colby was stopping and had quite a talk with him before the other members of the party arrived. . . . I was under the impression that any offer they had to make would be on a cash basis at not less than $12.00 per acre. During the discussion at the meeting it developed that they had no intention of purchasing on a cash basis or of making any offer in which a total cash payment would be made for the land. When I asked them to submit their proposition it was in accordance with the following cable which I sent you on April 5, "Met Colby and two Texas men St. Louis. These men declined purchase Matador for cash but suggested classifying land in three classes and stated price for each class. We to remove cattle promptly and give them five years to dispose property, selling sections for which they might find purchasers and reserving right at any stated period if found they could not dispose of more land at profit to turn balance unsold back to Company. Effect would be whenever they found good profit could not be made and all best lands sold the Company would be left with poorest land mixed in with settlers and no cattle to graze. The Company meantime would pay all the taxes on unsold land. No cash put up except as lands sold."
>
> I am sure the proposition set forth in the cable would not be acceptable to you in any way for it certainly is not to me. . . . In

addition to the terms given in my cable they reserve the right to dispose of the land in any size plot, and this might mean that they could sell the land in 40-acre lots. Then they require of us that we supply abstracts to the purchasers of any tract, which would mean that we might be called upon to supply eight or ten or possibly more abstracts to the section. This is entirely out of the question.

I suggested to the meeting that I would write you fully in regard to their proposition and further stated that I would ask you, and another member of the Board if you desire, to come to New York as soon as convenient for you—at least earlier than you usually come over in the fall—and discuss the matter with them. I do not feel that we could possibly come to any agreement with these gentlemen unless they are prepared to make us a much more reasonable proposition.[26]

The discovery that the "Colby group" was not prepared to make a purchase but wanted to act as agents in selling for the company did not terminate the negotiations but did place them on a different basis. The Dundee directors, in a special meeting, recognizing that it would be difficult, if not impossible, to find a single purchaser for all the land because of the size of the Matador holdings and the large sum required to finance such a transaction, decided that the best plan would be to set aside, one at a time, 100,000-acre tracts and allow developers such as Colby's associates to handle the sales. The company would thus have time to dispose of its cattle as its range diminished.

Guinness, who was acting as intermediary between the company and Colby, was notified that the directors were interested in disposing of the Matador Division lands only and that the Alamositas property was not to be considered in any proposal.[27]

Following the board's decision to keep the door open to negotiations, Mackenzie made investigations concerning the financial

[26] Mackenzie to Mackay, April 6, 1926.

[27] Mackay to Guinness, April 29, 1926. The discovery of oil and gas along the Canadian River seventy miles east of the Alamositas Division accounted for the decision to confine land sales to the Matador Division.

standings of the Colby group and found that both Burleson and Colby had good reputations and that "Mr. Reed . . . was the party who would take hold of the property." Letters from various banks placed Reed's worth at "about $1,500,000" and vouched for his character and ability. The manager's appraisal of the group was sent to Mackay in May:

> I do not think Mr. Burleson is to have anything to do with [the proposal], and he merely came [to St. Louis] to help Mr. Reed in the negotiations. I think, however, that Mr. Reed did not require this as he is fully capable of looking after his own interests. I was very much impressed with what I saw of Reed. He seems a very shrewd business man, and so far as I could see, perfectly capable of carrying out anything he would undertake. I have no doubt Mr. Colby is equally reliable and capable in his own line, but I do not think he knows anything about a business of this kind, although in our conversation he seemed very conservative in any suggestion he had to make.[28]

Mackenzie was also aware that the Matador and its personnel were being analyzed by the prospective buyers:

> They inquired if I was interested in the Company and I told them I was but I did not tell them to what extent, and when they asked me if I was willing to sell I unhesitatingly replied that I was working for the Matador Company and that my first consideration was its best interests. . . . I think the motive for asking all these questions was, first, to find out whether I would represent matters properly to you, and second, if I had any selfish motive, either in recommending the sale or not recommending the sale.

When arrangements were made by Guinness for Colby and his associates to inspect the Matador Division in May, Reed seized the opportunity to invite Mackenzie to visit the properties which the Yellow House Land Company had developed near Littlefield, Texas; the Austin entrepreneur felt that Mackenzie

[28] Mackenzie to Mackay, May 14, 1926.

needed to be convinced that a development program involving the sale of land to settlers could be carried out successfully. No demonstration was needed, however, and Mackenzie did not accept the invitation, since he had other evidence of Reed's ability to colonize agricultural lands.[29]

The role which Guinness was playing in the negotiations was something of a puzzle to the manager. Colby had frequently insisted that Guinness, as a large stockholder in the company, would influence the board's decision on whatever proposal was ultimately made, but when Mackenzie learned from Mackay that Guinness and his close friends held only 2,092 shares among them, he concluded that Guinness was interested only in earning a commission from the sale and had no care for the company's welfare.

By the end of June, Mackenzie was disgusted with the whole matter. Colby had proposed that an American company be formed to purchase the shares of the Matador, and this plan had been rejected by the board. Next he developed a scheme to purchase the company's property for cash but dropped the idea promptly when he was told that the land and cattle were worth approximately $10,450,000. After he had escorted the Colby group on a second trip to the ranches, Mackenzie reported to

[29] "Mr. M. H. Reed is a valued customer of this institution. We understand that the Yellow House Land Company is a corporation formed by Mr. Reed and two of his associates, they having purchased from the [George W.] Littlefield Estate approximately 250,000 acres of land in Lamb and Hockley counties, Texas, which they have subdivided and sold off in tracts of approximately 177 acres each. From what we hear we believe that the land company has disposed of nearly all of its holdings to actual settlers. The Littlefield estate has retained vendor's lien for the unpaid purchase price due them and the Yellow House Land Company, in re-selling, has had the purchasers assume the first lien and give them second lien notes for their equity. They appear to have been very successful, having been fortunate in that the past two crop seasons have been most favorable to them. We have no statement before us of the Yellow House Land Company, but we consider its affairs in very capable hands, and they should be responsible." R. C. Roberdeau, president, American National Bank, Austin, to J. C. Houston, vice-president, First National Bank, Denver, May 18, 1926.

the board that the visitors had even resorted to flattery in their attempts to secure his support of their proposals:

> They approached me on every angle that you could imagine. One suggestion was that if they bought the cattle along with the land that they would require somebody to help them run the cattle and dispose of them as the pasture was reduced in acreage by sale, and suggested that John or myself or both of us would help them in this matter. I replied that they should forget all about this for the present, as I had only one object in view and that was to see that the Company was served to the best of my ability.
>
> At one stage of the game they told me that I looked twenty years younger for my age than anybody of their acquaintance and then when they found out that I would not be a party to helping them after the sale, they inquired what was to become of the Company if I were to drop off in a year or so. I replied that they need not worry about that, that in all my experience of life, the conclusion I had arrived at was that the dropping off of any one man did not stop the wheels of business.[30]

Failing to find satisfaction in his dealings with Mackenzie, Reed suggested that he should go to Scotland to lay his proposals before the board. Mackenzie replied that such a trip would be a waste of time, and in this the Dundee directors concurred, though they left the way open to further bargaining:

> We should prefer that these gentlemen make an advance upon their terms before paying a visit to this side, otherwise their journey will be fruitless. At the same time, we are not prepared to discourage their coming if they are very keen about it, because very often in a large negotiation of this sort difficulties can be cleared out of the way in the course of conversation, and parties get closer together.[31]

In August the board reviewed the situation and concluded that negotiations should be suspended until Mackay made his

---

[30] Mackenzie to Mackay, Irons and Co., June 28, 1926.
[31] Mackay to Mackenzie, July 6, 1926.

annual visit to the ranches. At the time this decision was made, it was contemplated that James C. Johnston, a director, would accompany the chairman to America so that a quorum of the board would be present in the United States if developments warranted board action. However, since proposals acceptable to the company were not forthcoming, the Colby negotiations were considered closed by the end of the year, and Mackay's report to the shareholders early in 1927 covered the matter tersely: "We have had inquiries from certain groups to see whether all our lands could be bought, but the terms suggested were not of a nature to lead the Board to make a recommendation to you; to any responsible inquirer we have said that everything we possess is open for sale at the proper price, but that a great property like yours, built up by nearly half a century of effort, is not going to be scrapped."[32]

The coolness toward land-sale proposals which was displayed by the Dundee board during the latter half of 1926 was due primarily to the oil boom which developed in the northern Panhandle during that year and which stimulated speculation in land and leases throughout the area. Mackay, on a visit to Amarillo in November, 1925, was apprised of the increased activity in drilling which was then taking place, but not until the prolific Borger field was opened early in the following year did the Panhandle oil and gas region take on the proportions of a boom. Within days after the Dixon Creek Oil and Refining Company brought in its No. 1 Smith on January 11, the advance guard of the oil companies—geologists and lease agents—appeared at Alamositas and sought permission to "prospect for oil." Mackenzie, who had little knowledge of oil leases, turned down all applications and refused to allow geologists to enter the ranch; he had been notified that Mackay was negotiating with Shell Oil representatives in London and that the reply to all inquires made at Alamositas should be that the company was in no position to

[32] Report of Proceedings, Forty-fifth Annual General Meeting of Shareholders, 5.

make proposals. But when the chairman's discussions with the Shell company extended into the summer, Mackenzie became impatient and complained that "we are practically bored to death by parties seeking leases on the Company property not only at Alamositas but on the Matador Division, and if the Shell Company were to commence operations, either geological or drilling, it would put a stop to all inquiries about leases."[33]

The delay in concluding an agreement with the Shell company was explained by the secretary's office early in August:

> Since our last letter to you there has been a good deal of discussion with the Shell group. . . . It appears that the geological formations at Alamositas are different from what were assumed when our negotiations with that company were entered upon. The experts declare that the strata do not lend themselves to positive results when the instruments used for the geophysical tests are applied. They say that the formations at Matador would be more suitable but that, if applied in Oldham County, the results would almost certainly be negative. . . .
>
> The Shell Company have now agreed to take 100,000 acres on the east side of the pasture [Alamositas] and pay us the bonus, twenty-five cents per acre, and one year's rental for the privilege of testing 100,000 acres. . . .
>
> In view of the foregoing the Board think it would be a good thing for us to make arrangements with other large groups to take up acreage out of the remaining 250,000 acres. As you have many applications coming before you, you might sift out those which you think worthy of consideration and send us particulars.[34]

In October the Matador entered into a contract with a Shell subsidiary, the Roxana Petroleum Corporation; the terms were those agreed upon in the summer with what the Dundee office called "the Shell group" and were summarized in the chairman's annual report to the company:

[33] Mackenzie to Mackay, Irons and Co., July 20, 1926.
[34] Mackay, Irons and Co. to Mackenzie, August 3, 1926.

There is one entirely new item of income . . . upon which you may expect me to say something. I mean the sum of £6,416 which we received for granting to one of the large oil companies the right to test for oil upon 100,000 acres of land in the Alamositas Ranch. I should not wish you to get the notion that this payment proves the presence of oil on the Company's property. I wish it did. All it implies is that a speculative possibility is there. A wide area in the Panhandle of Texas is being explored for oil and in its centre a very considerable oil field has been proved. Naturally there is much excitement, especially as the proven field is extending in two or three directions. The usual thing has happened. Big companies and little companies, groups and individuals from all over the country have flocked to the Panhandle and entered into contracts with the owners of land for the right to test for oil or the right to trade in leases. We have made a contract giving the right to test for oil only. A bonus was paid to us on signing the contract, and a rental is payable monthly until certain tests have been begun. There is a right of withdrawal in favor of the lessee, and, of course, there is provision that a royalty will be paid to the Matador should oil be found. I think it inadvisable to go further into the details of the contract, because we may have further applications to deal with. Whether oil is found on our property or not, the fact that within no great distance of our Alamositas property a great community of people have come together is going to have an influence upon our land values. We visited a town [Borger] in the heart of the oil field which was said to have 10,000 souls, and yet less than a year before our visit not a single building existed there. Mushroom towns have often a short existence, but what promises permanence to some of these communities is the solid fact that an extensive oil field has been proved, and that capital is providing millions of dollars to develop it.[35]

The Roxana company surrendered its lease in August, 1927, without having drilled a single well; its geologists considered the territory covered by the lease unpromising, an opinion

[35] Report of Proceedings, Forty-fifth Annual General Meeting of Shareholders, 4-5.

shared by the Standard Oil Company of California. The latter had indicated some interest in leasing the western part of the Alamositas Division early in 1927 and had made a geological survey of the region, but decided that the results of its study did not justify leasing any of the land owned by the Matador.

In May, Murdo Mackenzie opened negotiations with E. R. Perry, president of the Exploration Company of Texas, concerning the leasing of the company's land in Motley, Cottle, and Floyd counties. Perry's organization, newly created at San Angelo and backed by Pittsburgh capital, proposed to take five-year oil and gas leases on eight blocks of land in the three counties and to drill a four-thousand-foot test well near the center of each block; the Matador would receive a one-eighth royalty from production, and the Exploration Company would be entitled to sell leases on acreage around the wells to responsible oil companies and, in addition, would attempt to sell leases on the remainder of the Matador Division—that portion outside the blocks—for a 10 per cent commission.

Conferences among Perry, Mackenzie, and S. H. Cowan during the summer resulted in the preparation of a contract which contained terms slightly different from those originally proposed; the test wells were reduced to six, and the Exploration Company agreed to pay a bonus of fifty cents an acre on 330,000 acres for the first year and a rental at the same rate for the second year. What followed by way of rentals would depend upon the results of the first two years' exploration.

In March, 1928, six months after the contract was signed, the board chairman reported to the shareholders:

> An agreement has been entered into . . . covering three-fourths of our land at the Matador Ranch. In the counties of Cottle, Motley, and Floyd, we own about 330,000 acres and all of these lands are in the contract. The geologist of the contracting company has certified the presence of an anticline plunging westward through the three counties named and an anticline or folding of the strata is necessary for the storing of oil should the rock

prove oil-bearing. The contracting company has interested quite a number of the larger oil companies in this big test of a new and unproven area. A new operating company will be formed by the group and the Matador contract will be transferred to it along with some other minor contracts while all the respective companies will subscribe their respective shares of the capital. Ten test wells will be drilled of which at least six will be on Matador land. It will take some time to carry out these tests but two wells on our land are now drilling and the remaining four should be under way in a few weeks. Unless oil is found at a shallower depth, the wells must be drilled to a depth of 4,000 feet each.

Meantime it is of interest to know that we were paid last July 165,000 dollars as a bonus for one year. In July next we are promised a similar sum to cover the period until July, 1929. What may follow thereafter depends upon the success of the exploration.[36]

In the following year Mackay notified the company that three of the wells had been completed and abandoned, and in 1930 he reported that the Exploration Company had completed its contract by drilling six wells to a depth of four thousand feet but that, "unfortunately for it and for us," no oil had been found. When the Exploration Company failed to find support for continuing testing activities, it surrendered its leases in August, 1930.

In 1927, when the Matador Division lands were leased for exploratory drilling, the company had withdrawn from sale its properties in Motley, Cottle, and Floyd counties pending completion of the tests. This action was taken because the board "always had an uneasy feeling, in offering land, that perhaps oil might be proved in blocks sold at simple farming values." By 1930 the directors were willing to concede that no oil existed, "at least to a depth of 4,000 feet," and offered to sell "as before" to farmers; but this time there was no demand, for the stock market collapse in the fall of 1929 had brought an end to speculative

[36] Report of Proceedings, Forty-sixth Annual General Meeting of Shareholders, 5.

192

buying on the part of the small land investor and a drought had parched the agricultural areas of the Southwest. The Great Depression was on, and it combined with World War II to bring land sales to a standstill during a sixteen-year period— 1930 through 1945. The slight variations in the company's land totals during this era were due to the transfer of small tracts to the state for highway construction and to reconveyances to the Matador of acreage purchased in the 1920's on the installment plan.

The fact that the company foreclosed on less than two thousand acres during the period of drought and depression was attributed to two factors—financial assistance by the government which permitted farmers to pay off or reduce mortgages on their farms, and the company's own policy of giving a mortgagee opportunity to refinance his obligation and allowing deferment of payments. In connection with the latter, it might be pointed out that a change in the company's attitude toward settlers and toward the community became apparent with the construction of the Quanah, Acme and Pacific Railroad early in MacBain's administration. The need for good public relations—"doing good and getting credit for it"—was particularly important at the Matador Division; and the company, in helping to construct the Motley County Railroad and in subscribing liberally to war bond drives, demonstrated its willingness to co-operate with the local people.

"In response to a public appeal" the board approved the construction of a swimming pool at Roaring Springs in 1929. Two factors entered into the directors' decision to open this facility to the people of the area:

> We possess in this spring one of the purest waters to be found anywhere in the State of Texas. It gushes in considerable volume from a rock formation of conglomerate situated about ten miles from the headquarters. If the spring were near a large city the water would probably be bottled for its purity. In a "dry and thirsty" land the spring has long been envied for use as a bathing

pool and our Manager feared that some day it might be appropriated by a public authority, thus placing the control of the water, important to our cattle, in alien hands. We have spent about $12,000 in making a concrete lined pool below the fall, and in providing dressing-rooms and the other equipment necessary for bathers. Some further but minor expenditure will be required this year for rest and refreshment purposes, fencing, etc. A caretaker armed with police authority keeps order. The pool was not opened until the end of August [1929], so that the season was very short, but crowds of people attended and bathed, some coming from great distances. We think that our neighbours appreciate this endeavour of the company to meet a public want. A suitable charge is made for admission to the pool and it should take care of the expenses and yield a fair return upon the outlay.[37]

In its relations with its employees the Matador company gave additional evidence of its ability to adjust to the times. When Alexander Mackay wrote in February, 1920, that "the war, followed by general restlessness, [had] dispersed the old-time cowboys," he was referring not only to the labor shortage on the ranches but to a growing tendency on the part of hands to sue for damages when they were injured in the company's service. It had been the custom to retain an injured man on the payroll until he was able to work again, but when *The Cattleman*, a monthly publication of the Texas Cattle Raisers Association, carried an article stating that the workmen's compensation law enacted by the Thirty-fifth Legislature in 1917 applied to ranch owners who employed three or more men, MacBain and Jackson concluded that "the Matador Company's best interest would be served by becoming a member of some reliable employer's insurance company." The application to the Texas Employers' Insurance Company of Dallas was approved, and a policy covering the Matador's ranching operations in Motley, Dickens, Floyd, Cottle, and Oldham counties was issued. Under this pol-

[37] Report of Proceedings, Forty-eighth Annual General Meeting of Shareholders, 6–7.

H. F. Mitchell and Murdo Mackenzie at Alamositas, 1923

Matador Division range, 1928

Counting steers for shipment, Matador Division, 1928

Swimming pool, Roaring Springs, Matador Division, 1929

Matador calves, Denver, 1930

John Mackenzie

Changing mounts, Alamositas Division, 1949

Loading pens, Murdo, Alamositas Division, 1949

icy the insurance company was liable for surgeons' fees and hospital and drug bills; and in the event a man was incapacitated by an accident, compensation amounting to 60 per cent of his weekly wage was paid. The premium rate was 2.5 per cent of the monthly payroll; for purposes of determining the premium, wages and the cost of board, estimated at $20.00 a man, were added to establish the monthly payroll. For example, "the Matador division payroll for July [1920] amounted to $2,038.25 to which add $20.00 per man per month for board—$880.00, making a total of $2,918.25 at 2½%, the premium shows to be $72.95 for the month."[38]

To show that his action in taking out the policy was justified, the manager reported that in a period of twelve weeks following the effective date of the policy, six accidents had occurred—four at the Matador Division and two at Alamositas; at the latter division both injuries were serious and were reported by Mitchell:

> A horse fell with Walter Rumans on the 6th August and broke one ankle all to pieces and tore the breast bone loose from the collar bone and broke two ribs on the left side and injured his lung. He now has pneumonia and the doctor says that he just has a fighting chance to recover. The accident happened in the Alamositas pasture and I sent him to the sanitarium in Amarillo.
>
> A horse pitched Jack Windell off today and broke his leg above the ankle; we brought him in this evening and sent him to Channing.[39]

By far the greatest number of injuries reported on the Matador ranges involved accidents with horses. In each injury rated as "serious" or in case of a death, efforts were made to record the circumstances and the events—"the full particulars"—from eyewitnesses and others close to the scene. As an illustration, on September 1, 1928, Murdo Mackenzie reported to Mackay, Irons and Company that a rider had been killed at the Alamo-

[38] MacBain to Mackay, Irons and Co., August 11, 1920.
[39] Mitchell to MacBain, quoted in MacBain to Mackay, Irons and Co., August 11, 1920.

sitas Division. While he anticipated that a claim would be made against the company, he was certain that the Matador could not be held "liable for any responsibility on account of the accident," and forwarded copies of statements sworn to before a notary public:

> I, Herbert Collins, wagon boss for the Matador Land and Cattle Company, Ltd. ranch near Channing, Texas, being duly sworn, make the following statement in regard to the death of Ralph Dayton:
>
> At the time of the accident Ralph Dayton held the position of "Night Hawk" with the outfit, which means that about sunset each night his duties were to take all of the horses belonging with the outfit and herd them all night, and bring them into camp about daylight each morning. Then he was off duty until the horses were turned over to him again at night.
>
> The night of August 16–17 the outfit was camped at "Blue Goose" and Dayton herded the horses as usual and brought them into camp the morning of August 17. He was then off duty until night, and had all the day for rest and sleep.
>
> When the outfit is to be moved during the day from one camping place to another, the "Night Hawk" after eating breakfast sometimes rides on to the next camping place where he can sleep and rest undisturbed. The outfit was to move from "Blue Goose" to the Dipping Vat Camp on August 17th, so after breakfast Dayton rode over to the Dipping Vat Camp. H. F. Parker and Tom McDougal were working at this camp.
>
> After leaving Blue Goose camp, Dayton was off duty until night when the horses would be turned over to him again. In the meantime he had taken one of the Dipping Vat Camp horses to ride on his own pleasure and had an accident and was killed.
>
> At the time of his accident and death Dayton was off duty and not engaged in any work of the Matador Company. The horse he was riding did not belong in his mount, and Dayton was riding him without my knowledge or consent.[40]

[40] Copy, affidavit by Herbert Collins, August 27, 1928.

H. F. Parker of Channing, Texas, made the following statement in regard to the death of Dayton:

About 7 o'clock on the morning of August 17th Ralph Dayton
rode over from Blue Goose Camp to Dipping Vat Camp where
Tom McDougal and myself were working. Soon after his arrival,
Dayton, McDougal and myself decided to ride to Adrian, a distance of about 14 miles. Dayton turned his horse loose and rode
one of the horses belonging at Dipping Vat Camp. We all left
for Adrian about 8 o'clock A.M., returning to Dipping Vat Camp
about 2:30 P.M.

A little later Dayton and myself saddled up two other horses
belonging at Dipping Vat Camp and rode to a pool of water in a
canyon about 2 miles west of the vats and went in swimming.
After our swim we decided to hunt for some wild grapes in a
little canyon with steep, rocky sides. In trying to get out of the
canyon we found a place that was barely passable; I rode up the
bluff first. The horse Dayton was on refused to take the bluff and
Dayton was urging him to go up it. I called to Dayton saying,
"That horse is a little mean, you had better get off and lead him
up." Dayton made no reply but continued to urge the horse. The
horse started to go up and when part way, either slipped or
whirled around to turn back and gave a couple of jumps. Dayton
lost his position in the saddle, his left foot ran through the stirrup
and he fell to the right side of the horse. He caught the saddle
horn with one hand, but seemed to lose his hold, and the horse
ran. This was about 5 P.M. Dayton and his horse were in the
canyon, but I had ridden my horse out of the canyon. By the
time I got back into the canyon Dayton and his horse were out
of sight. I tried to find the horse but the country was rough and
broken and it was about 6 o'clock P.M. before I found it. The
horse, still dragging Dayton, was very tired and standing quietly
alongside a fence. Dayton was dead. The saddle had turned
under the horse. I pulled Dayton's boot off, laid the body by the
fence, and went to Dipping Vat Camp for help.[41]

These documents were undoubtedly instrumental in securing
a decision in favor of the company when Ralph Dayton's mother

[41] Copy, affidavit by H. F. Parker, August 27, 1928.

filed suit for damages against the Matador. In March, 1930, Mackenzie notified the secretary's office of the decision but recommended that, since further action might be brought, the sum of $750 be paid to the mother "in full payment of any claim which she might have against the Company and on condition that her attorneys not receive one cent of the money paid to her." On March 14, 1930, Mrs. Elsa Adlia Amstead, Dayton's mother, acknowledged receipt of $750 from the company in satisfaction of all claims arising from the accidental death of her son, and the manager reported matter was closed:

> I am glad to get rid of this case, not that I was afraid of trying the case, no matter under what claim, but we could not employ an attorney to fight any case which they might bring for a less amount than we are paying her, and it will ease our minds considerably that the matter is settled for all time. I hope we may never again have a suit of this kind.[42]

The concern which the Matador officials had for the employees and the latter group's response—loyalty to the company—were put to the test during the depression of the 1930's, for in the face of drought and low livestock prices the directors might have given way to panic, reduced their herds, cut the working force, and slashed wages. As it was, every effort was made to save the cattle and to keep on the payroll those men who had served the company faithfully; in return, the ranch personnel took pay cuts and stayed with the organization.

The stock exchange panic which heralded the beginning of the depression late in 1929 had no noticeable effect on the company's business operations in that year; cattle sales were made prior to the Wall Street disaster and the prices for two-year-old steers were the highest received to that time for livestock of this class. Early in 1930, however, it became apparent that lower levels were forthcoming, since "forward sales"—contracts for de-

[42] Mackenzie to Mackay, March 17, 1930. A copy of the receipt, duly witnessed, accompanied the letter.

livery late in the year—were lagging and big stocks of dead meat, carried over from the previous year, lay in the packers' warehouses. Mackay warned the shareholders on April 1, 1930, that the outlook indicated lower prices for the year and that the Matador should be prepared for a further decline of market values; but he, along with most business leaders, misgauged the depths of the depression:

It must be acknowledged that the country [the United States] came through its financial troubles with credit to its bankers and to the leaders of large industrial undertakings. The investment market has now acquired a somewhat healthier tone by the elimination of much fictitious value in securities, and one can say that quotations rest again more generally upon earning power. Productive industry suffered less than might have been expected in view of the tremendous shock to credit. Luxury trades were naturally hardest hit but, as general commodity stocks were held everywhere in short supply, ordinary production had to go on, although on a somewhat reduced scale. Confidence is growing that much of the unemployed labour of the country may find employment again as the year advances, and that the second half of 1930 may show normal industrial activity. We are naturally interested in this question, because consumption of meat and its products is reduced when trading is slack and there is much unemployment.[43]

A year later Mackay admitted that the hopeful indications of improvement in the preceding year had not led to recovery and that trade conditions had worsened and had ended in utter stagnation:

The Western States had also to bear a special blow in a widespread and disastrous drought which, by the destruction of crops and livestock not only ruined many farmers but reduced them and their families to the verge of starvation. Bread queues in town and country alike, were a disturbing feature in the Western world.

[43] Report of Proceedings, Forty-eighth Annual General Meeting of Shareholders, 5–6.

One is happy to think that the worst of these troubles are over. Recovery may be slow, but there are signs which warrant the belief that improvement has already taken place, and that during the rest of the year the movements towards normal conditions may continue.[44]

Whatever hopes were held by Mackay and the other directors that 1931 would see an upturn in prices were dashed during the latter half of the year, and the chairman, in his annual report, qualified each remark which contained any trace of optimism:

I regret . . . that the results of the year's operations have proved for the first time in many years very unsatisfactory.

There is little need to remind you that the United States is passing through an economic depression on a vast scale. . . . The fall in the value of all commodities and services was great and sudden, and further declines have gone on ever since. There are some signs that the bottom may have been reached in the major commodity prices, but one cannot speak with confidence. . . .

The agricultural industry in which we are specially interested has had a particularly hard time. Diminished wages and earnings throughout the country enforced drastic economies in household management, such as the American people in their years of prosperity have not known. Extravagant and often wasteful in their food consumption, they encouraged the farmer and the cattleman to produce on a scale suitable only for a time of prosperity. When the belts had to be tightened, the producer was left with grains, meat, fruits, and vegetables for which there was no profitable demand, and he is facing, for the time being, the problem of getting rid of his surplus and restricting the volume of his products.[45]

For the first time since 1893 the American operations showed a loss—£32,278—in 1931; primarily responsible for this debit balance were the costs of feed and pasturage, for the drought had

[44] Report of Proceedings, Forty-ninth Annual General Meeting of Shareholders, 3.

[45] Report of Proceedings, Fiftieth Annual General Meeting of Shareholders, 3–4.

necessitated the removal of over ten thousand head of cattle from the company's ranges in 1930 and 1931 and upwards of 200,000 acres at the Matador Division were cleared of stock for a period of nearly two years.[46] Had not rains in 1932 and 1933 brought a partial restoration of the grass at Alamositas and at Matador, the operating losses in those years—£7,236 in 1932 and £1,642 in 1933—might have exceeded the 1931 figure, since cattle prices were "little other than disastrous." Table 6 shows the average price per head received by the company in each year from 1929 through 1939; it indicates the sudden drop following the stock market crash, the further decline in 1932 and 1933, and the upward turn prior to the wartime boom. While these figures do not reflect precisely the national livestock market quotations during the period, since the weights of Matador cattle were affected by local conditions of drought, they do mirror the general level of cattle prices.

TABLE 6*

YEAR	AVERAGE PRICE, ALL CATTLE SOLD
1929	$66.41
1930	39.83
1931	39.16
1932	24.67
1933	23.23
1934	25.03
1935	25.99
1936	43.25
1937	43.76
1938	41.98
1939	45.44

* From the annual reports for the years listed.

[46] In 1930, A. A. Spaugh of Manville, Wyoming, took 4,000 steers for summer pasturing; 3,000 heifers were fed at Grand Island, Nebraska; 2,500 two-year-old steers were sent to Coker, Nebraska, and placed on pastures controlled by Guy Combs of Hershey, Nebraska; and 3,500 heifers were pastured near Cuervo, New Mexico. Similar arrangements were made in 1931.

By 1934 the company's reserve fund was exhausted, and it became desirable to secure a loan to cover the advances made by American bankers and to provide additional working capital. In April, 1934, a loan of $300,000 was obtained from the Southwestern Life Insurance Company of Dallas, plus an additional loan in June of $200,000 from the same organization. The loans, which called for interest payment at the rate of 6 per cent a year, were secured by a mortgage over the entire Alamositas Division —394,285 acres.[47] In 1937 and 1938 payments to Southwestern Life reduced the debt, and in 1939 the balance was paid.

The working capital obtained through the Southwestern Life loan gave the Matador the flexibility needed to cope with the drought and the dust storms of the mid-thirties, for feed costs increased phenomenally as high winds and dust ruined crops as well as range grass. To save the herd, it was necessary to scatter the cattle again, and shipping and feed-pen charges soared once more.

Table 7 shows, in the "Balance" column, the profit or loss from American operations for each year from 1931 through 1939, along with the dividends paid to the shareholders.

TABLE 7*

Year	Balance		Dividend
1931	£32,278	(debit)	0%
1932	7,236	"	0
1933	1,642	"	0
1934	5,321	"	0
1935	6,258	"	0
1936	7,984	(credit)	0
1937	20,730	"	3
1938	19,769	"	5
1939	63,227	"	10

* From the annual reports for the years listed.

On May 19, 1936, Alexander Mackay presided at the forty-

[47] Fifty-second Annual Report, 5.

fourth annual meeting of the shareholders and reported on the previous year's activities and the current year's prospects; his analysis of the company's position was realistic and his forecast was mildly optimistic:

> I can hardly see any real activity . . . until the country has emerged more completely from the general depression which has now lasted for five or six years. That recovery is going forward, few if any people now deny, but the improvement is slow and hindered greatly by so much party politics being mixed up with business. This is specially apparent in a year like the present when the election for President takes place. Nevertheless in spite of this disturbing feature, the country is slowly climbing back toward normal trading conditions. . . . It is to be deplored however that there are still ten or twelve millions of workers unemployed and that the drain upon the nation's resources to support them is so great that the budget remains unbalanced. Until the national leaders have completed this gigantic task, there will be delay in the rate of progress; but there can be no doubt that in time America with its vast natural resources and facilities for production will reach again a new era of prosperity. . . .
> It is a little difficult to forecast the results of our trading for the current year, owing to so many uncertainties in the market position and otherwise. But it is reasonably possible to say that we shall be able to present a much better balance sheet than is now before you.

Unfortunately, the chairman did not live to see the "better balance sheet" which was presented at the end of the year, for on May 23—four days after the annual meeting—Alexander Mackay suddenly died at his home at Oban at the age of eighty.[48] In a tribute to Mackay, George Bonar sketched the role which he had played in the company's history:

> Mr. Mackay's record in the Company's service is a very remarkable one. The Company was founded in 1882 when Mr. Mackay became its first Secretary, later becoming a Director,

[48] W. L. Pattullo to Murdo Mackenzie, June 12, 1936.

and acting for a long period of years as its Chairman. It is not too much to say that in the minds of shareholders . . . the name of Mackay has become inseparable from that of Matador. For the long period of 54 years he was devoted to its interests. Like all companies of its kind, the Matador has suffered from time to time from the adverse factors to which its form of business is peculiarly liable, but through good times and bad times Mr. Mackay faithfully, loyally and skillfully guided the fortunes of the Company, and it is in no small measure due to him that, while most of the other companies formed in this country during the same period of American development have gone out of business in more or less reduced circumstances, the Matador still remains, and has on the average earned for its shareholders a fair return on their investment. We shall miss his guiding hand in the affairs of the Company, and those of us who knew him intimately mourn the loss of an outstanding personality and a great-hearted gentleman.[49]

Shortly after the death of his friend, Murdo Mackenzie expressed a desire to retire from the active management of the company. He was then eighty-seven years old and, though seemingly possessed of an iron constitution, was reluctant to undertake the arduous and frequent examination of the company's properties which he considered so necessary. At the annual meeting of the shareholders in May, 1937, approval was given to the appointment of John Mackenzie to the manager's position, and Murdo Mackenzie was re-elected to the board of directors.

In 1938 there was announced a shift in company policy—a change which was to have a significant effect on the Matador's career during the following thirteen years—the selection of another director who lived in the United States. The reasons for this action were stated to the shareholders in March, 1938, by Chairman Bonar:

In the course of the past year we have been able to find suitable men to fill the vacancies in the Directorate. . . . Our general

[49] Report of Proceedings, Fifty-fifth Annual General Meeting of Shareholders, 3.

management in Texas, as you all know, is in most capable hands, but we have felt for some time past, in view of the fundamental changes which have taken place in the U.S.A. in recent years, that it was too much to leave on the shoulders of the management alone the major questions of Company policy which might arise from an increasing rate of taxation and from some of the new legislation, and that, of the two vacancies [in 1938] one should be filled, if possible, by a Director located in Texas who is well versed in such matters. We have been very fortunate in finding such a man in Mr. Harry P. Drought, of San Antonio, who has acted for many years for the Alliance Trust Company as one of their Texas agents and who, in addition to his wide knowledge of land questions is, by virtue of his legal training and experience, familiar with these new questions that now so much concern us. We arranged that Mr. Mackenzie should become acquainted with Mr. Drought before there was any talk of an appointment and when in Texas I was glad to find that Mr. Mackenzie very sincerely welcomed both the idea and the man. We are quite certain that their collaboration on the spot will be found to be of great benefit to the Company.[50]

Drought's report on his first visit to the ranches was read to the shareholders since it contained "the impressions of a mind fresh to the company's problems"; likewise, it revealed the new director's familiarity with the western cattle industry:

Accompanied by the manager, I spent a week on the Alamositas and Matador ranches in Texas. Favorable weather and hard driving enabled me to see as much of the Alamositas as was necessary to give me a fairly accurate idea of all of it, and I was able to inspect most of the Matador. However, the Matador's irregular shape made it impossible for me to get over more than a comparatively small part of the acreage in Dickens County or to gain other than a very general knowledge of the acreage in Cottle County. Those parts of it which I did not have an opportunity to study will receive first attention on my next trip.

It is gratifying to be able to say that as a result of this inspec-

50 Report of Proceedings, Fifty-sixth Annual General Meeting of Shareholders, 7–8.

tion, I have no unfavorable criticism to offer. The lands as a whole are far above the average ranch land in Texas, and with the exception of some land on the ridges in the Turtle Hole pasture, which it is now planned to retire from pasturage for awhile, there was an unusually good stand of grass for the end of winter. Indeed, the cattle which have subsisted entirely on grass during the winter are in remarkably good condition for this time of the year.

Green is beginning to show on the pastures now, particularly below the cap rock on the Matador ranch. Any severe weather is improbable this month, and if none occurs by the first of next month there should be new grass in every pasture. Fortunately precipitation has been more than sufficient to give it growth, and additional rains have fallen since my visit.

Although I had always understood that the Matador herds were unusually fine, yet I was surprised by their high quality, which could only be attained by consistently careful and intelligent breeding. I am inclined to believe that the Matador cattle deserve their reputation of being the finest commercial Herefords to be found. The Sale of Steers recently reported to you by the manager is the subject of congratulatory comment at the cattlemen's convention now being held in San Antonio, and is the outstanding sale in Texas so far this year. . . .

I am tempted to write at length about the horses on the ranch, but I shall content myself with the statement that I am quite sure there is no ranch in Texas on which better horses for ranch purposes can be found. Such sales of horses as are made confirm this opinion, and I am pleased with the manner in which the management is taking advantage of the present fad for palomino horses, even though I suspect that it was instrumental in developing the fad, thus slighting my favorites, the dappled chestnut sorrels.

The management of the ranches is, of course, excellent, but I was impressed by the character and qualifications of the employed personnel. The superintendents of the Alamositas and of the Matador are able ranch executives, and each apparently does his job without unnecessary fuss or effort, but quietly, smoothly and capably. Their subordinates are considerably above the usual ranch hand type, and their interests and the

Matador's seem to be the same. The men are an energetic, hard-working, clean sort, and appear contented with their employment and environment.

The management has wisely taken advantage of the federal range program, including the construction of earthen tanks. I had practical opportunity to see many of these and they seem to be placed in practical locations and below ample watersheds. The intention is to take advantage of any similar plan which the federal government may carry forward this year, and it is hoped that additional dams can be constructed. The increased water supply thus obtained will extend the range of grazing cattle during the dry periods and will add substantially to the value of the pastures in which the dams are built.

Exploratory work under the oil lease of the Matador ranch has started but it is still in the initial stage.

The Matador ranches are properties which, under normal conditions, should be consistently profitable, and of which the stockholders may well be proud.[51]

It is well that men of experience were available to take over the guidance and management of the company's affairs in the late 1930's, for the "old guard" was disappearing. Following Mackay's death, George Bonar, who had been a director since 1922, was elected to the chairmanship, a position which he filled for only a year before his own death. In 1939, W. D. Macdougall, who was manager of the Alliance Trust Company of Dundee when he was appointed to the Matador directorate in 1925, was elected chairman of the board. At Alamositas, Emmett L. Roberds, who had been one of Mackenzie's division managers in Brazil during the second decade of the century and who had replaced H. F. Mitchell in 1926, indicated his desire to step down from the superintendent's post at the "North Ranch" in 1939. The vacancy thus created was filled by A. W. Rickels.

On May 30, 1939, Murdo Mackenzie died in Denver, and with his passing an era ended. Few men had been as intimately associated with the cattle industry as he had during the period of

[51] Drought to Mackay, Irons and Co., March 10, 1938.

transition from the open range to fenced ranching to feed-lot operations; and few, if any, had a stronger hand in shaping the industry's development. His career and character were sketched by Macdougall in 1940:

> He was a man of wide knowledge and sterling capacity. After gaining valuable experience in law, banking and estate work in Scotland he left for the United States in 1885 to undertake the management of the large holdings of the Prairie Land and Cattle Company. In 1890 he joined the Matador, and with a few years interval in charge of cattle interests in Brazil, he remained with us till his death. The Matador herd was his real life work and his pride, and we have to acknowledge today how largely it owes its present condition and status to his care. He took a leading position in the cattle industry of the United States, and from coast to coast wherever cattle men met his name was known and honoured. He was a past president of the American National Life Stock Association and was a power in it and other organizations. His personal friendship with President Theodore Roosevelt enabled him to carry to that powerful personage the stockmen's plea for redress from excessive freight rates. He was generally credited with the successful passage of the Bill which entrusted the Interstate Commerce Commission with the power to fix rates of interstate freights, and the President appointed him a member of the National Commission for the conservation of natural resources, and so on. Through his character and courage, his industry and integrity, he was entitled to be regarded as a type of those Scotsmen who have made their country respected in foreign lands.[52]

When he succeeded his father as general manager and, in 1940, as a director, John Mackenzie brought the experience and qualifications needed to meet the responsibilities of these positions. He was six years old when Murdo Mackenzie became

[52] Report of Proceedings, Fifty-eighth Annual General Meeting of Shareholders, 3–4. It was in 1890 that Mackenzie agreed to accept the position of manager, though his contract with the Matador did not become effective until January, 1891.

manager of the Matador, and during his boyhood and youth spent the summers on the ranches. After finishing school, he worked on the Cheyenne River Division and then at the Trinidad office under John MacBain. Along with James Burr, he left the Matador in 1911 to go to Brazil, where he remained until 1923, when he returned to Denver to become his father's assistant in the management of the company's operations in America. With a thorough knowledge of cattle and the cattle business, John Mackenzie was the natural and ideal selection for the position of manager. He and H. P. Drought co-operated cordially in promoting the company's interests during a period of strenuous activity—World War II.

In addition to the uncertainties of weather and market—natural risks accepted by the cattleman—the Matador was confronted by a new hazard with the outbreak of hostilities between Great Britain and Germany. Taxation—not new in itself—bore down with such force on the company that it became a matter of concern second only to the welfare of the herd. In disposing of the profits for 1939, the directors had to recommend the placing of 47 per cent of the profits to the tax account, while allowing a dividend of only 10 per cent:

> The most striking feature of these appropriations is the provision for taxation. . . .
> American Federal Income Tax and Excess Profits Tax, British Excess Profits Tax and British Income Tax, all combine to take away the major part of our earnings. Into these technical matters it would be out of place for me to enter now in detail, but I think we may record here an acknowledgment of the care and thought which they impose on our officials and advisers and our confidence that they will do everything in their power to lighten the burden. Incidentally, Excess Profits Tax—the heaviest item in our taxation—bears most unjustly on a Company like this, which has this year made a recovery from depression for reasons unconnected with the war. Those Companies which have experienced nothing but continuous prosperity escape the tax altogether, while a company that has had losses finds the greater part of its

recovered profit taken from it. The operation of the tax is most unjust and penalizes enterprise and energy.[53]

Despite this threat to its fiscal health, the Matador found itself in an excellent position as the decade drew to an end. It had withstood the blows of drought and depression, its lands were free of encumbrance, and its herds were unsurpassed in quality; those in authority at all levels possessed experience and were loyal to the traditions developed by the company in over a half-century of operations.

[53] Report of Proceedings, Fifty-eighth Annual General Meeting of Shareholders, 4–5.

~6~
The End of an Era

THE STORY of the Matador company during the last twelve years of its existence is largely, though not exclusively, an account of high income and soaring taxes, for as livestock prices rose throughout the 1940's to bring impressive profits, governmental levies—British and American—increased correspondingly. In Table 8 are found the profits, before taxes, and the dividends for the years listed.

TABLE 8*

YEAR	PROFIT	DIVIDEND
1940	£ 79,368†	12½%
1941	89,873†	12½‡
1942	95,555†	15‡
1943	98,107†	15‡
1944	72,673†	15‡
1945	119,323†	20‡
1946	126,551†	20§
1947	225,414§	20‖
1948	291,552§	20‖
1949	243,695#	20‖
1950	404,695**	35¶

* From the annual reports for the years listed.
† Exchange basis—$4.87 to the pound sterling.
‡ Does not include interim dividend of 5%.
§ Exchange basis—$4.035 to the pound sterling.
‖ Does not include interim dividend of 10%.
Exchange basis—$3.58 to pound sterling.
** Exchange basis—$2.80 to the pound sterling.
¶ Does not include interim dividends of 5% and 10%.

In 1882, when the Dundee Scots acquired the property of the Matador Cattle Company of Texas, the pound sterling was valued at $4.90 for the purpose of determining the purchase price; from that time until 1947 the company's accounts were prepared on the basis of an exchange rate of $4.87 to £1.00. In 1947, however, a more realistic rate was used, and with the devaluation of the pound to $2.80 in September, 1949, an average value for that year was employed in preparing the accounts.

Because of the uncertainties accompanying each year's tax bill, the company announced the annual profits as listed above, then transferred to the tax reserve a sum estimated to be sufficient to meet tax payments. The transfers made during the period 1940–50 are shown in Table 9.

TABLE 9*

YEAR	TRANSFERRED TO TAXATION RESERVE
1940	£ 60,000
1941	75,000
1942	80,000
1943	80,000
1944	50,000
1945	95,000
1946	95,000
1947	160,000
1948	170,000
1949	120,000
1950	227,000

* From the annual reports for the years listed.

Promise of relief from "the blight of double taxation" came in 1945, when the governments of the United States and Great Britain made a provisional agreement under which the dual tax liabilities of such organizations as the Matador could be adjusted; but because of the peculiar tax laws of each country and the puzzling interdependence of the two systems, little was achieved until 1949.

In 1942 the capital of the company was divided from fifty thousand shares of six pounds each into three hundred thousand shares of one pound each; this was the first change in the capital structure since 1896 and was followed by a major rearrangement of the capital in 1948 after a proposal, submitted by Chairman Macdougall, was approved by the shareholders:

> It is quite anomalous that the Capital of a Company in such a position [as ours] should be represented by shares of 13/4 paid up with uncalled liability of 6/8 per share. We have accordingly consulted with our legal advisers with the view of taking such steps as may be necessary to pay up this liability out of Reserves and transform all the Company's shares into fully paid up £1 shares. There are a moderate number of shares on which the holders have paid in advance in anticipation of calls, and the present holders of these shares will, of course, be entitled to repayment of these advances. I need not warn you that this desirable capital operation does not, in a business such as ours (dependent on the two most uncertain things in the world—weather and prices), indicate any promise of an increase in the total amount distributed by way of dividend in future years.[1]

On December 7, 1948, the Court of Sessions in Edinburgh sanctioned the rearrangement and the reduction of capital according to the following scheme:

> On December 31, 1947 the capital of the company was:
>
> | | | |
> |---|---|---|
> | Authorized—300,000 shares of £1.00 each | | £300,000 |
> | Issued—300,000 shares of £1.00 each, 13/4d paid | | £200,000 |
> | Prepayment by shareholders of uncalled capital | | 23,606 |
> | | | £223,606 |

The existing capital was reduced from £300,000 to £200,000 (a) by repaying 6/8d per share which had been prepaid on

[1] Statement by the Chairman, Sixty-fifth Annual General Meeting of Shareholders, April 15, 1947.

213

70,818 shares, equaling £23,606, and (b) by canceling the un-called capital of 6/8d per share on 300,000 shares.

After the repayment of 6/8d per share on the fully paid shares, all the shares of the company (300,000) became fully paid shares of 13/4d each, equaling £200,000. These shares were subdivided into 800,000 shares of 5/– each fully paid in the ratio of eight shares of 5/– each (40/–) for three shares of 13/4d each (40/–).

The capital was then increased from £200,000 to £300,000 which permitted the creation of 400,000 shares of 5/– each for issue. Thus in 1948 the statement on capital read:

Authorized—1,200,000 shares of 5/– each	£300,000
Issued and fully paid—800,000 shares of 5/–	£200,000
Unissued—400,000 shares of 5/–	100,000
	£300,000

As Macdougall pointed out, revisions in the capital structure had nothing to do with the profits earned or dividends declared by the company; receipts from cattle sales constituted the major portion of each year's income, though land sales immediately after the war—25,000 acres in 1946 and 45,000 acres in 1947—brought substantial credits to the land account. The average prices realized for all classes of cattle marketed from 1940 through 1950 are shown in Table 10; in the period covered these were reflected in the company's books as increases in income, in profits, in dividends, and in taxes.

TABLE 10*

YEAR	NUMBER MARKETED, ALL CLASSES	AVERAGE PRICE†
1940	14,406	$ 47.68
1941	13,628	54.10
1942	13,213	61.86
1943	10,030	78.65
1944	9,924	69.89
1945	13,204	72.44
1946	16,104	79.56

1947	16,049	98.25
1948	13,670	120.44
1949	10,471	120.60
1950	10,922	138.77

* From the annual reports for the years listed.
† After deducting cost of outside pasturage and feed lot charges.

The returns indicated above, all of which "brought satisfaction to the board," were due in some measure to the practice of sending hundreds of steers to feed lots and outside pastures for fattening prior to shipping them to market. Originally undertaken as emergency action to save the cattle from starvation during the droughts of the early 1930's, the placing of two- and three-year-olds on selected grassland and in large feed lots brought two advantages—an increase in weight and conservation of the ranges at Alamositas and Matador. In connection with the latter item, it should be pointed out that, following the decision in the early 1920's to withdraw from the northern divisions, the herd strength was not cut in direct proportion to the grazing areas surrendered, though some reduction was effected (Appendix B).

In contracting for pasturage, the company customarily paid the landowner on the basis of the weight gained by the cattle during their stay on the pasture. For example, in 1940, under an agreement with W. C. Harris of Sterling, Colorado, the Matador paid four cents a pound for the gain on steers carried for fifteen months on pastures which Harris controlled in Wyoming and three cents a pound for the gain on steers pastured from spring until fall. In the same year Harris agreed to take fifteen hundred steers at his feed lots in Sterling "on the usual cost-plus basis" for a five-month period:

The Harris Grain Company has contracted for 500,000 pounds of barley at ninety cents per hundredweight, and 12,000 bushels of wheat at ninety-five cents per hundred. This grain will be set aside for feeding our cattle and billed to us at cost plus 10 cents per hundred to cover cost of buying, storing, grinding and

215

shrinkage in grinding and mixing. The cattle will be fed a balanced ration of grain, mill run, bran, dry beet pulp, soy bean oil meal or linseed oil meal or cotton seed cake and alfalfa or wild hay and molasses meal. They are also contracting alfalfa hay at around $8.00 per ton in the stack. The cost of feeding the steers will be handled in the usual manner and statements rendered twice monthly, payment to be made as the cattle are marketed.[2]

Illustrative of the gainful nature of feed-lot operations was the report on 157 steers which were shipped from Alamositas to Sterling on August 10, 1940. These weighed off the cars at an average of 803 pounds and after 103 days attained an average weight of 1,135 pounds, an average gain of 332 pounds, or 3.2 pounds a head per day. One hundred and fifty-six head were marketed—one steer died in the feed lot—and brought $16,709.11. After deducting the payment for feed—$4,582.46—the shipment netted the Matador $12,126.65, or $77.73 a head.

Fundamental to the success of the company's operations during the war were the extra efforts put forth by its employees in America. The labor shortage, brought about by the draft and the lure of high wages in defense plants, threw a heavy burden on the superintendents and the older men who remained on the ranches; roundup crews were shorthanded, windmills and fences had to be maintained, and the care and control of thousands of cattle scattered over vast areas required the attention of skilled and experienced riders. The Dundee directors came to appreciate the energy and efficiency with which the ranch personnel met and overcame the problems which arose; to give appropriate recognition, the board singled out individuals for special mention at the annual shareholders' meetings:

This labour trouble and all the troubles incident to it and these war times generally have been faced not only by our General Manager but by his lieutenants, Mr. Reilly, the Superintendent at Matador, Mr. Stevens at Alamositas and others, including Mr. Payne, the range foreman at Matador, with a loyalty and effi-

[2] John Mackenzie to Mackay, Irons and Co., August 27, 1940.

ciency which we cannot praise too highly. I am sure that this Annual Meeting of the Company will desire to be associated with the message of appreciation which the Board have already sent to Mr. Mackenzie on behalf of himself and all those working under him.[3]

John V. Stevens, who replaced A. W. Rickels at Alamositas in 1940, was young and energetic and drove himself relentlessly in setting an example for those who worked under him. To visit each camp and pasture in the division was not easy, for though the land lay in a solid block and the only roads on it were company roads, the Canadian River presented a barrier to vehicular travel at times; within the ranch there were two principal crossings, both fords and both impassable during a flood or a rise in the river. Since the headquarters were near Murdo, north of the river, travel to and from the south pastures—the major part of the property—involved use of the highway bridge some thirty miles east of the ranch.

Excerpts from the Alamositas diary for 1942 illustrate the nature of Stevens' activities and those of his subordinates:

January 1. Clarence on south side scattering groceries and supplies. Everett went to all camps on north side of river looking at mills and fixing gateposts. Stevens worked on books then went to Amarillo to see about buying retreaded tires. None to buy. To buy have to carry old carcasses and have retreaded. Coldest day in 2 years: 6 degrees at 6:30 A.M.

January 5. Clarence lined cattle car with paper for shipment of show calves. Hauled oat hay to Murdo for calves. Bob Page helped. Lined car from bottom to top on east side.

Stevens went via Channing to camps out west, cutting ice at Popham Camp. Cut ice several places. Woody and I went through steers and cut ice. . . . Bulls at new farm looking fine. Returned via old freight road. Calf in ice, coyotes eating while alive at Halfway Mill. Cloudy and snowing, 5 degrees.

[3] Report of Proceedings, Sixty-third Annual General Meeting of Shareholders, 2.

January 7. Clarence, Virgil and Bob killed beef in A.M. then helped load show calves for Denver. Stevens attended to loading of show calves, went via Amarillo to south side, located tank at Las Achies, then went to Vat Camp, saw cowboys at Trujillo Camp. Having trouble with steer gathering. Bad, cold day; 7 degrees.

January 29. Clarence, Everett and Lindsey Montgomery went to Hartley to catch bus for Lubbock to take physical examination. Stevens took Mr. Davies of American Meat Packing Institute to Hollicott Camp to see purebred cattle. Curley breaking young mules and young horses. Cattle doing fine.

January 31. Clarence got back from Lubbock; reported passing his physical then hauled load of feed to New Farm. Everett passed his physical and went to Popham Camp to leather mill. 20 degrees; partly cloudy, windy and cold.

February 8. Everett returned from Amarillo and packed and moved all of his things. Going to Lubbock to try for Air Force but is quitting his job.

Stevens and Bill Smithers drove out in the West Trujillo pasture to the river. Returned to Vat Camp for lunch. Cowboys gathering calves to wean. Returned via Alamositas to river; had to be pulled across river.

June 4. Budd worked on crossing at Rito Blanco; Virgil went across river and fixed well in new pasture. Stevens spent the day looking for hogs and for hands.

June 9. Stevens went from south side to Tucumcari, talked to 2 boys about work. May not show up. Had another rain on east side of ranch.

June 16. Virgil went to Pedrosa and worked on 2 mills, Red Tower and Line Mill. Line Mill motor busted; Stevens went to Old Farm, carried Mr. Gray to bring back horse. Then crossed river and went to Alamositas Camp and Vat Camp for lunch. Boys have all mares gathered, working steers.

September 12. Bud went with Virgil to work on water troughs at Scab Mill. Stevens did chores then went to Cruise pasture and helped boys work steers. Cut out 169 to ship. In P.M. wrote letters and mailed them. Mr. Mackenzie arrived from Matador.

November 6.   Harvey hauled feed from Hollicott. We finally got a car of cake and he hauled two loads. Stevens went to south side, crossed river. Boys had 30 bulls from Alamositas pasture; then went through Alamositas. Met Hiram Sweeney and had lunch at Vat Camp. Returned via Alamositas Camp. Got back to river and it was up big. Had to return via Amarillo.

Cows and calves are doing fine. Bulls are failing and saddle horses are failing.

When Maurice Reilly died unexpectedly on June 15, 1946, Johnny Stevens moved to the Matador Division to become the fifth and last superintendent at the Ballard Springs headquarters. In August, Roland Howe was appointed to fill the superintendent's post at Alamositas.

The last major addition to the Matador organization in America occurred in 1947, when John Mackenzie, Jr., was appointed assistant manager. Announcement of this action was made by Macdougall in April, 1948:

> Mr. [John] Mackenzie is still in his prime as a cattleman, but we must look to the future, and it is right that he should have a colleague and successor. Fortunately, he has an able and intelligent son who naturally has been in touch with the ranches since boyhood and has also had the benefit of a legal training, an excellent thing for any business man. We have now appointed him Assistant Manager, and we extend a warm welcome to John, Junior, confident that he will eventually worthily carry on the fine tradition set by his father and before him his grandfather, Murdo Mackenzie.[4]

In view of the excellent profits and mounting dividends announced by the company during the decade of the 1940's, rumors that the Matador would be sold came as a surprise when they were circulated late in 1950. Actually, as early as October stock market observers noted the rise in Matador shares—from 49/3*d* in the spring to 87/6*d* in the fall—on the London exchange and

---

[4] Statement by the Chairman, Sixty-sixth Annual General Meeting of Shareholders, April 6, 1948.

surmised that a "take-over" was in the offing and that American oil interests were involved. There was talk that a bid of £5.00 would be made for the 5/- shares, and it was pointed out that such an offer could hardly be turned down, since the yield from dividends—even at 40 or 50 per cent—was actually very small and constituted no real inducement to the shareholder to retain his stock.

In the middle of November, 1950, trading in Matador shares was halted on the London exchange at the request of Chairman Macdougall. "The finding of oil several miles from Matador ranch land" was credited with inspiring the upward climb in the company's stock, although the nearest completion known at the time was in Dickens County and was located a considerable distance from Matador property.[5]

On November 25, 26, and 27, both ranches were inspected by appraisers representing Appraisal Associates of Texas, a Dallas concern, and on March 14, 1951, the report of the evaluation was sent to John Mackenzie, who was then in Dundee. The Associates disclaimed that their evaluation study was an appraisal because of the brevity of the inspection and recommended that, before any important decisions regarding the market value of the ranches were made, a complete appraisal of the properties should be conducted. At the same time, in a cover letter to their report, Appraisal Associates stated, "It is the considered judgment of the appraisers that the probable market value of the Texas ranches of the Matador Land and Cattle Company, Ltd., consisting of 791,707 acres as of March 14, 1951, is $19,800,000, subject to the limitations of this valuation study."[6]

On February 10, 1951, the secretaries sent to each Matador stockholder an announcement that the directors had been ap-

[5] Lubbock *Morning Avalanche*, November 17, 1950. The item concerning Macdougall's action appeared under a Dundee dateline. Though the Humble Oil and Refining Company had been given a long-term lease on the Matador Division in 1937 with the stipulation that it drill one well per year, no oil had been found by 1950.

[6] Appraisal Associates to John Mackenzie, March 14, 1951.

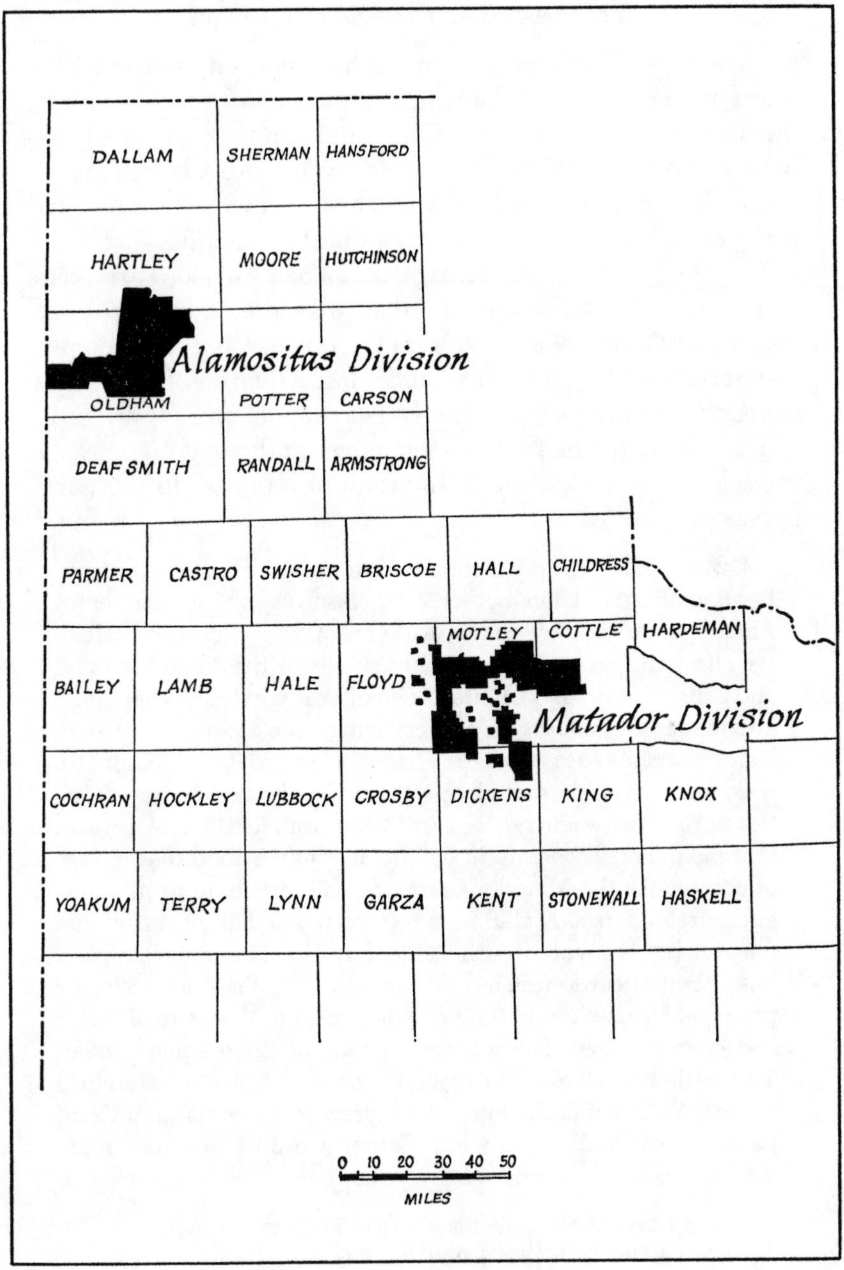

The Matador and Alamositas Divisions, 1950

proached by American interests "which desired to discuss the terms of an offer which they might make . . . for the purchase of the whole of the shares in the Company" and that it seemed likely that an offer would be made which would provide a cash payment "slightly in excess of the market price of £8 10/– and would allow the retention . . . of an interest in the mineral rights."[7]

In an Associated Press release under a San Angelo, Texas, date line, it was reported on April 6 that "a syndicate in New York" was prepared to make an offer on the ranches and that the purchaser planned to sell the land and retain a quarter of the royalty or sell the royalty for cash and the land at auction.[8]

The company's first official statement on the negotiations and the sale of its stock came in the form of a release to the newspapers on June 16:

> Lazard Brothers and Company, Limited, 11 Old Broad Street, London, England, on behalf of themselves and a number of American corporations have made an offer of $23.70 per share for all of the 800,000 outstanding shares of the Matador Land and Cattle Company, Limited. The offer is conditioned upon its acceptance by holders of 90 per cent of the shares or by such lesser percentage as Lazard Brothers may determine. British resident shareholders will be permitted by the exchange authorities to re-invest their proceeds in American securities. American shareholders will be paid in dollars. It is understood that in case of acceptance the Matador Company will distribute to the present shareholders of Matador an interest in one-half of the oil and mineral rights owned by the Matador. The Matador Company has operated cattle ranches in the United States since 1882. Its principal ranches are in the Panhandle area of the State of Texas and comprise over 800,000 acres or about 1,200 square miles. The cattle herds are said to total about 47,000 head of Hereford cattle. The General Manager and a director of the Matador Company is John Mackenzie whose father Murdo Mackenzie managed the ranches for about forty years.

[7] Mackay, Irons and Co. to the Shareholders, February 10, 1951.
[8] Lubbock *Morning Avalanche*, April 6, 1951.

In July, 1951, the offer from Lazard Frères was accepted, and on July 31, 1951, the transfer was carried through.[9] Actually, the company did not sell its property in this transaction; the "sale" was effected by the purchasers' acquiring from many different stockholders practically all of the shares of stock in the corporation. In other words, the shareholders sold their corporation which owned the lands and herds.[10] The land involved in the purchase included approximately 395,000 acres at Alamositas, some 400,000 acres at Matador, and about 4,600 acres at Malta, Montana. The herd, including 1,400 horses, was rated at 46,746 head at the end of 1950.

On July 16, 1951, the Toreador Royalty Corporation was incorporated under the laws of the state of Delaware. To this organization the former Matador stockholders conveyed an undivided one-half of the mineral rights on the ranch property and received pro rata shares in the new concern. Among the Toreador officials were several persons who had been associated with the Matador—Sam Wiley of the Denver office became the new corporation's secretary and James Wright of Dundee served as a director; Wright had been appointed to the Matador board in 1944 and was a central figure in the reorganization of the company's capital structure in 1948 and in the negotiations with Lazard Frères.

While the principal factor which prompted each Matador shareholder to part with his stock was undoubtedly the price offered—$23.70 for a seventy-cent share—British residents received an added advantage, for permission was granted them

[9] John Mackenzie to Pearce, January 28, 1952. Had all the shares been sold, the purchase price would have been $18,960,000.

[10] According to the Matador's "Final Dividend" list dated April 16, 1951, the largest single block of stock—39,120 shares—was held by the "Executors of Alexander Mackay"; the address shown was "Mrs. Edith M. M. Donovan, Glencruitten, Oban." Mrs. Donovan was one of Alexander Mackay's daughters. Sixty residents of the United States holding a total of 139,844 shares were recipients of the final dividend; the remainder of the shares were held by residents of the United Kingdom.

to reinvest their proceeds in American securities since payment was made in dollars.

When the breakup of the Matador ranches began in 1951—for Lazard Frères started the liquidation process immediately—the last of the great foreign-owned cattle companies devoted exclusively to the production of beef disappeared. The career of the Matador was unique in that this company survived to the middle of the twentieth century, though it experienced the same vicissitudes which drove other organizations of its kind into bankruptcy or into colonizing activities. That it persisted was due to four features: "a knowledge of good land, a reliance on the best-bred cattle, an ample source of reserves, and a sound tradition of business management."[11] To these should be added the character of the men who managed the American properties —Henry H. Campbell, Murdo Mackenzie, John MacBain, and John Mackenzie—for they developed the company's business and built its wealth.

As the Matador went out of existence and a way of life ended, the sentiments of many on both sides of the Atlantic were aptly and appropriately expressed by Harry Drought:

> And so the great Matador Company is going into voluntary liquidation. I consider myself very fortunate to have been a part of its fine organization. Regardless of how advantageous to the shareholders the sale may have been, there are many heartaches caused by this conclusion. The Company, however, will live forever in the history of the Southwest. We were connected with a cattle empire and our pride in it outweighed our desire for profits.[12]

[11] Haley, *Heraldry of the Range*, 22.
[12] Drought to James Wright, August 28, 1951.

Epilogue

To FACILITATE the breakup of the vast range lands acquired through their purchase of the Matador stock in 1951, Lazard Frères and associates formed fifteen corporations and divided the land and cattle among them. Five of these new concerns—the Adrian Cattle Corporation, the Alamositas Cattle Corporation, the Canadian River Cattle Corporation, the Pedrosa Cattle Corporation, and the Trujillo Cattle Corporation—took over the properties at the "north ranch," the Alamositas Division. The Matador Division, the "south ranch," was partitioned among the following: the Bear Creek Cattle Corporation, the Dickens Cattle Corporation, the Harnica Cattle Corporation, the Mott Cattle Corporation, the Pease River Cattle Corporation, the Red Lake Cattle Corporation, the Rodatam Cattle Corporation, the Tee-Pee Cattle Corporation, the Turtle Hole Cattle Corporation, and the Wolf Creek Cattle Corporation. In size, the tracts originally assigned to the new companies varied from approximately 96,000 acres, held by the Canadian River Corporation, to about 16,000 acres, owned by the Dickens Corporation.

During the 1950's the corporations were purchased by individuals or groups of individuals; in turn, these owners began cattle-raising operations of their own or disposed of their lands in marketable and manageable units to ranchers and farmers. For example, in January, 1956, it was reported that R. H. Fulton of Lubbock, Texas, had purchased the capital stock of the Ca-

225

nadian River Cattle Corporation and that he would operate the ranch thus acquired.[1] On the south ranch the Rock Island Oil and Refining Company obtained the Wolf Creek, TeePee, and Rodatam corporations, and a group headed by Coyal Francis of Wichita Falls purchased the Harnica, Bear Creek, and Turtle Hole corporations. Of the latter associates, only Francis and John V. Stevens currently (1963) hold land formerly owned by the Matador Company.[2]

In general, the lands lying within the old Alamositas Division remain in the hands of comparatively few people, while the former Matador Division has been divided into many small ranches and some tracts suitable for agriculture have been sold to farmers.

[1] Lubbock *Avalanche-Journal*, January 4, 1956. The Alamositas Division headquarters lay on the property obtained by Fulton.

[2] Stevens to Pearce, July 18, 1963; personal interview. The Matador Division headquarters lay on the Rodatam corporation's property.

Appendix A: Personnel

MEMBERS, BOARD OF DIRECTORS, 1882–1951
William Robertson, Dundee, 1882–99; Chairman, 1882–99.[1]
Alfred M. Britton, Ft. Worth, Texas, 1882–85.
Robert Fleming, Dundee, 1882–89.
George Halley, Dundee, 1882–1904.
John Robertson, Dundee, 1882–1906.
William Smith, Benholm Castle, Kincardinshire, 1882–1902.
David McIntyre, Dundee, 1886–1912; Chairman, 1910–12.
David Wilkie, Kirriemuir, 1900–14; Chairman, 1912–14.
James H. Halley, Dundee, 1906–25.
J. Nicoll Smith, Dundee, 1906–21.
Sir Francis Webster, Arbroath, 1906–24.
Alexander Mackay, Dundee, 1912–36; Chairman, 1915–36.
Charles J. M. Wilkie, Kirriemuir, 1915–20.
Murdo Mackenzie, Denver, Colorado, 1918–39.
James C. Johnston, Edinburgh, 1921–34.
George Bonar, Dundee, 1922–38; Chairman, 1937–38.
W. D. Macdougall, Dundee, 1925–51; Chairman, 1939–51.
H. P. Drought, San Antonio, Texas, 1938–51.
Lewis F. Robertson, Dundee, 1938–51.
W. L. Pattullo, Dundee, 1939–44.
John Mackenzie, Denver, Colorado, 1940–51.
James Wright, Dundee, 1944–51.

[1] From 1900 through 1909 no chairman was indicated in the annual reports.

Secretaries, 1882–1951

Alexander Mackay, C. A. (Mackay and Mess), 1882–1900.
Alexander Mackay, C. A. (Mackay and Irons), 1901–1902.
Alexander Mackay, C. A. (Mackay, Irons and Co.), 1903–11.
Mackay, Irons and Co., C. A., 1912–51.

Managers in America, 1882–1951

Alfred M. Britton, Ft. Worth, Texas, 1882–85.
William F. Sommerville, Ft. Worth, Texas, 1885–90.
Murdo Mackenzie, Trinidad, Colorado, 1891–1911.
John MacBain, Trinidad and Denver, Colorado, 1912–22.
Murdo Mackenzie, Denver, Colorado, 1922–36.
John Mackenzie, Denver, Colorado, 1937–51.

Ranch Superintendents

Matador Division (Motley County, Texas), 1882–1951
Henry H. Campbell, 1882–90.
Arthur G. Ligertwood, 1891–1909.
J. M. Jackson, 1910–23.
Maurice J. Reilly, 1923–46.
John V. Stevens, 1946–51.
Alamositas Division (Oldham and Hartley Counties, Texas), 1902–51
Dave Somerville, 1902–1904.
David George (Dode) Mackenzie, 1904–1906.
H. Frank Mitchell, 1906–26.
E. L. Roberds, 1926–39.
A. W. Rickels, 1939–40.
John V. Stevens, 1940–46.
Roland Howe, 1946–51.
Canadian Division (Swift Current, Saskatchewan), 1905–21
Dave Somerville, 1905–12.
J. R. Lair, 1913–21.
South Dakota Division (Cheyenne River Indian Reservation), 1904–14

Dave Somerville, 1904–1905.
H. Frank Mitchell, 1905–1906.
David George (Dode) Mackenzie, 1906–1909.
James Burr, 1910–11.
James M. (Mat) Walker, 1911–14.
Montana Division (Ft. Belknap Indian Reservation), 1913–28
James M. (Mat) Walker, 1913–19.
Maurice J. Reilly, 1920–23.
J. D. Reid, 1923–28.
South Dakota Division (Pine Ridge Indian Reservation), 1921–26
J. B. Henson, 1921 (in charge pro tem).
R. G. Reid, 1921–26.

Appendix B: Statistics

Year	Land Owned (Acres)*	Herd Strength*	Calf Brand*	Cattle Sales*
1883	374,717	76,600	20,844	4,816
1884	419,179	94,017	24,136	8,587
1885	424,296	94,441	19,501	17,508
1886	435,336	95,066	21,226	12,947
1887	435,101	96,545	22,456	14,605
1888	435,421	96,353	16,198	13,429
1889	435,722	95,904	17,002	14,945
1890	444,657	97,781	16,756	16,668
1891	445,457	†	14,484	9,173
1892	446,737	70,200	14,293	8,527
1893	452,497	58,016	5,309	9,238
1894	452,497	58,259	9,066	6,377
1895	453,157	61,333	13,321	4,827
1896	450,876	60,450	14,629	6,088
1897	450,876	61,180	16,204	8,417
1898	459,056	63,940	16,477	8,980
1899	477,456	64,492	13,821	7,615
1900	483,609	67,415	16,506	8,153
1901	484,959	69,213	17,335	9,812
1902	711,320	69,256	14,098	9,018

* From the annual reports for the years listed.
† Not published.

Appendix B: Statistics

Year	Land Owned (Acres)*	Herd Strength*	Calf Brand*	Cattle Sales*
1903	727,560	63,724	9,931	9,640
1904	740,803	63,464	11,169	9,543
1905	744,535	63,628	11,814	8,597
1906	749,941	64,530	13,588	6,873
1907	743,995	65,683	13,569	7,349
1908	745,581	71,133	17,128	7,051
1909	751,806	71,339	13,872	8,388
1910	752,737	70,482	14,948	8,772
1911	754,775	70,462	16,214	10,367
1912	755,969	70,629	15,987	8,958
1913	755,809	71,516	14,485	7,331
1914	768,849	66,577	12,632	10,856
1915	756,516	69,105	16,896	8,731
1916	879,735	72,403	15,771	8,636
1917	†	72,992	16,280	8,681
1918	†	72,160	14,702	8,101
1919	†	68,190	10,714	7,370
1920	†	69,632	17,066	9,221
1921	†	70,634	17,103	11,215
1922	837,621	69,018	14,139	10,037
1923	†	66,239	10,569	9,163
1924	†	64,977	14,096	9,517
1925	†	65,619	16,017	10,904
1926	†	62,316	15,943	13,512
1927	†	54,478	16,048	20,547
1928	†	54,387	15,270	14,129
1929	877,620	54,518	15,432	11,518
1930	877,555	51,784	14,532	14,233
1931	877,306	49,292	11,698	10,999
1932	877,306	49,815	14,044	11,184
1933	878,841	52,566	16,122	11,391

* From the annual reports for the years listed.
† Not published.

The Matador Land and Cattle Company

Year	Land Owned (Acres)*	Herd Strength*	Calf Brand*	Cattle Sales*
1934	878,816	49,151	14,287	15,419
1935	878,748	46,144	7,987	10,133
1936	878,725	49,166	13,035	7,946
1937	878,711	49,105	13,463	10,060
1938	878,791	51,309	15,134	8,819
1939	878,791	51,227	15,070	13,970
1940	878,791	51,028	15,198	14,406
1941	878,791	50,328	15,328	13,628
1942	878,764	49,409	14,874	13,213
1943	878,764	51,296	14,500	10,030
1944	878,764	51,164	12,855	9,924
1945	878,625	51,034	13,500	13,204
1946	853,128	48,439	14,200	16,104
1947	808,000	45,949	13,000	16,049
1948	808,000	45,057	12,500	13,670
1949	808,000	45,210	11,500	10,471
1950	†	46,746	13,500	10,922

* From the annual reports for the years listed.
† Not published.

Bibliography

The Matador Papers

THE FILES kept by the Matador Land and Cattle Company, Ltd., at the Dundee and the Denver offices and at the Matador and Alamositas divisions constitute the Matador Papers in the Southwest Collection at Texas Technological College at Lubbock. Consisting of over four hundred thousand separate items—letters, diaries, ledgers, tally-books, reports, and legal documents— the papers have provided the major source of information in the writing of this book.

Other Unpublished Material

Collinson, Frank. "The First Cattle Ranch on Tongue River, Motley County, Texas." MS in archives, Panhandle-Plains Historical Society, Canyon, Texas, c.1936.

Harper, Carl. "Movements toward Railroad Building on the South Plains of Texas." Unpublished Master's thesis, Department of History, Texas Technological College, 1935.

McDowell, Grace C. "The Matador Ranch." Unpublished MS in archives, Panhandle-Plains Historical Society, Canyon, Texas, 1935.

Published Material

Beale, Joseph H. and Bruce Wyman. *Railroad Rate Regulation.* 2d ed. New York, Baker, Voorhis and Company, 1915.

Bolton, Herbert E. *Coronado, Knight of Pueblos and Plains*. New York, Whittlesey House, 1949.

Broadhurst, William L. *Ground Water in High Plains in Texas*. Austin, Board of Water Engineers, Progress Report No. 6, 1946.

Cambridge History of the British Empire, VI. Cambridge, University Press, 1930.

Campbell, Harry H. *The Early History of Motley County*. San Antonio, The Naylor Co., 1958.

Carroll, H. Bailey. "The Texan Santa Fe Trail," *Panhandle-Plains Historical Review*, Vol. XXIV (1951).

Carter, Robert G. *On the Border with MacKenzie*. Washington, Eynon Printing Co., Inc., 1935.

Craig, John A. "Among the Matadors." Reprint, originally published in *The Weekly Live Stock Report*, Chicago, n.d. [*c.* 1902].

Dictionary of American Biography, XXII. New York, Charles Scribner's Sons, 1958.

Edminster, Lynn Ramsay. *The Cattle Industry and the Tariff*. New York, The Macmillan Company, 1926.

Frink, Maurice, W. Turrentine Jackson, and Agnes Wright Spring. *When Grass Was King*. Boulder, University of Colorado Press, 1956.

Haley, J. Evetts. *Charles Goodnight, Cowman and Plainsman*. Boston, Houghton Mifflin Company, 1936. (Reprinted by the University of Oklahoma Press in 1949.)

———. *Fort Concho and the Texas Frontier*. San Angelo, San Angelo *Standard-Times*, 1952.

———. *The Heraldry of the Range*. Canyon, Panhandle-Plains Historical Society, 1949.

———. *The XIT Ranch of Texas*. Revised ed. Norman, University of Oklahoma Press, 1953.

Handbook of Texas. 2 vols. Austin, The Texas State Historical Association, 1952.

Holden, William Curry. *The Spur Ranch*. Boston, Christopher Publishing House, 1934.

Hunt, Frazier. *Cap Mossman, Last of the Great Cowmen*. New York, Hastings House, 1951.

Kansas City *Times*, May 27, 1941.

Lubbock *Morning Avalanche*, November 17, 1950; April 6, 1951.

Mackenzie, Murdo. "The Matador Ranch," *Panhandle-Plains Historical Review*, Vol. XXI (1948).

Marvin, Donald M. "The Tariff Relationship of the United States and Canada," *Annals of the American Academy of Political and Social Science*, Vol. CXLI (1928).

New York *Times*, December 12, 1909.

Riordan, M. "Murdo Mackenzie, Range King," *The Westerner* (Denver), Vol. 6 (1943), Nos. 9, 10, 11; Vol. 7 (1944), Nos. 1, 2.

Rister, Carl C. *Fort Griffin on the Texas Frontier*. Norman, University of Oklahoma Press, 1956.

Sanders, Alvin H. *The Story of the Herefords*. Chicago, The Breeder's Gazette, 1914.

"Scottish Capital Abroad," *Blackwood's Edinburgh Magazine*, Vol. CXXXVI (1884).

Sheffy, L. F. *The Life and Times of Timothy Dwight Hobart*. Canyon, Texas, Panhandle-Plains Historical Society, 1950.

U. S. Congress, Senate. *Regulation of Railway Rates*. Hearings before the Committee on Interstate Commerce, Senate of the United States. 59 Cong., 1 sess. (1905), *Sen. Doc. 243*, XVI. Washington, Government Printing Office, 1906.

Wallace, Ernest. *Charles DeMorse, Pioneer Editor and Statesman*. Lubbock, Texas Tech Press, 1943.

Wentworth, Edward N. "A Search for Cattle Trails in Matto Grosso," *Agricultural History*, Vol. XXVI (1952).

Index

Index

Mackenzie, Colonel Ranald S.: 5
Mackenzie, William: 34
Malta, Montana: 173, 174, 223
Managers, in America: 228
Martin, Charles F.: 105
Matador, Motley County, Texas: 55, 115, 132, 133, 134, 139
Matador Cattle Company of Texas: 7, 49; sold to Scots, 10–11
Matador Division: 114, 131, 145, 147, 152, 158, 177, 184, 185, 205, 206, 216, 219, 225, 226, 226n.; headquarters described, 116; land consolidation on, 120; railroad through, 128, 132–40; land sales at, 149; oil explorations on, 154, 156, 189, 191–92
Matador Land and Cattle Co., Ltd.: vii, 11–12, 15, 49, 50; land policy, 50–55; adopts northern feeding program, 54; withdraws from North, 169, 172–74; valuation of properties, 220; sale and liquidation, 222–24, 225–26
Matador shares: on London exchange, 219–220
Matador steers: take grand champion prizes, 112
Mauck, Captain Clarence: 5
Memorandum of Association: of Matador Land and Cattle Co., Ltd., 12, 13; altered, 15
Mess and Mackay, Chartered Accountants: 12
Middle Pease River: 5, 115
Milk River: 142, 144, 145
Milwaukee Railroad: see Chicago, Milwaukee and St. Paul Railroad
Missouri River: 95, 96, 98
Mitchell, H. Frank: 83, 141, 144, 164, 195, 207
Montana Division: 146, 164, 178; closed, 174; see also Fort Belknap Indian Reservation
Moreau River: 95, 98

Moscoso, Luis de: 4
Mossman, Burton C. "Cap": 97, 98
Motley County, Texas: viii, 3, 11, 26, 31, 50, 56, 86, 130, 131, 134, 136, 152, 191–92, 194; first settlement in, 5; railroad through, 132–40
Motley County Railroad: 139, 139n., 193
Mott Cattle Corporation: 225
Murdo: railroad switch at Alamositas Division, 86, 94, 145, 217

National Live Stock Association: 103–105
National Packing Company: 101
Neff, Pat: 179
"Nesters": 117–18
Newcastle Land and Live Stock Company: 164, 167
Nichols, John W.: 8
North Pease River: 65
North Sea: 23
Northern Trail: 30

Oban, Scotland: 203, 223n.
Oil: explorations for, 153–58, 188–92, 220n.
Oklahoma Panhandle: 30, 47
Oldham County, Texas: 79n., 85, 86, 147, 153n., 189, 194
Omaha, Nebraska: 31
Orin, Wyoming: 48, 64
Ottawa, Canada: 86, 88, 93, 151

Paducah, Texas: 132, 133, 137, 145
Pampa, Texas: 76
Panhandle, Carson County, Texas: 44
Panhandle Stock Association: 33
Parker, H. F.: 196–97
Parliamentary commission: 10; report of, 34
Pattullo, W. L.: 111
Pease River: 3, 6n.
Pease River Cattle Corporation: 225
Pecos River: 4, 6

241

THE MATADOR LAND AND CATTLE COMPANY

has been set in eleven-point Caledonia, with two points of space between the lines. Caledonia is an original type design by W. A. Dwiggins, cut in 1940 for the Linotype as a refinement of Scotch faces of the early nineteenth century. Handset Bulmer was selected for chapter titles and display to complement the transitional characteristics of Caledonia.

University of Oklahoma Press

Norman